WHAT THEY SAID ABOUT THE ENGLISH EDITION:

"THE REPORT ON DONALD DUCK THAT WALT DISNEY DOESN'T WANT YOU TO READ .....
Last June [1975], a shipment of the English edition was seized by the U.S. Customs Bureau as a possible 'infringement' on Disney's copyrights. After a year of deliberation, Customs ruled that importing the book does not constitute 'piracy'."

Jim Hoberman, *Village Voice*

The Center for Constitutional Rights, the lawyers who successfully defended the publisher said:
" .... the seizure of the books is a classic case of abuse of the laws to suppress political dissent and unpopular opinions."

Docket Report 1976-1977

".... an eyeopener for those of us who grew up on Donald Duck and the Mickey Mouse Club..... This exposé should be in libraries as another example of America's role in world politics."

Lavonne Jacobsen, *Booklegger*

"It has become a handbook of de-colonisation. It examines the meaning of Walt Disney comics: in doing this one thing precisely and profoundly, it illuminates a global situation. The clinical writings of Franz Fanon worked in a similar way."

John Berger, *New Society*

"Closes a long standing gap in the subject of imperialism and ideology in Latin America."

Arturo Torrecilla, *Insurgent Sociologist*

"*The* popular classic study on cultural imperialism, and children's literature."

Ian Segal

HOW TO READ DONALD DUCK

IMPERIALIST IDEOLOGY IN THE DISNEY COMIC

ARIEL DORFMAN,
Chilean literary critic and novelist, was born in 1942.
He has written extensively on literature and ideology,
particularly children's literature. Before the
fascist coup, he was Professor of Spanish American Literature
at the University of Chile. He narrowly escaped the
fascist repression, and is now living in exile.
Among his publications are *Imaginación y violencia en America,*
essays on the Latin American novel;
Superman y sus Amigos del Alma (with Manuel Jofre);
Ensayos Quemados en Chile; and a prize-winning novel on the
Chilean revolution, *Moros en la costa.*

ARMAND MATTELART,
sociologist, was born in Belgium in 1936, and lived in
Chile from 1962 to the fascist coup in 1973. He has written
extensively on cultural imperialism and the role of
the mass media in the developing countries. Before the
fascist coup, he was Professor of Mass Communications and
Ideology at the University of Chile, and head of the
Mass Communications Division of the Chilean state publishing
house Quimantú. He was expelled during the fascist
coup, and is now living in exile. His most recent books are
Mass Media, Idéologies et Mouvement Révolutionnaire:
Chili 1970–1973, and
Multinationales et systèmes de communication. In 1975 he
directed a feature-length film on Chile,
La Spirale, and is co-editor (with Seth Siegelaub)
of the 2-volume anthology,
Communication and Class Struggle.

DAVID KUNZLE,
art historian, has written extensively on the comics,
including the definitive volume *The Early Comic Strip* (1973),
and on political posters, including
U.S. Posters of Protest 1966–1970. He has also written
on the art of revolutionary Chile, and has recently
completed a book *Fashion and Fetishism*. He is presently
working on a study of the art
of revolutionary Cuba.

HOW TO READ DONALD DUCK

IMPERIALIST IDEOLOGY IN THE DISNEY COMIC

ARIEL DORFMAN
ARMAND MATTELART

TRANSLATION AND INTRODUCTION BY
DAVID KUNZLE

WITH APPENDIX BY
JOHN SHELTON LAWRENCE

international general, new york

How to Read Donald Duck
was originally published in Chile as *Para Leer al Pato Donald*
by Ediciones Universitarias de Valparaíso, in 1971.

A Latin American edition was published, under the same
title, by Siglo Veintiuno Editores, Buenos Aires, 1972; the
Italian edition, *Come Leggere Paperino*, by Feltrinelli
Editore, Milan, 1972; the Portuguese edition,
Para Ler o Pato Donald, by Iniciativas Editoriais, Lisbon, 1975;
the French, *Donald l'imposteur,* Alain Moreau, Paris,
1976; the Swedish, *Konsten Att Lasa Kalle Anka,*
Stockholm, UF-Forlaget, 1977; the German,
Walt Disneys "Dritte Welt", Basis Verlag, Berlin, 1977;
the Danish, *Anders And i den tredje verden,* Informations
Forlag Aps, 1978, with editions in
Dutch, Greek, Finnish, and Japanese.

For information please address
International General, Post Office Box 350,
New York, N.Y. 10013, USA.

ISBN: 088477-023-0
Second Edition, Enlarged
First Printing (1984)
Printed in Hungary

CONTENTS

PREFACE TO THE ENGLISH EDITION

To say that this book was burnt in Chile should not come as a surprise to anyone. Hundreds of books were destroyed, and thousands more prohibited and censored.

It was written in the middle of 1971, in the middle of the Chilean revolutionary process. Copper had been rescued, the land was being returned to the peasantry, the whole Chilean people were recovering the industries that during the twentieth century had been the means of enrichment for Mr. Rockefeller, Grace, Guggenheim, and Morgan. Because this process was intolerable to the United States government and its multinational corporations, it had to be stopped. They organized a plan, which at the time was suspected, and since has been confirmed by Mr. Kissinger, Ford and Colby to have been directed and financed by the United States intelligence services. Their objective: to overthrow the constitutional government of Chile. To realize their objective, an "invisible blockade" was imposed: credits were denied, spare parts purchased for industrial machinery were not sent, and later, the Chilean State bank accounts in the U.S. were blocked, and an embargo preventing the sale of Chilean copper throughout the world was organized.

There were, however, two items which were not blocked: planes, tanks, ships and technical assistance for the Chilean armed forces; and magazines, TV serials, advertising, and public opinion polls for the Chilean mass media, which continued, for the most part, to be in the hands of the small group which was losing its privileges. To maintain them, with those of the U.S., their media prepared the climate for the bourgeois insurrection which finally materialized some years later on the 11th of September 1973. Each day, with expert U.S. advice, in each newspaper, each weekly, each monthly magazine, each news dispatch, each movie, and each comic book, their arsenal of psychological warfare was fortified. In the words of General Pinochet, the point was to "conquer the minds," while in the words of Donald Duck (in the magazine *Disneylandia* published in December 1971, coinciding with the first mass rallies of native fascism, the so-called "march of the empty pots and pans") the point was to "restore the king."

But the people did not want the restoration of the king nor of the businessman. The popular Chilean cultural offensive, which accompanied the social and economic liberation, took multiple forms: wall paintings, popular papers, TV programs, motion pictures, theater, songs, literature. In all areas of human activity, with differing degrees of intensity, the people expressed their will. Perhaps the most important arm of this offensive, was the work of the State Publishing House "Quimantú," a word meaning "Sunshine of Knowledge" in the language of the native Chilean Mapuche indians. In two and a half years it published five million books; twice the amount which had been published in all of Chile during the past seventy years. In addition, it transformed the content of some of the magazines it had inherited from before the Popular Unity government, and created new ones. It is in this multi-faceted context, with a people on the march to cultural liberation – a process which also meant criticizing the "mass" cultural merchandise exported so profitably by the U.S. to the Third World – that *How to Read Donald Duck* was generated. We simply answered a practical need; it was *not* an academic exercise.

For the mad dog warriors on that September 11th, there were no paintings on the walls. There were only enormous "stains" which dirtied the city and memory. They, using the fascist youth brigades, whitewashed all the singing, many-colored walls of the nation. They broke records, murdered singers, destroyed radios and printing presses, emprisoned and executed journalists, so that nothing would be left to remind anybody of anything about the struggle for national liberation.

But it was not enough to clean these cultural "stains" from the street. The most important task was to eliminate all those who bore the "stain" inside themselves, the fighters, workers, peasants, employees, students, and patriotic soldiers, to eliminate these creators of a new life, to eliminate this new life which grew, and for which we all created.

This book, conceived for the Chilean people, and our urgent needs, produced in the midst of our struggle, is now being published far from Chile in the uncleland of Disney, behind the barbed wire network of ITT.

Mr. Disney, we are returning your Duck. Feathers plucked and well-roasted. Look inside, you can see the handwriting on the wall, our hands still writing on the wall:

Donald, Go Home!

Dorfman and Mattelart
January 1975,
in exile

INTRODUCTION TO THE ENGLISH EDITION

David Kunzle

The Walt Disney World logo
is a terrestrial globe wearing Mickey Mouse ears,
enclosed in the letter D

The names of the Presidents change; that of Disney remains. Forty-six years after the birth of Mickey Mouse, eight years after the death of his master, Disney's may be the most widely known North American name in the world. He is, arguably, the century's most important figure in bourgeois popular culture. He has done more than any single person to disseminate around the world certain myths upon which that culture has thrived, notably that of an "innocence" supposedly universal, beyond place, beyond time — and beyond criticism.

The myth of U.S. political "innocence" is at last being dismantled, and the reality which it masks lies in significant areas exposed to public view. But the Great American Dream of cultural innocence still holds a global imagination in thrall. The first major breach into the Disney part of this dream was made by Richard Schickel's *The Disney Version: The Life, Times, Art and Commerce of Walt Disney* (1968). But even this analysis, penetrating and caustic as it is, in many respects remains prey to the illusion that Disney productions, even at their worst, are somehow redeemed by the fact that, made in "innocent fun," they are socially harmless.

Disney is no mean conjuror, and it has taken the eye of a Dorfman and Mattelart to expose the magician's sleight of hand, to reveal the scowl of capitalist ideology behind the laughing mask, the iron fist beneath the Mouse's glove. The value of their work lies in the light it throws not so much upon a particular group of comics, or even a particular cultural entrepreneur, but on the way in which capitalist and imperialist values are supported by its culture. And the very simplicity of the comic has enabled the authors to make simply visible a very complicated process.

While many cultural critics in the United States bridle at the magician's unctuous patter, and shrink from his bland fakery, they fail to recognize just what he is faking, and the extent to which it is not just things, but people he manipulates. It is not merely animatronic robots that he molds, but human beings as well. Unfortunately, the army of media critics have focused over the past decades principally on the "sex-and-violence" films, "horror comics" and the peculiar inanities of the TV comedy, as the great bludgeons of the popular sensibility. If important sectors of the intelligentsia in the U.S. have been lulled into silent complicity with Disney, it can only be because they share his basic values and see the broad public as enjoying the same cultural privileges; but this complicity becomes postively criminal when their common ideology is imposed upon non-capitalist, underdeveloped countries, ignoring the grotesque disparity between the Disney dream of wealth and leisure, and the *real* needs in the Third World.

It is no accident that the first thoroughgoing analysis of the Disney ideology should come from one of the most economically and culturally dependent colonies of the U.S. empire. *How to Read Donald Duck* was born in the heat of the struggle to free Chile from that dependency; and it has since become, with its eleven Latin American editions, a most potent instrument for the interpretation of bourgeois media in the Third World.

Until 1970, Chile was completely in pawn to U.S. corporate interests; its foreign debt was the second highest per capita in the world. And even under the Popular Unity government (1970–1973), which initiated the peaceful road to socialism, it proved easier to nationalize copper than to free the mass media from U.S. influence. The most popular TV channel in Chile imported about half its material from the U.S. (including *FBI, Mission Impossible, Disneyland*, etc.), and until June 1972, eighty percent of the films shown in the cinemas (Chile had virtually no native film industry) came from the U.S. The major chain of newspapers and magazines, including *El Mercurio*, was owned by Agustin Edwards, a Vice-President of Pepsi Cola, who also controlled many of the largest industrial corporations in Chile, while he was a resident in Miami. With so much of the mass media serving conservative interests, the government of the Popular Unity tried to reach the people through certain alternative media, such as the poster, the mural and a new kind of comic book.*

The ubiquitous magazine and newspaper kiosks of Chile were emblazoned with the garish covers of U.S. and U.S.–style comics (including some no longer known in the metropolitan country): *Superman, The Lone Ranger, Red Ryder, Flash Gordon*, etc. – and, of course, the various Disney magazines. In few countries of the world did Disney so completely dominate the so-called "children's comic" market, a term which in Chile (as in much of the Third World) includes magazines also read by adults. But under the aegis of the Popular Unity government publishing house Quimantú, there developed a forceful resistance to the Disney hegemony.

As part of this cultural offensive, *How to Read Donald Duck* became a bestseller on publication in late 1971, and subsequently in other Latin American editions; and, as a practical alternative there was created, in *Cabro Chico (Little Kid*, upon which Dorfman and Mattelart also collaborated), a delightful children's comic designed to drive a wedge of new values into the U.S.–disnified cultural climate of old. Both ventures had to compete in a market where the bourgeois media were long entrenched and had established their own strictly commercial criteria for the struggle, and both were too successful not to have aroused the hostility of the bourgeois press. *El Mercurio*, the leading reactionary mass daily in Chile, under the headline "Warning to Parents"**, denounced them as part of a government "plot" to seize control of education and the media, "brainwash" the young, inject them with "subtle ideological contraband," and "poison" their minds against Disney characters. The article referred repeatedly to "mentors both Chilean and foreign" (i.e. the authors of the present work, whose names are of German–Jewish and Belgian origin) in an appeal to the crudest kind of xenophobia.

The Chilean bourgeois press resorted to the grossest lies, distortions and scare campaigns in order to undermine confidence in the Popular Unity government, accusing the government of doing what they aspired to do themselves: censor and silence the voice of their opponents. And seeing that, despite their machinations, popular

*Cf. Herbert Schiller and Dallas Smythe "Chile: An End to Cultural Colonialism" *Society*, March 1972, pp. 35–39, 61. And David Kunzle "Art of the New Chile: Mural, poster and comic book in a 'revolutionary process' " in *Art and Architecture in the Service of Politics*, edited by Henry Millon and Linda Nochlin, forthcoming from the MIT Press.

***El Mercurio* (Santiago de Chile), 13 August 1971. The passage below is slightly abridged from that published on pages 80–81 in the Chilean edition of *How to Read Donald Duck:*

"Among the objectives pursued by the Popular Unity government appears to be the creation of a new mentality in the younger generation. In order to achieve this purpose, typical of all Marxist societies, the authorities are intervening in education and the advertising media and resorting to various expedients.

"Persons responsible to the Government maintain that education shall be one of the means calculated to achieve this purpose. A severe critique is thus being instituted at this level against teaching methods, textbooks, and the attitude of broad sectors of the nation's teachers who refuse to become an instrument of propaganda.

"We register no surprise at the emphasis placed upon changing the mentality of school children, who in their immaturity can not detect the subtle ideological contraband to which they are being subject.

"There are however other lines of access being forged to the juvenile mind, notably the magazines and publications which the State publishing house has just launched, under literary mentors both Chilean and foreign, but in either case of proven Marxist militancy. "It should be stressed that not even the vehicles of juvenile recreation and amusement are exempt from this process, which aims to diminish the popularity of consecrated characters of world literature, and at the same time replace them with new models cooked up by the Popular Unity propaganda experts.

"For sometime now the pseudo-sociologists have been clamoring, in their tortuous jargon, against certain comic books with an international circulation, judged to be disastrous in that they represent vehicles of intellectual colonization for those who are exposed to them . . . Since clumsy forms of propaganda would not be acceptable to parents and guardians, children are systematically given carefully distilled doses of propaganda from an early age, in order to channel them in later years in Marxist directions.

"Juvenile literature has also been exploited so that the parents themselves should be exposed to ideological indoctrination, for which purpose special adult supplements are included. It is illustrative of Marxist procedures that a State enterprise should sponsor initiatives of this kind, with the collaboration of foreign personnel.

"The program of the Popular Unity demands that the communications media should be educational in spirit. Now we are discovering that this "education" is no more than the instrument for doctrinaire proselytization imposed from the tenderest years in so insidious and deceitful a form, that many people have no idea of the real purposes being pursued by these publications."

It is now widely known, even in the U.S., that *El Mercurio* was CIA funded: "Approximately half the CIA funds (one million dollars) were funnelled to the opposition press, notably the nation's lead daily, *El Mercurio*." (*Time*, September 30, 1974, p.29).

support for the government grew louder every day, they called upon the military to intervene by force of arms.

On September 11, 1973 the Chilean armed forces executed, with U.S. aid, the bloodiest counterrevolution in the history of the continent. Tens of thousands of workers and government supporters were killed. All art and literature favorable to the Popular Unity was immediately suppressed. Murals were destroyed. There were public bonfires of books, posters and comics.*

Intellectuals of the Left were hunted down, jailed, tortured and killed. Among those persecuted, the authors of this book.

The "state of war" declared by the Junta to exist in Chile, has been openly declared by the Disney comic too. In a recent issue, the Allende government, symbolized by murderous vultures called Marx and Hegel (meaning perhaps, Engels), is being driven off by naked force: "Ha! Firearms are the only things these lousy birds are afraid of."

*In autumn 1973, UNESCO voted by 32 to 2 to condemn the book-burning in Chile. The U.S. (with Taiwan) voted with the Junta.

How to Read Donald Duck, is now, of course, banned in Chile. To be found in possession of a copy is to risk one's life. By "cleansing" Chile of every trace of Marxist or popular art and literature, the Junta are protecting the cultural envoys of their imperial masters. They know what kind of culture best serves their interests, that Mickey and Donald will help keep them in power, hold socialism at bay, restore "virtue and innocence" to a "corrupted" Chile.

How to Read Donald Duck is an enraged, satirical and politically impassioned book. The authors' passion also derives from a sense of personal victimization, for they themselves, brought up on Disney comics and films, were injected with the Disney ideology which they now reject. But this book is much more than that: it is not just Latin American water off a duck's back. The system of domination which the U.S. culture imposes so disastrously abroad, also has deleterious effects at home, not least among those who work for Disney, that is, those who *produce* his ideology. The circumstances in which Disney products are made ensure that his employees reproduce in their lives and work relations the same system of exploitation to which they, as well as the consumer, are subject.

* * *

To locate Disney correctly in the capitalist system would require a detailed analysis of the working conditions at Disney Productions and Walt Disney World. Such a study (which would, necessarily, break through the wall of secrecy behind which Disney* operates), does not yet exist, but we may begin to piece together such information as may be gleaned about the circumstances in which the comics are created, and the people who create them; their relationship to their work, and to Disney.

Disney does not take the comics seriously. He hardly even admits publicly of their existence.** He is far too concerned with the promotion of films and the amusement parks, his two most profitable enterprises. The comics tag along as an "ancillary activity" of interest only insofar as a new comic title (currently *Robin Hood*) can be used to help keep the name of a new film in the limelight. Royalties from comics constitute a small declining fraction of the revenue from Publications, which constitute a small fraction of the revenue from Ancillary Activities, which constitute a small fraction of the total corporate revenue. While Disney's share of the market in "educational" and children's books in other formats has increased dramatically, his cut of the total U.S. comics cake has surely shrunk.

But in foreign lands the Disney comics trade is still a mouse that roars. Many parts of the world, without access to Disney's films or television shows, know the Disney characters from the comics alone. Those too poor to buy a ticket to the cinema, can always get hold of a comic, if not by purchase, then by borrowing it from a friend. In the U.S. moreover, comic book circulation figures are an inadequate index of the cultural influence of comic book characters. Since no new comedy cartoon shorts have been made of Mickey Mouse since 1948, and of Donald Duck since 1955 (the TV shows carry reruns), it is only in the comic that one finds original stories with the classic characters devised over the last two decades. It is thus the comic books and strips which sustain old favorites in the public consciousness (in the U.S. and abroad) and keep it receptive to the massive merchandizing operations which exploit the popularity of those characters.

Disney, like the missionary Peace Corpsman or "good-will ambassador" of his Public Relations men, has learned the native lingoes – he is fluent in eighteen of them at the moment. In Latin America he speaks Spanish and Portuguese; and he speaks it from magazines which are slightly different, in other ways, from those produced elsewhere and at home. There are, indeed, at least four different Spanish language editions of the Disney comic. The differences between them do not affect the basic content, and to determine the precise significance of such differences would require an excessive amount of research; but the fact of their existence points up some structural peculiarities in this little corner of Disney's

*If we continue to refer to Disney Productions after the death of Walt as "Disney" and "he", we do so in response to the fact that his spirit, that of U.S. corporate capitalism, continues to dominate the organization.

**Neither comic book nor syndicated newspaper strip is mentioned in the company's *Annual Report* for 1973. They presumably fall within the category Publications, which constitutes 17% of the group "Ancillary Activities." This group, of which Character Merchandizing, and Music and Records (27% each) are the major constituents, showed an extraordinary increase in activity (up 28% over the previous year, up 228% over the last four years, the contribution of Publications being proportionate), so as to bring its share of the total corporate revenue of $385 million up to 10%.

Written solicitation with Disney Productions regarding income from comic books proved unavailing. The following data has been culled from the press:

The total monthly circulation of Disney comics throughout the world was given in 1962 at 50 million, covering 50 countries and 15 different languages (*Newsweek*, 31 December 1962, pp.48–51). These have now risen to 18: Arabic, Chinese, Danish, Dutch, English, Finnish, Flemish, French, German, Hebrew, Italian, Japanese, Norwegian, Portuguese, Serbo-Croatian, Spanish, Swedish, and Thai. The number of countries served must have risen sharply in the later fifties, to judge by the figures published in 1954 (*Time*, 27 December, p. 42): 30 million copies of a "single title" (*Walt Disney's Comics and Stories*) were being bought in 26 countries every month.

In the United States, discounting special "one-shot" periodicals keyed to current films, the following 14 comic book titles are now being published under Disney's name: *Aristokittens, Beagle Boys, Chip and Dale, Daisy and Donald, Donald Duck, Huey Dewey and Louie Junior Woodchucks, Mickey Mouse, Moby Duck, Scamp, Supergoof, Uncle Scrooge, Walt Disney Showcase, Walt Disney's Comics and Stories, Walt Disney's Comics Digest*. It should be stressed that while the number of Disney titles has recently increased, their individual size has diminished considerably, as has, presumably, their circulation.

empire. For the Disney comic, more than his other media, systematically relies on foreign labor in all stages of the production process. The native contributes directly to his own colonization.*

Like other multinational corporations, Disney's has found it profitable to decentralize operations, allowing considerable organizational and production leeway to its foreign subsidiaries or "franchises," which are usually locked into the giant popular press conglomerates of their respective countries, like Mondadori in Italy or International Press Corporation in Britain. The Chilean edition, like other foreign editions, draws its material from several outside sources apart from the U.S. Clearly, it is in the interests of the metropolis that the various foreign subsidiaries should render mutual assistance to each other, exchanging stories they have imported or produced themselves. Even when foreign editors do not find it convenient to commission stories locally, they can select the type of story, and combination of stories ("story mix") which they consider suited to particular public taste and particular marketing conditions, in the country or countries they are serving. They also edit (for instance, delete scenes considered offensive or inappropriate to the national sensibility**), have dialogues more or less accurately translated, more or less freely adapted, and add local color (in the literal sense: the pages arrive at the foreign press ready photographed onto black and white transparencies ("mats"), requiring the addition of color as well as dialogue in the local idiom). Some characters like Rockerduck, a freespending millionaire rival of Scrooge; Fethry Duck, a "beatnik" type; and 0.0. Duck, a silly spy; are known only, or chiefly from the foreign editions, and never caught on at home. The Italians in particular have proven adept in the creation of indigenous characters.

Expressed preferences of foreign editors reveal certain broad differences in taste. Brazil and Italy tend towards more physical violence, more blood and guts; Chile, evidently tends (like Scandinavia, Germany and Holland), to more quiet adventures, aimed (apparently) at a younger age group. Since the military are now in control of education and the mass media in Chile, and are known to be importing Brazilian techniques of repression, one may expect them to also introduce the more violent, Brazilian style of Disney comic.

The tremendous and increasing popularity of Disney abroad is not matched, proportionately, in the home market, where sales have been dropping, to a degree probably exceeding that of other comic classics, ever since the peak reached in the early '50s. Competition from television is usually cited as a major cause of the slump in the comics market; logistical difficulties of distribution are another; and a third factor, affecting Disney in particular, may be sought in the whole cultural shift of the last two decades, which has transformed the taste of so many of the younger children as well as teenagers in the U.S., and which Disney media appear in many respects to have ignored. If the Disney formula has been successfully preserved in the films and amusement parks even within this changing climate, it is by virtue of an increasingly heavy cloak of technical gimmickry which has been thrown over the old content. Thus the comics, bound today to the same production technology (coloring, printing, etc.) as when they started thirty-five years ago, have been unable to keep up with the new entertainment tricks.

The factors which sent the comics trade into its commercial decline in the U.S. have not weighed to anything like the same extent in the less developed nations of the world. The "cultural lag," an expression of dominance of the metropolitan center over its colonized areas, is a familiar phenomenon; even in the U.S., Disney comics sell proportionately better in the Midwest and South.

Fueling the foreign market from within the U.S. has in recent years run into some difficulties. The less profitable domestic market, which Disney does not directly control and

*Some statistics will reveal the character and extent of foreign participation in the Disney comic, as well as the depth of Disney's penetration into the Latin American continent. The Chilean edition, which also serves neighboring Peru, Paraguay and Argentina, used, in a recent year, for its four comics titles (one weekly, three biweeklies) totalling 800,000 copies sold per month: 4,400 pages of Disney material, of which well over a third came direct from Disney studios, just over a third from Disney's U.S. franchise, Western Publishing Company, less than a quarter from Italy, and a small fraction from Brazil and Denmark. The Mexican edition (which uses only half as many pages as the Chile group) takes almost exclusively from the U.S. On the other hand, Brazil, with five titles totalling over two million copies sold per month, is fairly dependent upon Italy (1,000 out of 5,000 pages) and generates 1,100 pages of its own material. Another Latin American edition is that of Colombia. Italy is perhaps the most self-sufficient country of all, producing itself over half of its 5,600 annual pages. France's *Journal de Mickey*, which sells around 340,000 copies weekly, consists of about half Disney and half non-Disney material.

There is a direct reverse flow back to the mother country in *Disneyland*, a comic for younger readers with more stylish drawing started about 1971, produced entirely in England, and distributed by Fawcett in the U.S. This, and *Donald and Mickey*, the other major Disney comic serving the non-U.S. English-speaking world, sell around 200,000 copies per week each in the United Kingdom.

**A collection of such editorial changes might reveal some of the finer and perhaps more surprising nuances of cultural preference. The social sensibility of the Swedes, for instance, was offended by the inclusion of some realistic scenes of poverty in which the ducklings try to buy gifts for the poor ("Christmas for Shacktown" 1952). By cutting such scenes, the editors rendered the story almost incomprehensible.

A country with a totally different cultural tradition, such as Taiwan, cannot use Disney comics in their original form at all, and changes the very essence of favorite characters. Thus Donald becomes a responsible, model parent, admired and obeyed by his little nephews.

which now relies heavily on reprints, might conceivably be allowed to wind down altogether. As the domestic market shrinks, Disney pushes harder abroad, in the familiar mechanism of imperialist capitalism. As the foreign market expands, he is under increasing pressure to keep it dependent upon supply from the U.S. (despite or because of the fact that the colonies show, as we have seen, signs of independent productive capacity). But Disney is faced with a recruitment problem, as old workhorses of the profession, like Carl Barks, retire, and others become disillusioned with the low pay and restrictive conditions.

Disney has responded to the need to revitalize domestic production on behalf of the foreign market in a characteristic way: by tightening the rein on worker and product, to ensure that they adhere rigidly to established criteria. Where Disney can exercise direct control, the control must be total.

Prospective freelancers for Disney receive from the Publications Division a sheaf of Comic Book Art Specifications, designed in the first instance for the Comic Book Overseas Program. (Western Publishing, which is not primarily beholden to the foreign market, and which is also trying to attract new talent, although perhaps less strenuously, operates by unwritten and less inflexible rules). Instead of inviting the invention of new characters and new locales, the Comic Book Art Specifications do exactly the opposite: they insist that only the established characters be used, and moreover, that there be "no upward mobility. The subsidiary figures should never become stars in our stories, they are just extras." This severe injunction seems calculated to repress exactly what in the past gave a certain growth potential and flexibility to the Duckburg cast, whereby a minor character was upgraded into a major one, and might even aspire to a comic book of his own. Nor do these established characters have any room to manoeuvre even within the hierarchical structure where they are immutably fixed; for they are restricted to "a set pattern of behavior which must be complied with." The authoritarian tone of this instruction to the story writer seems expressly designed to crush any kind of creative manipulation on his part. He is also discouraged from localizing the action in any way, for Duckburg is explicitly stated to be *not* in the U.S., but "everywhere and nowhere." All taint of specific geographical location must be expunged, as must all taint of dialect in the language.

Not only sex, but love is prohibited (the relationship between Mickey and Minnie, or Donald and Daisy, is "platonic" — but not a platonic form of love). The gun laws outlaw all firearms but "antique cannons and blunderbusses;" (other) firearms may, under certain circumstances, be waved as a threat, but never used. There are to be no "dirty, realistic business tricks," no "social differences,"* or "political ideas." Above all, race and racial stereotyping is abolished: "Natives should never be depicted as negroes, Malayans, or singled out as belonging to any particular human race, and under no circumstances should they be characterized as dumb, ugly, inferior or criminal."

As is evident from the analysis in this book, and as is obvious to anyone at all familiar with the comics, none of these rules (with the exception of the sexual prohibition) have been observed in the past, in either Duck or Mouse stories. Indeed, they have been flouted, time and again. Duckburg is identifiable as a typical small Californian or Midwestern town, within easy reach of forest and desert (like Hemet, California, where Carl Barks, the creator of the best Donald Duck stories lived); the comics are full of Americanisms, in custom and language. Detective Mickey carries a revolver when on assignment, and often gets shot at. Uncle Scrooge is often guilty of blatantly dirty business tricks, and although defined by the Specifications as "*not* a bad man", he constantly behaves in the most reprehensible manner (for which he is properly reprehended by the younger ducks). The stories are replete with the "social differences" between rich and penniless (Scrooge and Donald), between virtuous Ducks and unshaven thieves; political ideas frequently come to the fore; and, of course, natives are often characterized as dumb, ugly, inferior and criminal.

The Specifications seem to represent a fantasy on the studios' part, a fantasy of control, of a purity which was never really present. The public is supposed to think of the comics, as of Disney in general, in this way; yet the past success of the comics with the public, and their unique character vis-a-vis other comics, has undubitably depended on the prominence given to certain capitalist socio-political realities, like financial greed, dirty business tricks, and the denigration of foreign peoples.

Since a large proportion of the comics stories were always largely produced and published outside the Studios, their content has never, in fact, been under as tight control as the other Disney media. They have clearly benefitted from this. It could be argued that some of the best "non-Disney Disney" stories, those by the creator of **Uncle Scrooge**, Carl Barks, reveal more than a simplistic, wholly reactionary Disney ideology. There are elements of satire in Barks' work which one seeks in vain in any other corner of the world of Disney, just as Barks has elements of social realism which one seeks in vain in any other corner of the world of comics. One of the most intelligent students of Barks, Dave Wagner, goes so far as to say that "Barks is the only exception to the uniform reactionary

*The contradiction here is nakedly exposed in the version of the Specifications distributed by the Scandinavian Disney publishers: ". . . no social differences (poor kids, arrogant manager, humble servant) . . . Donald Duck, in relation to Uncle Scrooge, is . . . underpaid . . . grossly exploited in unpleasant jobs . . ."

tendencies of the (postwar) Disney empire."* But the relationship of Barks to the Disney comics as a whole is a problematical one; if he is responsible for the best of the Duck stories, he is not responsible for all of them, any more than he is responsible for the non-Duck stories; and even those of his stories selected for the foreign editions are sometimes subjected to subtle but significant changes of content. It could be proven that Disney's bite is worse than his Barks. The handful of U.S. critics who have addressed themselves to the Disney comic have singled out the work of Barks as the superior artist. But the picture which emerges from the U.S. perspective (whether that of a liberal, such as Mike Barrier, or a Marxist, such as Wagner) is that Barks, while in the main clearly conservative in his political philosophy, also reveals himself at times as a liberal, and represents with clarity and considerable wit, the contradictions and perhaps, even some of the anguish, from which U.S. society is suffering. Barks is thus elevated to the ranks of elite bourgeois writing and art, and it is at this level, rather than that of the mass media hack, that criticism in the U.S. addresses itself. At his best, Barks represents a self-conscious guilty bourgeois ideology, from which the mask of innocence occasionally drops (this is especially true of his later works, when he deals increasedly with certain social realities, such as foreign wars, and pollution, etc).

This outline analysis of the problem of the Disney comic and its relationship to a comparatively sophisticated U.S. audience, demands treatment in depth which I hope to undertake elsewhere. It is strictly irrelevant to the position of Dorfman and Mattelart, and to the Third World struggle for cultural independence.

* * *

Dorfman and Mattelart's book studies the Disney productions and their effects on the world. It cannot be a coincidence that much of what they observe in the relationships between the Disney characters can also be found, and maybe, even explained, in the organization of work within the Disney industry.

The system at Disney Productions seems to be designed to prevent the artist from feeling any pride, or gaining any recognition, other than corporate, for his work. Once the contract is signed, the artist's idea becomes Disney's idea. He is its owner, therefore its creator, for all purposes. It says so, black and white, in the contract: "all art work prepared for our comics magazines is considered work done for hire, and *we are the creators thereof for all purposes*" (stress added). There could hardly be a clearer statement of the manner in which the capitalist engrosses the labor of his workers. In return for a small fee or wage, he takes from them both the profit and the glory.

Walt Disney, the man who never by his own admission learned to draw, and never even tried to put pencil to paper after around 1926, who could not even sign his name as it appeared on his products, acquired the reputation of being (in the words of a justly famous and otherwise most perceptive political cartoonist) "the most significant figure in graphic art since Leonardo."** The man who ruthlessly pillaged and distorted the children's literature of the world, is hailed (in the citation for the President's Medal of Freedom, awarded to Disney in 1964) as the "creator of an American folklore." Throughout his career, Disney systematically suppressed or diminished the credit due to his artists and writers. Even when obliged by Union regulations to list them in the titles, Disney made sure his was the only name to receive real prominence. When a top animator was individually awarded an Oscar for a short, it was Disney who stepped forward to receive it.

While the world applauds Disney, it is left in ignorance of those whose work is the cornerstone of his empire: of the immensely industrious, prolific and inventive Ub Iwerks, whose technical and artistic innovations run from the multi-plane camera to the character of Mickey himself; of Ward Kimball, whose genius was admitted by Disney himself and who somehow survived Disney's stated policy of ridding the studios of "anyone showing signs of genius."*** And of course, Carl Barks, creator of Uncle Scrooge and many other favorite "Disney" characters, of over 300 of the best "Disney" comics stories, of 7,000 pages of "Disney" artwork paid at an average $11.50 per page, not one signed with his name, and selling at their peak from 3–5 million copies; while his employers, trying carefully to keep him ignorant of the true extent of this astonishing commercial success, preserved him from individual fame and from his numerous fans who enquired in vain after his name.

Disney thought of himself as a "pollinator" of people. He was indisputably a fine story editor. He knew how to coordinate labor; above all, he knew how to market ideas. In capitalist economics, both labor and ideas become his property. From the humble inker to the full-fledged animator, from the poor student working as a Disneyland trash-picker to the highly skilled "animatronics" technician, all surrender their labor to the great impresario.

Like the natives and the nephews in the comics, Disney workers must surrender to the millionaire Uncle Scrooge McDisney their treasures — the surplus value of their physical and

---

*Private communication, 4 July 1974. For Wagner's article on Barks, see "Donald Duck: An Interview" *Radical America*, VII, 1, 1973, pp. 1–19.

**David Low, "Leonardo da Disney," in the *New Republic*, 5 January 1942, pp. 16–18; reprinted in the same magazine, 22 November 1954.

***Cited in *Walt Disney*, compiled by the editors of *Wisdom*, (Beverly Hills, Calif.), XXXII, December 1959.

mental resources. To judge from the anecdotes abounding from the last years of his life, which testify to a pathological parsimony, Uncle Walt was identifying in small as well as big ways less and less with the unmaterialistic Mickey (always used as the personal and corporate symbol), and more and more with Barks' miser, McDuck.

Literature, too, has been obliged to pour its treasures into the great Disney moneybin. Disney was, as Gilbert Seldes put it many years ago, the "rapacious strip-miner" in the "goldmine of legend and myth." He ensured that the famous fairy tales became *his*: *his* Peter Pan, not Barrie's, *his* Pinocchio, not Collodi's. Authors no longer living, on whose works copyright has elapsed, are of course totally at the mercy of such a predator; but living authors also, confronted by a Disney contract, find that the law is of little avail. Even those favorable to Disney have expressed shock at the manner in which he rides roughshod over the writers of material he plans to turn into a film. The writer of at least one book original has publicly denounced Disney's brutality.* The rape is both artistic and financial, psychological and material. A typical contract with an author excludes him or her from any cut in the gross, from royalties, from any share in the "merchandizing bonanza" opened up by the successful Disney film. Disney sews up all the rights for all purposes, and usually for a paltry sum.**

In contrast, to defend the properties he amassed, Disney has always employed what his daughter termed a "regular corps of attorneys"*** whose business it is to pursue and punish any person or organization, however small, which dares to borrow a character, a technique, an idea patented by Disney. The man who expropriated so much from others will not countenance any kind of petty theft against himself. The law has successfully protected Disney against such pilfering, but in recent years, it has had a more heinous crime to deal with: theft compounded by sacrilege. Outsiders who transpose Disney characters, Disney footage or Disney comic books into unflattering contexts, are pursued by the full rigor of the law. The publisher of an "underground" poster satirizing Disney puritanism by showing his cartoon characters engaged in various kinds of sexual enterprise,**** was sued, successfully, for tens of thousands of dollars worth of damages; and an "underground" comic book artist who dared to show Mickey Mouse taking drugs, is being prosecuted in similar fashion.

Film is a collective process, essentially teamwork. A good animated cartoon requires the conjunction of many talents. Disney's longstanding public relations image of his studio as one great, happy, democratic family, is no more than a smoke screen to conceal the rigidly hierarchical structure, with very poorly paid inkers and colorers (mostly women) at the bottom of the scale, and top animators (male, of course) earning five times as much as their assistants. In one instance where a top animator objected, on behalf of his assistant, to this gross wage differential, he was fired forthwith.

People were a commodity over which Disney needed absolute control. If a good artist left the studio for another job, he was considered by Disney, if not actually as a thief who had robbed him, then as an accomplice to theft; and he was never forgiven. Disney was the authoritarian father figure, quick to punish youthful rebellion. In post-war years, however, as he grew in fame, wealth, power, and distance, he was no longer regarded by even the most innocent employee as a father figure, but as an uncle – the rich uncle. Always "Walt" to everyone, he had everyone "walt" in.***** "There's only one S.O.B. in the studio," he said, "and that's me."

For his workers to express solidarity against him was a subversion of his legitimate authority. When members of the Disney studio acted to join an AFL-CIO affiliated union, he fired them and accused them of being Communist or Communist sympathisers. Later, in the McCarthy period, he cooperated with the FBI and HUAC (House Unamerican Activities Committee) in the prosecution of an ex-employee for "Communism."

Ever since 1935, when the League of Nations recognized Mickey Mouse as an "International Symbol of Good Will", Disney has been an outspoken political figure, and one who has always been able to count upon government help. When the Second World War cut off the extremely lucrative European market, which contributed a good half of the corporate income, the U.S. government helped him turn to Latin America. Washington hastened the solution of the strike which was crippling his studio, and at a time when Disney was literally on the verge of bankruptcy, began to commission propaganda

---

*Cited in Schickel, p. 297

**Cf. Bill Davidson, "The Fantastic Walt Disney" in *Saturday Evening Post*, 7 November 1964, pp. 67–74.

***Diane Daisy Miller, *The Story of Walt Disney*, New York, 1956, p. 139ff.

****Reproduced in David Kunzle, *Posters of Protest* (catalogue for an exhibition held at the University of California, Santa Barbara, Art Galleries, February 1970), fig. 116. Even the publisher of a Japanese magazine carrying a translated extract of this work and a reproduction of the poster, has been threatened by the long arm of Disney law. Ironically, cheap pirated copies of the poster abound; I even picked one up in a bookstore in Mexico City. Its popularity in Latin America is further attested by the delight it aroused when exhibited as part of the U.S. Posters of Protest show, in the Palace of Fine Arts, Santiago de Chile (September 1972).

*****i.e. "walled in" The pun is that of a studio hand, cited in "Father Goose", *Time*, 27 December 1954, p. 42.

films, which became his mainstay for the duration of the war. Nelson Rockefeller, then Coordinator of Latin American Affairs, arranged for Disney to go as a "good-will ambassador" to the hemisphere, and make a film in order to win over hearts and minds vulnerable to Nazi propaganda. The film, called *Saludos Amigos,* quite apart from its function as a commercial for Disney, was a diplomatic lesson served upon Latin America, and one which is still considered valid today. The live-action travelogue footage of "ambassador" Disney and his artists touring the continent, is interspersed with animated sections on "life" in Brazil, Argentina, Peru and Chile, which define Latin America as the U.S. wishes to see it, and as the local peoples are supposed to see it themselves. They are symbolized by comic parrots, merry sambas, luxury beaches and goofy gauchos, and (to show that even the primitives can be modern) a little Chilean plane which braves the terrors of the Andes in order to deliver a single tourist's greeting card. The reduction of Latin America to a series of picture postcards was taken further in a later film, *The Three Caballeros*, and also permeates the comic book stories set in that part of the world.

During the Depression, Disney favorites such as Mickey Mouse and the Three Little Pigs were gratefully received by critics as fitting symbols of courageous optimism in the face of great difficulties. Disney always pooh-poohed the idea that his work contained any particular kind of political message, and proudly pointed (as proof of his innocence) to the diversity of political ideologies sympathetic to him. Mickey, noted the proud parent, was "one matter upon which the Chinese and Japanese agree." "Mr. Mussolini, Mr. King George and Mr. President Roosevelt" all loved the Mouse; and if Hitler disapproved (Nazi propaganda considered all kinds of mice, even Disney's, to be dirty creatures) — "Well," scolded Walt, "Mickey is going to save Mr. A. Hitler from drowning or something one day. Just wait and see if he doesn't. Then won't Mr. A. Hitler be ashamed!"* Come the war, however, Disney was using the Mouse not to save Hitler, but to damn him. Mickey became a favorite armed forces mascot; fittingly, the climactic event of the European war, the Normandy landings, were code-named Mickey Mouse.

Among Disney's numerous wartime propaganda films, the most controversial and in many ways the most important was *Victory through Air Power*. Undertaken on Disney's own initiative, this was designed to support Major Alexander Seversky's theory of the "effectiveness" (i.e. damage-to-cost ratio) of strategic bombing, including that of population centers. It would be unfair to project back onto Disney our own guilt over Dresden and Hiroshima, but it is noteworthy that even at the time a film critic was shocked by Disney's "gay dreams of holocaust."** And it is consistent that the maker of such a film should later give active and financial support to some noted proponents of massive strategic and terror bombing of Vietnam, such as Goldwater and Reagan. Disney's support for Goldwater in 1964 was more than the public gesture of a wealthy conservative; he went so far as to wear a Goldwater button while being invested by Johnson with the President's Medal of Freedom. In the 1959 presidential campaign, he was arrogant enough to bully his employees to give money to the Nixon campaign fund, whether they were Republicans or not.

Disney knew how to adapt to changing cultural climates. His postwar Mouse went "straight;" like the U.S., he became policeman to the world. As a comic he was supplanted by the Duck. Donald Duck represented a new kind of comedy, suited to a new age: a symbol not of courage and wit, as Mickey had been to the '30s, but an example of heroic failure, the guy whose constant efforts towards gold and glory are doomed to eternal defeat. Such a character was appropriate to the age of capitalism at its apogee, an age presented (by the media) as one of opportunity and plenty, with fabulous wealth awarded to the fortunate and the ruthless competitor, like Uncle Scrooge, and dangled as a bait before the eyes of the unfortunate and the losers in the game.

The ascendancy of the Duck family did not however mean that Mickey had lost his magic. From darkest Africa *Time* magazine reported the story of a district officer in the Belgian Congo, coming upon a group of terrified natives screaming "Mikimus." They were fleeing from a local witchdoctor, whose "usual voo had lost its do, and in the emergency, he had invoked, by making a few passes with needle and thread, the familiar spirit of that infinitely greater magician who has cast his spell upon the entire world — Walt Disney."***The natives are here cast, by *Time*, in the same degraded role assigned to them by the comics themselves.

Back home, meanwhile, the white magic of Disney seemed to be threatened by the virulent black magic of a very different kind of comic. The excesses of the "horror comic" brought a major part of the comic book industry into disrepute, and under the fierce scrutiny of moralists, educators and child psychologists all over the U.S. and Europe, who saw it as an arena for the horrors of sexual vice, sadism and extreme physical violence of all kinds.****

Disney, of course, emerged not just morally unscathed, but positively victorious. He became a model for the harmless comic demanded by the new Comics Code Authority. He was now Mr. Clean, Mr. Decency, Mr. Innocent Middle America, in an otherwise rapidly degenerating

*Cited by Schickel, p. 132.

**Schickel, p. 233.

****Time*, 27 December 1954, p. 42.

****Cf. Frederic Wertham, *Seduction of the Innocent*, 1954.

culture. He was championed by the most reactionary educational officials, such as California State Superintendant of Public Instruction, Dr. Max Rafferty, as "the greatest educator of this century — greater than John Dewey or James Conant or all the rest of us put together."* Disney meanwhile (for all his honorary degrees from Harvard, Yale, etc.) continued, as he had always done, to express public contempt for the concepts of "Education," "Intellect," "Art," and the very idea that he was "teaching" anybody anything.

The public Disney myth has been fabricated not only from the man's works but also from autobiographical data and personal pronouncements. Disney never separated himself from his work; and there are certain formative circumstances of his life upon which he himself liked to enlarge, and which through biographies and interviews, have contributed to the public image of both Disney and Disney Productions. This public image was also the man's self-image; and both fed into and upon a dominant North American self-image. A major part of his vast audience interpret their lives as he interpreted his. His innocence is their innocence, and vice-versa; his rejection of reality is theirs; his yearning for purity is theirs too. Their aspirations are the same as his; they, like he, started out in life poor, and worked hard in order to become rich; and if he became rich and they didn't, well, maybe luck just wasn't on their side.

* * *

Walter Elias Disney was born in Chicago in 1901. When he was four, his father, who had been unable to make a decent living in that city as a carpenter and small building contractor, moved to a farm near Marceline, Missouri. Later, Walt was to idealize life there, and remember it as a kind of Eden (although he had to help in the work), as a necessary refuge from the evil world, for he agreed with his father that "after boys reached a certain age they are best removed from the corruptive influences of the big city and subjected to the wholesome atmosphere of the country.**

But after four years of unsuccessful farming, Elias Disney sold his property, and the family returned to the city — this time, Kansas City. There, in addition to his schooling, the eight year old Walt was forced by his father into brutally hard, unpaid work*** as a newspaper delivery boy, getting up at 3:30 every morning and walking for hours in dark, snowbound streets. The memory haunted him all his life. His father was also in the habit of giving him, for no good reason, beatings with a leather strap, to which Walt submitted "to humor him and keep him happy." This phrase in itself suggests a conscious attempt, on the part of the adult, to avoid confronting the oppressive reality of his childhood.

Walt's mother, meanwhile, is conspicuously absent from his memories, as is his younger sister. All his three elder brothers ran away from home, and it is a remarkable fact that after he became famous, Walt Disney had nothing to do with either of his parents, or, indeed, any of his family except Roy. His brother Roy, eight years older than himself and throughout his career his financial manager, was from the very beginning a kind of parent substitute, an uncle father-figure. The elimination of true parents, especially the mother, from the comics, and the incidence in the films of mothers dead at the start, or dying in the course of events, or cast as wicked stepmothers (*Bambi, Snow White* and expecially *Dumbo*);****must have held great personal meaning for Disney. The theme has of course long been a constant of world folk-literature, but the manner in which it is handled by Disney may tell us a great deal about 20th century bourgeois culture. Peculiar to Disney comics, surely, is the fact that the mother is not even, technically, missing; she is simply non-existent as a concept. It is possible that Disney truly hated his childhood, and feared and resented his parents, but could never admit it, seeking through his works to escape from the bitter social realities associated with his upbringing. If he hated being a child, one can also understand why he always insisted that his films and amusement parks were designed in the first place for adults, not children, why he was pleased at the statistics which showed that for every one child visitor to Disneyland, there were four adults, and why he always complained at getting the awards for Best *Children's* Film.

As Dorfman and Mattelart show, the child in the Disney comic is really a mask for adult anxieties; he is an adult self-image. Most critics are agreed that Disney shows little or no understanding of the "real child," or real childhood psychology and problems.

Disney has also, necessarily, eliminated the biological link between the parent and child — sexuality. The raunchy touch, the barnyard humor of his early films, has long since been sanitized. Disney was the only man in Hollywood to whom you could not tell a dirty joke. His sense of humor, if it existed at all (and many writers on the man have expressed doubts on this

---

*Schickel, p. 298.

**Cited in Schickel, p. 35.

***i.e. his father added the money he earned to the household budget. Newspaper delivery is one of the few legally sanctioned forms of child labor still surviving today. Most parents nowadays (presumably) let their children keep the money they earn, and regard the job as a useful form of early ideological training, in which the child learns the value and necessity of making a minute personal "profit" out of the labor which enriches the millionaire newspaper publisher.

****According to Richard Schickel, *Dumbo* is "the most overt statement of a theme that is implicit in almost all the Disney features — the absence of a mother" (p. 225).

score) was always of a markedly "bathroom" or anal kind. Coy anality is the Disney substitute for sexuality; this is notorious in the films, and observable in the comics also. The world of Disney, inside and outside the comics, is a male one. The Disney organization excludes women from positions of importance. Disney freely admitted "Girls bored me. They still do."* He had very few intimate relationships with women; his daughter's biography contains no hint that there was any real intimacy even within the family circle. Walt's account of his courtship of his wife establishes it as a purely commercial transaction.** Walt had hired Lillian Bounds as an inker because she would work for less money than anyone else; he married her (when his brother Roy married, and moved out) because he needed a new room-mate, and a cook.

But just as Disney avoided the reality of sex and children, so he avoided that of nature. The man who made the world's most publicized nature films, whose work expresses a yearning to return to the purity of natural, rustic living, avoided the countryside. He hardly ever left Los Angeles. His own garden at home was filled with railroad tracks and stock (this was his big hobby). He was interested in nature only in order to tame it, control it, cleanse it. Disneyland and Walt Disney World are monuments to his desire for total control of his environment, and at the end of his life he was planning to turn vast areas of California's loveliest "unspoiled" mountains, at Mineral King, into a 35 million dollar playground. He had no sense of the special non-human character of animals, or of the wilderness; his concern with nature was to anthropomorphize it.

Disney liked to claim that his genius, his creativity "sprouted from mother earth."*** Nature was the source of his genius, his genius was the source of his wealth, and his wealth grew like a product of nature, like corn. What made his golden cornfield grow? Dollars. "Dollars," said Disney, in a remark worthy of Uncle Scrooge McDuck, "are like fertiliser – they make things grow."****

As Dorfman and Mattelart observe, it is Disney's ambition to render the past like the present, and the present like the past, and project both onto the future. Disney has patented – "sewn up all the rights on" – tomorrow as well as today. For, in the jargon of the media, "he has made tomorrow come true today," and "enables one to actually experience the future." His future is currently taking shape in Walt Disney World in Orlando, Florida; an amusement park which covers an area of once virgin land twice the size of Manhattan, which in its first year attracted 10.7 million visitors (about the number who visit Washington, D.C. annually). With its own laws, it is a state within a state. It boasts of the fifth largest submarine fleet in the world. Distinguished bourgeois architects, town planners, critics and land speculators have hailed Walt Disney World as the solution to the problems of our cities, a prototype for living in the future. EPCOT (Experimental Prototype Community of Tomorrow), now in the course of construction, will be, in the words of a well-known critic***** "a *working* community, a vast, living, ever-changing laboratory of urban design . . . (which) understandably . . . evades a good many problems – housing, schools, employment, politics and so on . . . They are in the fun business." Of course.

The Disney parks have brought the fantasies of the "future" and the "fun" of the comics one step nearer to capitalist "reality." "In Disneyland (the happiest place on earth)," says Public Relations, "you can encounter 'wild' animals and native 'savages' who often display their hostility to your invasion of their jungle privacy . . . From stockades in Adventureland, you can actually shoot at Indians."

Meanwhile, out there in the *real* real world, the "savages" *are* fighting back.

*Schickel, p. 48. Cf. "Top management's roster lists very few Jews, very few Catholics. No blacks. No women." cited by D. Keith Mono. "A Real Mickey Mouse Operation" *Playboy*, December 1973, p. 328.

**His daughter's words (Miller, op. cit., p. 98) bear repeating: "Father (was) a low-pressure swain with a relaxed selling technique. That's the way he described it to me . . . (he was) an unabashed sentimentalist . . . (but) to hear him talk about marrying Mother, you'd think he was after a lifetime's supply of her sister's fried chicken." His proposal came in this form: " 'Which do you think we ought to pay for first, the car or the ring?' " They bought the ring, and on the cheap, because it was probably "hot" (stolen). According to *Look* magazine (15 July 1955, p. 29), "Lillian Bounds was paid so little, she sometimes didn't bother to cash her paycheck. This endeared her greatly to Roy . . . (who) urged Walt to use his charm to persuade the lady to cash even fewer checks."

****Time*, 27 December 1954, p. 42.

*****Newsweek*, 31 December 1962, pp. 48–51.

*****Peter Blake, in an article for the *Architectural Forum*, June 1972 (Stress added).

HOW TO READ DONALD DUCK

APOLOGY FOR DUCKOLOGY

The reader of this book may feel disconcerted, not so much because one of his idols turns out to have feet of clay, but rather because the kind of language we use here is intended to break with the false solemnity which generally cloaks scientific investigation. In order to attain knowledge, which is a form of power, we cannot continue to endorse, with blinded vision and stilted jargon, the initiation rituals with which our spiritual high priests seek to legitimize and protect their exclusive privileges of thought and expression. Even when denouncing prevailing fallacies, investigators tend to fall with their language into the same kind of mystification which they hope to destroy. This fear of breaking the confines of language, of the future as a conscious force of the imagination, of a close and lasting contact with the reader, this dread of appearing insignificant and naked before one's particular limited public, betrays an aversion for life and for reality as a whole. We do not want to be like the scientist who takes his umbrella with him to go study the rain.

We are not about to deny scientific rationalism. Nor do we aspire to some clumsy popularization. What we do hope to achieve is a more direct and practical means of communication, and to reconcile pleasure with knowledge.

The best critical endeavor incorporates, apart from its analysis of reality, a degree of methodological self-criticism. The problem here is not one of relative complexity or simplicity, but one of bringing the terms of criticism itself under scrutiny.

Readers will judge this experiment for themselves, preferably in an active, productive manner. It results from a joint effort; that of two researchers who until now have observed the preordained limits of their respective disciplines, the humanistic and social sciences, and who found themselves obliged to change their methods of interpretation and communication. Some, from the bias of their individualism, may rake this book over sentence by sentence, carving it up, assigning this part to that person, in the hopes of maybe restoring that social division of intellectual labor which leaves them so comfortably settled in their armchair or university chair. This work is not to be subjected to a letter-by-letter breakdown by some hysterical computer, but to be considered a joint effort of conception and writing.

Furthermore, it is part of an effort to achieve a wider, more massive distribution of the basic ideas contained in this book. Unfortunately, these ideas are not always easily accessible to all of the readers we would like to reach, given the educational level of our people. This is especially the case since the criticism contained in the book cannot follow the same popular channels which the bourgeoisie controls to propagate its own values.

We are grateful to the students of CEREN (Centro de Estudios de la Realidad Nacional, Center for the Study of Chilean Society, at the Catholic University), and to the seminar on "Subliterature and Ways to Combat it" (Department of Spanish, University of Chile) for the constant individual and collective contributions to our work.

Ariel Dorfman, member of the Juvenile and Educational Publications Division of Quimantú*, was able to participate in the development of this book thanks to the assignment offered to him by the Department of Spanish at the University of Chile. Armand Mattelart, head of Quimantú's Investigation and Evaluation of the Mass Media Section, and Research Professor of CEREN, participated in the book thanks to a similar dispensation.

4 September 1971,
First anniversary of the triumph of the
Popular Unity Government

* Popular Unity Government Printing House.

INTRODUCTION: INSTRUCTIONS ON HOW TO BECOME A GENERAL IN THE DISNEYLAND CLUB

"My dog has become a famous lifeguard and my nephews will be brigadier-generals. To what greater honor can one aspire?"

Donald Duck (D 422*)

"Baby frogs will be *big* frogs someday, which bring high prices on the market . . . I'm going to fix some special *frog food* and speed up the growth of those little hoppers!"

Donald Duck (D 451, CS 5/60)

It would be wrong to assume that Walt Disney is merely a business man. We are all familiar with the massive merchandising of his characters in films, watches, umbrellas, records, soaps, rocking chairs, neckties, lamps, etc. There are Disney strips in five thousand newspapers, translated into more than thirty languages, spread over a hundred countries. According to the magazine's own publicity puffs, in Chile alone, Disney comics reach and delight each week over a million readers. The former Zig-Zag Company, now bizarrely converted into Pinsel Publishing Enterprise (Juvenile Publications Company Ltd.), supplies them to a major part of the Latin American continent. From their national base of operations, where there is so much screaming about the trampling underfoot (the suppression, intimidation, restriction, repression, curbing, etc.)

*We use the following abbreviations: D = *Disneylandia*, F = *Fantasias*, TR = *Tio Rico* (Scrooge McDuck), TB = *Tribilin* (Goofy). These magazines are published in Chile by Empresa Editorial Zig-Zag (now Pinsel), with an average of two to four large- and medium-sized stories per issue. We obtained all available back issues and purchased current issues during the months following March 1971. Our sample is thus inevitably somewhat random:

Disneylandia: 185, 192, 210, 281, 292, 294, 297, 303, 329, 342, 347, 357, 364, 367, 370, 376, 377, 379, 381, 382, 383, 393, 400, 401, 421, 422, 423, 424, 431, 432, 433, 434, 436, 437, 439, 440, 441, 443, 444, 445, 446, 447, 448, 449, 451, 452, 453, 454, 455, 457.

Tio Rico: 40, 48, 53, 57, 61, 96, 99, 106, 108, 109, 110, 111, 113, 115, 116, 117, 119, 120, 128.

Fantasias: 57, 60, 68, 82, 140, 155, 160, 165, 168, 169, 170, 173, 174, 175, 176, 177, 178.

Tribilin: 62, 65, 78, 87, 92, 93, 96, 99, 100, 101, 103, 104, 106, 107.

(Translator's Note: Stories for which I have been able to locate the U.S. originals are coded thus: CS = (*Walt Disney's*) *Comics and Stories*; DA = *Duck Album*; DD = *Donald Duck*; GG = *Gyro Gearloose*; HDL = *Huey, Dewey and Louie, Junior Woodchucks*; and US = *Uncle Scrooge*.

The figures following represent the original date of issue; thus 7/67 means July 1967. Sometimes, however, when there is no monthly date, the issue number appears followed by the year.)

of the liberty of the press, this consortium, controlled by financiers and "philanthropists" of the previous Christian Democrat regime (1964-70), has just permitted itself the luxury of converting several of its publications from biweeklies to weekly magazines.

Apart from his stock exchange rating, Disney has been exalted as the inviolable common cultural heritage of contemporary man; his characters have been incorporated into every home, they hang on every wall, they decorate objects of every kind; they constitute a little less than a social environment inviting us all to join the great universal Disney family, which extends beyond all frontiers and ideologies, transcends differences between peoples and nations, and particularities of custom and language. Disney is the great supranational bridge across which all human beings may communicate with each other. And amidst so much sweetness and light, the registered trademark becomes invisible.

Disney is part – an immortal part, it would seem – of our common collective vision. It has been observed that in more than one country Mickey Mouse is more popular than the national hero of the day.

In Central America, AID (the U.S. Agency for International Development) – sponsored films promoting contraception feature the characters from "Magician of Fantasy." In Chile, after the earthquake of July 1971, the children of San Bernardo sent Disneyland comics and sweets to their stricken fellow children of San Antonio. And the year before, a Chilean women's magazine proposed giving Disney the Nobel Peace Prize.*

We need not be surprised, then, that any innuendo about the world of Disney should be interpreted as an affront to morality and civilization at large. Even to whisper anything against Walt is to undermine the happy and innocent palace of childhood, for which he is both guardian and guide.

No sooner had the first children's magazine been issued by the Chilean Popular Unity Government publishing house Quimantú, than the reactionary journals sprang to the defense of Disney:

"The voice of a newscaster struck deep into the microphone of a radio station in the capital. To the amazement of his listeners he announced that Walt Disney is to be banned in Chile. The government propaganda experts have come to the conclusion that Chilean children should not think, feel, love or suffer through animals.

"So, in place of Scrooge McDuck, Donald and nephews, instead of Goofy and Mickey Mouse, we children and grownups will have to get used to reading about our own society, which, to judge from the way it is painted by the writers and panegyrists of our age, is rough, bitter, cruel and hateful. It was Disney's magic to be able to stress the happy side of life, and there are always, in human society, characters who resemble those of Disney comics.

"Scrooge McDuck is the miserly millionaire of any country in the world, hoarding his money and suffering a heart attack every time someone tries to pinch a cent off him, but in spite of it all, capable of revealing human traits which redeem him in his nephews' eyes.

"Donald is the eternal enemy of work and lives dependent upon his powerful uncle. Goofy is the innocent and guileless common man, the eternal victim of his own clumsiness, which hurts no one and is always good for a laugh.

"Big Bad Wolf and Little Wolf are masterly means of teaching children pleasantly, not hatefully, the difference between good and evil. For Big Bad Wolf himself, when he gets a chance to gobble up the Three Little Pigs, suffers pangs of conscience and is unable to do his wicked deed.

"And finally, Mickey Mouse is Disney in a nutshell. What human being over the last forty years, at the mere presence of Mickey, has not felt his heart swell with emotion? Did we not see him once as the "Sorcerer's Apprentice" in an unforgettable cartoon which was the delight of children and grownups, which preserved every single note of the masterly music of Prokoviev [a reference no doubt to the music of Paul Dukas]. And what of *Fantasia*, that prodigious feat of cinematic art, with musicians, orchestras, decorations, flowers, and

* "At the time of his death (1966), a small, informal but worldwide group was promoting – with the covert assistance of his publicity department – his nomination for the Nobel Peace prize" (from Richard Schickel, *The Disney Version*, New York, 1968, p. 303). San Bernardo is a working-class suburb of greater Santiago; San Antonio a port in the central zone. (Trans.)

every animate being moving to the baton of Leopold Stokowski? And one scene, of the utmost splendor and realism, even showed elephants executing the most elegant performance of "The Dance of the Dragonflies" [a reference no doubt to the "Dance of the hours"].

"How can one assert that children do not learn from talking animals? Have they not been observed time and again engaging in tender dialogues with their pet dogs and cats, while the latter adapt to their masters and show with a purr or a twitch of the ears their understanding of the orders they are given? Are not fables full of valuable lessons in the way animals can teach us how to behave under the most difficult circumstances?

"There is one, for instance, by Tomas de Iriarte which serves as a warning against the danger of imposing too stringent principles upon those who work for the public. The mass does not always blindly accept what is offered to them."*

This pronouncement parrots some of the ideas prevailing in the media about childhood and children's literature. Above all, there is the implication that politics cannot enter into areas of "pure entertainment," especially those designed for children of tender years. Children's games have their own rules and laws, they move, supposedly, in an autonomous and asocial sphere like the Disney characters, with a psychology peculiar to creatures at a "privileged" age. Inasmuch as the sweet and docile child can be sheltered effectively from the evils of existence, from the petty rancors, the hatreds, and the political or ideological contamination of his elders, any attempt to politicize the sacred domaine of childhood threatens to introduce perversity where there once reigned happiness, innocence and fantasy. Since animals are also exempt from the vicissitudes of history and politics, they are convenient symbols of a world beyond socio-economic realities, and the animal characters can represent ordinary human types, common to all classes, countries and epochs. Disney thus establishes a moral background which draws the child down the proper ethical and aesthetic path. It is cruel and unnecessary to tear it away from its magic garden, for it is ruled by the Laws of Mother Nature; children *are* just like that and the makers of comic books, in their infinite wisdom, understand their behavior and their biologically-determined need for harmony. Thus, to attack Disney is to reject the unquestioned stereotype of the child, sanctified as the law in the name of the immutable human condition.

There are *automagic*** antibodies in Disney. They tend to neutralize criticism because they are the same values already instilled into people, in the tastes, reflexes and attitudes which inform everyday experience at all levels. Disney manages to subject these values to the extremest degree of commercial exploitation. The potential assailer is thus condemned in advance by what is known as "public opinion," that is, the thinking of people who have already been conditioned by the Disney message and have based their social and family life upon it.

The publication of this book will of course provoke a rash of hostile comment against the authors. To facilitate our adversaries' task, and in order to lend uniformity to their criteria, we offer the following model, which has been drawn up with due consideration for the philosophy of the journals to which the gentlemen of the press are so attached:

INSTRUCTIONS ON HOW TO EXPEL SOMEONE FROM THE DISNEYLAND CLUB

1. The authors of this book are to be defined as follows: indecent and immoral (while Disney's world is pure); hyper-complicated and hyper-sophisticated (while Walt is simple, open and sincere); members of a sinister elite (while Disney is the most popular man in the world); political agitators (while Disney is non-partisan, above politics); calculating and embittered (while Walt D. is spontaneous, emotional, loves to laugh and make laughter); subverters of youth and domestic peace (while W.D. teaches respect for parents, love of one's fellows and protection of

La Segunda (Santiago), 20 July 1971, p. 3. This daily belongs to the Mercurio group, which is controlled by Augustin Edwards, the major press and industrial monopolist in Chile. The writer of the article quoted worked as Public Relations officer for the American copper companies Braden and Kennecott. (cf. A. Mattelart "Estructura del poder informativo y dependencia" in "Los Medios de Comunicación de Masas: La Ideologia de la Prensa Liberal en Chile" *Cuadernos de la Realidad Nacional* (CEREN, Santiago), 3, Marzo de 1970).

** A word-play on the advertising slogan for a washing machine, which cleans "automagicamente" (automatically and magically) — Trans.

the weak); unpatriotic and antagonistic to the national spirit (while Mr Disney, being international, represents the best and dearest of our native traditions); and finally, cultivators of "Marxism-fiction," a theory imported from abroad by "wicked foreigners"* (while Unca Walt is against exploitation and promotes the classless society of the future).

2. Next, the authors of this book are to be accused of the very lowest of crimes: of daring to raise doubts about the child's imagination, that is, O horror!, to question the right of children to have a literature of their own, which interprets them so well, and is created on their behalf.

3. FINALLY, TO EXPEL SOMEONE FROM THE DISNEYLAND CLUB, ACCUSE HIM REPEATEDLY OF TRYING TO BRAINWASH CHILDREN WITH THE DOCTRINE OF COLORLESS SOCIAL REALISM, IMPOSED BY POLITICAL COMMISSARS.

There can be no doubt that children's literature is a genre like any other, monopolized by specialized subsectors within the culture industry. Some dedicate themselves to the adventure story, some to mystery, others to the erotic novel, etc. But at least the latter are directed towards an amorphous public, which buys at random. In the case of the children's genre, however, there is a virtually biologically captive, predetermined audience.

Children's comics are devised by adults, whose work is determined and justified by their idea of what a child is or should be. Often, they even cite "scientific" sources or ancient traditions ("it is popular wisdom, dating from time immemorial") in order to explain the nature of the public's needs. In reality, however, these adults are not about to tell stories which would jeopardize the future they are planning for their children.

So the comics show the child as a miniature adult, enjoying an idealized, gilded infancy which is really nothing but the adult projection of some magic era beyond the reach of the harsh discord of daily life. It is a plan for salvation which presupposes a primal stage within every existence, sheltered from contradictions and permitting imaginative escape. Juvenile literature, embodying purity, spontaneity, and natural virtue, while lacking in sex and violence, represents earthly paradise. It guarantees man's own redemption as an adult: as long as there are children, he will have the pretext and means for self-gratification with the spectacle of his own dreams. In his children's reading, man stages and performs over and over again the supposedly unproblematical scenes of his inner refuge. Regaling himself with his own legend, he falls into tautology; he admires himself in the mirror, thinking it to be a window. But the child playing down there in the garden is the purified adult looking back at himself.

So it is the adult who produces the comics, and the child who consumes them. The role of the apparent child actor, who reigns over this uncontaminated world, is at once that of audience and dummy for his father's ventriloquism. The father denies his progeny a voice of his own, and as in any authoritarian society, he establishes himself as the other's sole interpreter and spokesman. All the little fellow can do is to let his father represent him.

But wait a minute, gentlemen! Perhaps children really *are* like that?

Indeed, the adults set out to prove that this literature is essential to the child, satisfying his eager demands. But this is a closed circuit: children have been conditioned by the magazines and the culture which spawned them. They tend to reflect in their daily lives the characteristics they are supposed to possess, in order to win affection, acceptance, and rewards; in order to grow up properly and integrate into society. The Disney world is sustained by rewards and punishments; it hides an iron hand with the velvet glove. Considered, by definition, unfit to choose from the alternatives available to adults, the youngsters intuit "natural" behavior, happily accepting that their imagination be channelled into incontestable ethical and aesthetic ideals. Juvenile literature is justified by the children it has generated through a vicious circle.

Thus,adults create for themselves a childhood embodying their own angelical aspirations, which offer consolation, hope and a guarantee of a "better," but unchanging, future. This "new reality," this autonomous realm of magic, is artfully isolated from the reality of the everyday. Adult values are projected onto the child, as if childhood was a special domaine where these values could be protected uncritically. In Disney, the two strata —adult and child— are not to be considered as antagonistic; they fuse in a single embrace, and history becomes biology. The identity of parent and child inhibits the emer-

*Actual words of Little Wolf (D 210)

gence of true generational conflicts. The pure child will replace the corrupt father, preserving the latter's values. The future (the child) reaffirms the present (the adult), which, in turn, transmits the past. The apparent independence which the father benevolently bestows upon this little territory of his creation, is the very means of assuring his supremacy.

But there is more: this lovely, simple, smooth, translucent, chaste and pacific region, which has been promoted as Salvation, is unconsciously infiltrated by a multiplicity of adult conflicts and contradictions. This transparent world is designed both to conceal and reveal latent traces of real and painful tensions. The parent suffers this split consciousness without being aware of his inner turmoil. Nostalgically, he appropriates the "natural disposition" of the child in order to conceal the guilt arising from his own fall from grace; it is the price of redemption for his own condition. By the standards of his angelic model, he must judge himself guilty; as much as he needs this land of enchantment and salvation, he could never imagine it with the necessary purity. He could never turn into his own child. But this salvation only offers him an imperfect escape; it can never be so pure as to block off all his real life problems.

In juvenile literature, the adult, corroded by the trivia of everyday life blindly defends his image of youth and innocence. Because of this, it is perhaps the best (and least expected) place to study the disguises and truths of contemporary man. For the adult, in protecting his dream-image of youth, hides the fear that to penetrate it would destroy his dreams and reveal the reality it conceals.

Thus, *the imagination of the child is conceived as the past and future utopia of the adult.* But set up as an inner realm of fantasy, this model of his Origin and his Ideal Future Society lends itself to the free assimilation of all his woes. It enables the adult to partake of his own demons, provided they have been coated in the syrup of paradise, and that they travel there with the passport of innocence.

Mass culture has granted to contemporary man, in his constant need to visualize the reality about him, the means of feeding on his own problems without having to encounter all the difficulties of form and content presented by the modern art and literature of the elite. Man is offered knowledge without commitment, a self-colonization of his own imagination. By dominating the child, the father dominates himself. The relationship is a sado-masochistic one, not unlike that established between Donald and his nephews. Similarly, readers find themselves caught between their desire and their reality, and in their attempt to escape to a purer realm, they only travel further back into their own traumas.

Mass culture has opened up a whole range of new issues. While it certainly has had a levelling effect and has exposed a wider audience to a broader range of themes, it has simultaneously generated a cultural elite which has cut itself off more and more from the masses. Contrary to the democratic potential of mass culture, this elite has plunged mass culture into a suffocating complexity of solutions, approaches and techniques, each of which is comprehensible only to a narrow circle of readers. The creation of children's culture is part of this specialization process.

Child fantasy, although created by adults, becomes the exclusive reserve of children. The self-exiled father, once having created this specialized imaginary world, then revels in it through the keyhole. The father must be absent, and without direct jurisdiction, just as the child is without direct obligations. Coercion melts away in the magic palace of sweet harmony and repose – the palace raised and administered at a distance by the father, whose physical absence is designed to avoid direct confrontation with his progeny. This absence is the prerequisite of his omnipresence, his total invasion. Physical presence would be superfluous, even counterproductive, since the whole magazine is already his projection. He shows up instead as a favorite uncle handing out free magazines. Juvenile literature is a father surrogate. The model of paternal authority is at every point immanent, the implicit basis of its structure and very existence. The natural creativity of the child, which no one in his right mind can deny, is channelled through the apparent absence of the father into an adult-authoritarian vision of the real world. Paternalism *in absentia* is the indispensable vehicle for the defense and invisible control of the ostensibly autonomous childhood model. The comics, like television, in all vertically structured societies, rely upon distance as a means of authoritarian reinforcement.

The authoritarian relationship between the real life parent and child is repeated and reinforced within the fantasy world itself, and is the basis for all relations in the entire world of the comics. Later, we shall show how the relationship of child-readers to the magazine they con-

sume is generally based on and echoed in the way the characters experience their own fantasy world within the comic. Children will not only identify with Donald Duck because Donald's situation relates to their own life, but also because the way they read or the way they are exposed to it, imitates and prefigures the way Donald Duck lives out his own problems. Fiction reinforces, in a circular fashion, the manner in which the adult desires the comic be received and read.

Now that we have peeked into the parent-child relationship, let us be initiated into the Disney world, beginning with the great family of ducks and mice.

I. UNCLE, BUY ME A CONTRACEPTIVE . . .

Daisy: "If you teach me to skate this afternoon, I will give you something you have always wanted."
Donald: "You mean . . ."
Daisy: "Yes . . . My 1872 coin."
Nephews: "Wow! That would complete our coin collection, Unca Donald."

(D 433)

There is one basic product which is never stocked in the Disney store: parents. Disney's is a universe of uncles and grand-uncles, nephews and cousins; the male-female relationship is that of eternal fiancés. Scrooge McDuck is Donald's uncle, Grandma Duck is Donald's aunt (but not Scrooge's wife), and Donald is the uncle of Huey, Dewey, and Louie. Cousin Gladstone Gander is a "distant nephew" of Scrooge; he has a nephew of his own called Shamrock, who has two female cousins (DA 649, 1955). Then there are the more distant ancestors like grand-uncle Swashbuckle Duck, and Asa Duck, the great-great-great uncle of Grandma Duck; and (most distant of all) Don de Pato, who was associated with the Spanish Armada (DD 9/65). The various cousins include Gus Goose, Grandma Duck's idle farmhand, Moby Duck the sailor, and an exotic oriental branch with a Sheik and Mazuma Duck, "the richest bird in South Afduckstan," with nephews. The genealogy is tipped decisively in favor of the masculine sector. The ladies are spinsters, with the sole exception of Grandma Duck who is apparently widowed without her husband having died, since he appears just once (D 424) under the suggestive title "History Repeats Itself." There are also the cow Clarabelle (with a short-lived cousin, F 57), the hen Clara Cluck, the witch Magica de Spell, and naturally Minnie and Daisy, who, being the girl friends of the most important characters are accompanied by nieces of their own (Daisy's are called April, May, and June; she also has an uncle of her own, Uncle Dourduck, and Aunts Drusilla and Tizzy).

Since these women are not very susceptible to men or matrimonial bonds, the masculine sector is necessarily and perpetually composed of bachelors accompanied by nephews, who come and go. Mickey has Morty and Ferdy, Goofy has Gilbert (and an uncle "Tribilio," F 176), and Gyro Gearloose has Newton; even the Beagle Boys have uncles, aunts and nephews called the Beagle Brats (whose female cousins, the Beagle Babes, make the occasional appearance). It is predictable that any future demographic increase will have to be the result of extra-sexual factors.

Even more remarkable is the duplication — and triplication — in the baby department. There are four sets of triplets in this world: the nephews of Donald and the Beagle Boys, the nieces of Daisy, and the inevitable three piglets.

The quantity of twins is greater still. Mickey's nephews are an example, but the majority proliferate without attribution to any uncle: the chipmunks Chip and Dale, the mice Gus and Jaq. This is all the more significant in that there are innumerable other examples outside of Disney: Porky and Petunia and nephews; Woody Woodpecker and nephews; and the little pair of mice confronting the cat Tom.

The exception — Scamp and Big Bad Wolf — will be considered separately.

In this bleak world of family clans and solitary pairs, subject to the archaic prohibition of marriage within the tribe, and where each and every one has his own mortgaged house but never a home, the last vestige of parenthood, male or female, has been eliminated.

The advocates of Disney manage a hasty rationalization of these features into proof of innocence, chastity and proper restraint. Without resorting polemically to a thesis on infant sexual education already outmoded in the nineteenth century, and more suited to monastic cave dwellers than civilized people (admire our mercurial* style), it is evident that the absence of father and mother is not a matter of chance. One is forced to the paradoxical conclusion that in order to conceal normal sexuality from children, it is necessary to construct an aberrant world — one which, moreover (as we shall see later), suggestive of sexual games and innuendo. One may wrack one's brains trying to figure out the educational value of so many uncles and cousins; persumably they help eradicate the wicked taint of infant sexuality. But there are other reasons.

The much vaunted and very inviting fantasy world of Disney systematically cuts the earthly roots of his characters. Their charm supposedly lies in their familiarity, their resemblance to ordinary, common or garden variety of people who cross our path every day. But, in Disney, characters only function by virtue of a suppression of *real* and concrete factors; that is, their personal history, their birth and death, and their whole development in between, as they grow and change. Since they are not engendered by any biological act, Disney characters may aspire to immortality: whatever apparent, momentary sufferings are inflicted on them in the course of their adventures, they have been liberated, at least, from the curse of the body.

By eliminating a character's effective past, and at the same time denying him the opportunity of self-examination in respect to his present predicament, Disney denies him the only perspective from which he can look at himself, other than from the world in which he has always been submerged. The future cannot serve him either: reality is unchanging.

The generation gap is not only obliterated between the child, who reads the comic, and the parent, who buys it, but also within the comic itself by a process of substitution in which the uncles can always be replaced by the nephews. Since there is no father, constant replacement and displacement of the uncle is painless. Since he is not genetically responsible for the youngster, it is not treasonable to overrule him. It is as if the uncle were never really king, an appropriate term since we are dealing with fairy tales, but only regent, watching over the throne until its legitimate heir, the young Prince Charming, eventually comes to assume it.

But the physical absence of the father does not mean the absence of paternal power. Far from it, the relations between Disney characters are much more vertical and authoritarian than those of the most tyrannical real life home, where a harsh discipline can still be softened by sharing, love, mother, siblings, solidarity, and mutual aid. Moreover, in the real life home, the maturing child is always exposed to new alternatives and standards of behavior, as he responds to pressures from outside the family. But since power in Disney is wielded not by a father, but by an uncle, it becomes arbitrary.

Patriarchy in our society is defended, by the patriarchs, as a matter of biological predetermination (undoubtedly sustained by a social structure which institutionalizes the education of the child as primarily a family responsibility). Uncle-authority, on the other hand, not having been conferred by the father (the uncle's brothers and sisters, who must in theory have given birth to the nephews, simply do not exist), is of purely *de facto* origin, rather than a natural right. It is a contractual relationship masquerading as a natural relationship, a tyranny which does not even assume the responsibility of breeding. And one cannot rebel against it in the name of nature; one cannot say to an uncle "you

*"Mercurial" — akin to the style of *El Mercurio*, noted for its pompous moralism. (Trans.)

are a bad father."

Within this family perimeter, no one loves anyone else, there is never an expression of affection or loyalty towards another human being. In any moment of suffering, a person is alone; there is no disinterested or friendly helping hand. One encounters, at best, a sense of pity, derived from a view of the other as some cripple or beggar, some old down-and-out deserving of our charity. Let us take the most extreme example: the famous love between Mickey and Pluto. Although Mickey certainly shows a charitable kind of affection for his dog, the latter is always under the obligation to demonstrate his usefulness and heroism. In one episode (D 381), having behaved very badly and having been locked up in the cellar as punishment, Pluto redeems himself by catching a thief (there is always one around). The police give Mickey a hundred-dollar reward, and offer another hundred to buy the dog itself, but Mickey refuses to sell: "O.K. Pluto, you cost me around fifty dollars in damages this afternoon, but this reward leaves me with a good profit." Commercial relations are common coin here, even in so "maternal" a bond as that between Mickey and his bloodhound.

With Scrooge McDuck, it is of course worse. In one episode, the nephews, exhausted after six months scouring the Gobi desert on Scrooge's behalf, are upbraided for having taken so long, and are paid one dollar for their pains. They flee thankfully, in fear of yet more forced labor. It never occurs to them to object, to stay put and to demand better treatment.

But McDuck obliges them to depart once more, sick as they are, in search of a coin weighing several tons, for which the avaricious millionaire is evidently prepared to pay a few cents (TR 106, US 10/69). It turns out that the gigantic coin is a forgery and Scrooge has to buy the authentic one. Donald smiles in relief; "Now that you have the true Hunka Junka, Uncle Scrooge, we can all take a rest." The tyrant replies: "Not until you return that counterfeit hunk of junk and bring back my pennies!" The ducks are depicted in the last picture like slaves in ancient Egypt, pushing the rock to its destiny at the other end of the globe. Instead of coming to the realization that he ought to open his mouth to say *no*, Donald reaches the very opposite conclusion: "Me and my big mouth!" Not even a complaint is permitted against this unquestioned supremacy. What are the consequences of Daisy's Aunt Tizzy discovering a year later that Daisy had dared to attend a dance she disapproved of? "I'm going . . . and I am cutting *you* out of my will, Daisy! Goodbye!" (D 383, DD 7/67).

There is no room for love in this world. The youngsters admire a distant uncle (Unca Zak McWak) who invented a "spray to kill apple-worms." (D 455, DD 5/68). "The whole world is thankful to him for that . . . He's famous . . . and rich," the nephews exclaim. Donald sensibly replies "Bah! *Brains, fame*, and *fortune* aren't *everything.*" "Oh, no? What's left?" ask Huey, Dewey and Louie in unison. And Donald is at a loss for words: "er . . . um . . . let's see now . . . uh-h . . ."

So the child's "natural disposition" evidently serves Disney only insofar as it lends innocence to the adult world, and serves the myth of childhood. Meanwhile, it has been stripped of the true qualities of children: their unbounded, open (and therefore manipulable) trustfulness, their creative spontaneity (as Piaget has shown), their incredible capacity for unreserved, unconditional love, and their imagination which overflows around and through and within the objects which surround them. Beneath all the charm of the sweet little creatures of Disney, on the other hand, lurks the law of the jungle: envy, ruthlessness, cruelty, terror, blackmail, exploitation of the weak. Lacking vehicles for their natural affection, children learn through Disney fear and hatred.

It is not Disney's critics, but Disney himself who is to be accused of disrupting the home; it is Disney who is the worst enemy of family harmony.

Every Disney character stands either on one side or the other of the power demarcation line. All those below are bound to obedience, submission, discipline, humility. Those above are free to employ constant coercion: threats, moral and physical repression, and economic domination (i.e. control over the means of subsistence). The relationship of powerful to powerless is also expressed in a less aggressive, more paternalistic way, though gifts to the vassals. It is a world of permanent profit and bonus. It is only natural that the Duckburg Women's Clubs are always engaged in good works: the dispossessed eagerly accept whatever charity can be had for the begging.

The world of Disney is a nineteenth century orphanage. With this difference: there is no outside, and the orphans have nowhere to flee to. In spite of all their global travelling, and their crazy and feverish mobility, the characters remain trapped within, and doomed to return, to the same power structure. The elasticity of physical space conceals the true rigidity of the relationships within which the characters are imprisoned. The mere fact of being older or richer or more beautiful in this world confers authority. The less fortunate regard their subjection as natural. They spend all day complaining about the slavemaster, but they would rather obey his craziest order than challenge him.

This orphanage is further conditioned by the genesis of its inmates: not having been born, they cannot grow up. That is to say, they can never leave the institution through individual, biological evolution. This also facilitates unlimited manipulation and control of the population; the addition – and, if necessary, subtraction – of characters. Newcomers, whether a single figure or a pair of distant cousins, do not have to be the creation of an existing character. It is enough for the story writer to *think him up*, to invent him. The uncle-nephew structure permits the writer, who stands outside the magazine, to establish his mind as the only creative force, and the fount of all energy (just like the brainwaves and light bulbs issuing from every duck's head). Rejecting bodies as sources of existence, Disney inflicts upon his heroes the punishment that Origenes inflicted upon himself. He emasculates them, and deprives them of their true organs of relation to the universe: perception and generation. By means of this unconscious stratagem, the comics systematically and artfully reduce real people to abstractions. Disney is left in unrestricted control over his world of eunuch heroes, who are incapable of physical generation and who are forced to imitate their creator and spiritual father. Once again, the adult invades the comic, this time under the mantle of benevolent artistic genius. (We have nothing against artistic genius, by the way).

There can be no rebellion against the established order; the emasculated slave is condemned to subjection to others, as he is condemned to Disney.

Careful now. This world is inflexible, but may not show it. The hierarchical structure may not readily betray itself. But, should the system of implicit authoritarianism exceed itself or should its arbitrary character, based on the strength of will on one side and passivity on the other, become explicit and blatant, rebellion become mandatory. No matter that there be a king, as long as he governs while hiding his steel hand in a velvet glove. Should the metal show through, his overthrow becomes a necessity. For the smooth preservation of order, power should not be exaggerated beyond certain tacitly agreed limits. If these limits are transgressed revealing the arbitrary character of the arrangement, the balance has been disturbed, and must be restored. *Invariably*, those who step in are the youngsters. They act, however, neither to turn tyranny into spontaneity and freedom, nor to bring their creative imagination to bear on power, but in order to perpetuate the same order of adult domination. When the grownup misbehaves, the child takes over his sceptre. As long as the system works, no doubts are raised about it. But once it has failed, the child rebels demanding restoration of the betrayed values and the old hierarchy of domination. With their prudent takeover, their mature criticism, the youngsters uphold the same value system. Once again, real differences between father and child are passed over: the future is the same as the present, and the present the same as the past.

Since the child identifies with his counterpart in the magazine, he contributes to his own colonization. The rebellion of the little folk in the comics is sensed as a model for the child's own real rebellion against injustice; but by rebelling in the name of adult values, the readers are in fact internalizing them.

As we shall see, the obsessive persistence of the little creatures – astute, bright, competent, diligent and responsible – against the oversized animals – dull, incompetent, thoughtless, lying and weak – leads to a frequent, if only temporary, *inversion*. For example; Little Wolf is always locking up his father Big Bad Wolf, the chipmunks outwit the bear and the fox, the mice Gus and Jaq defeat the cat and the inevitable thief, the little bear Bongo braves the terrible "Quijada" (Jawbone), and the foal Gilbert becomes his uncle Goofy's teacher. Even the smart Mickey gets criticized by his nephews. These are but a few examples among many.

Thus, the only possible way of changing status is by having the representative of the adults (dominator) be transformed into the representative of the children (dominated). This happens whenever an adult commits the same errors he criticizes in children when they disturb the adult order. Similarly, the only change permitted to the child (dominated) is to turn himself into an adult (dominator). Once having created the myth of childish perfection, the adult then uses it as a substitute for his own "virtue" and "knowledge." But it is only himself he is admiring.

Let us consider a typical example (F 169): the duality in Donald Duck himself (he is illustrated as having a duplicate head three times during the course of the episode). Donald has reneged on a promise to take his nephews on holiday. When they remind him, he tries to slap them, and ends up deceiving them. But justice intervenes when Donald mistakenly starts beating up "Little Bean," a baby elephant, instead of his nephews. The judge condemns Donald to "serve his sentence in the open air," in the custody of his nephews, who are granted the full authority of the law to this effect. This is a perfect example of how the representative of childish submission is a substitute for the representative of paternal power. But, how did this substitution come about? Wasn't it Donald who first broke the law by cheating on his nephews, and they who responded with great restraint? First, they demanded Donald keep his promise, then they silently watched a situation develop in which he deluded himself. Without having to lie, they only began actively to hoax him when all previous tactics had failed. Donald's error was first to mistake a child's toy rubber elephant for a real one, then treat the real one as if it was a toy. Life for him is full of delusions, caused by his ethical error, his incapacity for moral judgement, and his deviation from paternal standards. As he forfeits authority and power, he also loses his sensory objectivity (mistaking a rubber elephant for a real one, and vice-versa). Without ever recognizing his errors, he is replaced by his nephews who, for their part, correct the problem and behave in exemplary adult fashion. By teaching their uncle a lesson, they reinforce the old code. They do not attempt to invalidate their subordinate status, but only demand that it be justly administered. The existing standards are equated to truth, goodness, authority and power.

Donald is a dual figure here because he retains the obligations of the adult on the one hand, while behaving like a child on the other. This extreme case where he is punished by a judge (generally it is a universal moral destiny) indicates his commitment to recover his original, single face, lest a generational struggle be unleashed which would reflect real change in the existing Duckburg values.

The nephews, moreover, hold the key for entry into the adult world, and they make good use of it: the Junior Woodchuck (Boy Scout) Handbook. It is a Golden Treasury of conventional wisdom. It has an answer to every situation, every period, every date, every action, every technical problem. Just follow the instructions on the can, to get out of any difficulty. It represents the accumulation of conventions permitting the child to control the future and trap it, so that it will not vary from the past, so that all will repeat itself. All courses of action have been pretested and approved by authority of the manual, which is the tribunal of history, the eternal law, sponsored and sanctified by those who will inherit the world. There can be no surprises here, for it has shaped the world in advance and forever. It's all written down there, in that rigid catechism, just put it into practice and carry on reading. Even the adversary is possessed of objective and just standards. The Handbook is one of the rare one-hundred-percent-perfect gimmicks in the complex world of Disney: out of forty-five instances in which it is used, it never fails once, beating in infallibility even the almost perfect Mickey.

But is there nothing which escapes this incessant transposition between adult and child, and vice-versa? Is there no way of stepping aside from this struggle for vertical subordination and the obsessive propagation of the system?

Indeed there is. There is horizontal movement, and it is always present. It operates among creatures of the same status and power level, who, among themselves, cannot be permanently dominated or dominators. All that is left to them – since solidarity among equals is prohibited – is to *compete*. Beat the other guy to it. Why beat him? To rise above him, momentarily, enter the dominators club, and advance a rung (like a Disneyland Club corporal or sergeant) on the ladder of mercantile value. Here the only permitted horizontal becomes the finishing-line of the race.

There is one sector of Disney society which is beyond the reach of criticism, and is never ousted by lesser creatures: the female. As in the male sector, the lineage also tends to be avuncular (for example, Daisy, her nieces and Aunt Tizzy, D 383, DD 7/67), except that the woman has no chance of switching roles in the dominator-dominated relationship. Indeed, she is never challenged because she plays her role to perfection, whether it be humble servant or constantly courted beauty queen; in either case, sub-

ordinate to the male. Her only power is the traditional one of seductress, which she exercises in the form of coquetry. She is denied any further role which might transcend her passive, domestic nature. There are women who contravene the "feminine code," but they are allied with the powers of darkness. The witch, Magica de Spell is a typical antagonist, but not even she abandons aspirations proper to her "feminine" nature. Women are left with only two alternatives (which are not really alternatives at all): to be Snow White or the Witch, the little girl housekeeper or the wicked stepmother. Her brew is of two kinds: the homely stew and the dreadful magic poison. And since she is always cooking for the male, her aim in life is to catch him by one brew or the other.

If you are no witch, don't worry ma'am: you can always keep busy with "feminine" occupations; dressmaker, secretary, interior decorator, nurse, florist, cosmetician, or air hostess. And if work is not your style, you can always become president of the local charity club. In all events, you can always fall back upon eternal coquetry — this is your common denominator, even with Grandma Duck (see D 347) and Madame Mim.

In his graphic visualization of this bunch of coquettes Disney resorts constantly to the Hollywood actress stereotype. Although they are sometimes heavily satirized, they remain a single archetype with their physical existence limited to the escape-hatch of amorous struggle (Disney reinforces the stereotype in his famous films for "the young" as for example, the fairies in *Pinocchio* and *Peter Pan*). Disney's moral stand as to the nature of this struggle is clearly stated, for example, in the scene where Daisy embodies infantile, Doris Day-style qualities against the Italianate vampiress Silvia.

Man is afraid of this kind of woman (who wouldn't be?). He eternally and fruitlessly courts her, takes her out, competes for her, wants to

rescue her, showers her with gifts. Just as the troubadours of courtly love were not permitted carnal contact with the women of their lords, so these eunuchs live in an eternal foreplay with their impossible virgins. Since they can never fully possess them, they are in constant fear of losing them. It is the compulsion of eternal frustration, of pleasure postponed for better domination. Woman's only retreat in a world where physical adventure, criticism and even motherhood has been denied her, is into her own sterile sexuality. She cannot even enjoy the humble domestic pleasures permitted to real-life women, as enslaved as they are – looking after a home and children. She is perpetually and uselessly waiting around, or running after some masculine idol, dazzled by the hope of finding at last a true man. Her only *raison d'etre* is to become a sexual object, infinitely solicited and postponed. She is frozen on the threshhold of satisfaction and repression among impotent people. She is denied pleasure, love, children, communication. She lives in a centripetal, introverted, egolatrous world; a parody of the island-individual. Her condition is solitude, which she can never recognize as such. The moment she questions her role, she will be struck from the cast of characters.

How hypocritical it is for Disney comics to announce: "We refuse to accept advertisements for products harmful to the moral and material health of children, such as cigarettes, alcoholic beverages, or gambling ... Our intention has always been to serve as a vehicle of healthy recreation and entertainment, amidst all the problems besetting us." All protestations to the contrary, Disney does present an implicit model of sexual education. By suppressing true sexual contact, coitus, possession and orgasm, Disney betrays how demonical and terrible he conceives them to be. He has created another aberration: an asexual sexuated world. The sexual innuendo is more evident in the drawing, than in the dialogue itself.

In this carefully preserved reservation, coquettes – male and female, young and old – try impotently to conceal the apparatus of sexual seduction under the uniform of the Salvation Army. Disney and the other libidinous defenders of childhood, clamor on the alters of youthful innocence, crying out against scandal, immorality, pornography, prostitution, indecency, and incitation to "precocious sensuality", when another youth magazine dares to launch a poster with a back view of a romantic and ethereal couple, nude. Listen to the sermon of Walt's creole imitators:

> "It must be recognized that in Chile we have reached incredible extremes in the matter of erotic propaganda, perversion and vice. It is manifest in those groups preaching individual moral escapism, and a break with all moral standards.
>
> "We hear much talk of the new man and the new society, but these concepts are often accompanied by filthy attitudes, indecent exhibitionism, and indulgence in sexual perversion.
>
> "One does not have to be a Puritan to pronounce strong censure upon this moral licentiousness, since it is well known that no healthy people and no lasting historical work can be based upon the moral disorder which threatens our youth with mortal poison. What ideals and what sacrifices can be asked of young people initiated into the vice of drugs and corrupted by aberrant practices or precocious sensuality? And if youth becomes incapable of accepting any ideal or sacrifice, how can one expect the country to resolve its problems of development and liberation, all of which presuppose great effort, and even a dose of heroism?
>
> "It is unfortunate, indeed, that immorality is being fostered by government-controlled publications. A few days ago a scandalous street poster announced the appearance of a youth magazine published on the official presses .... Without stout-hearted youth there is no real youth, but only premature and corrupt maturity. And without youth, the country has no future."*

*Editorial in *El Mercurio* (Santiago), 28 September 1971.

But why this unhealthy phobia of Disney's? Why has motherhood been expelled from his Eden? We shall have occasion to return to these questions later – and without recourse to the usual biographical or psychoanalytic (oedipal) explanations.

It is enough at this point to note that the paucity of women, their subordination and their mutilation, facilitates the roundabout of uncles, nephews, adults and children, and their constantly interchangeable roles which always assert the same values. Later we will examine how without a mother to intervene, there is no obstacle to showing the adult world as perverse and clumsy, thus preparing us for this replacement by the little ones who have already implicitly pledged allegiance to the adult flag.

Or, to use the exact words of Little Wolf (D 210):

"Gulp! Bad things always come in big packages!"

II. FROM THE CHILD TO THE NOBLE SAVAGE

"Gu!"
The Abominable Snow Man
(TR 113, US 6-8/56)

Disney relies upon the acceptability of his world as *natural*, that is to say, as at once normal, ordinary and true to the nature of the child. His depiction of women and children is predicated upon its supposed objectivity, although, as we have seen, he relentlessly twists the nature of every creature he approaches.

It is not by chance that the Disney world is populated with animals. Nature appears to pervade and determine the whole complex of social relations, while the animal-like traits provide the characters with a facade of innocence. It is, of course, true that children tend to identify with the playful, instinctive nature of animals. As they grow older, they begin to understand that the mature animal shares some of his own physical evolutionary traits. They were once, in some way, like this animal, going on all fours, unable to speak, etc. Thus the animal is considered as being the only living being in the universe inferior to the child,* one which the child has overtaken and is able to manipulate. The animal world is one of the areas where the creative imagination of the child can freely roam; and it is indisputable that many animal films have great pedagogic value, which educate a child's sensibility and senses.

The use of animals is not in itself either good or bad; it is the use to which they are put, it is the kind of being they incarnate that should be scrutinized. Disney uses animals to trap children, not to liberate them. The language he employs is nothing less than a form of manipulation. He invites children into a world which appears to offer freedom of movement and creation, into which they enter fearlessly, identifying with creatures as affectionate, trustful, and irresponsible as themselves, of whom no betrayal is to be expected, and with whom they can safely play and mingle. Then, once the little readers are caught within the pages of the comic, the doors close behind them. The animals become transformed, under the same zoological *form* and the same smiling mask, into monstrous human beings.

But this perversion of the true nature of animals and the superficial use of their physical

*Disney does not hesitate to exploit this relationship of biological superiority in order to militarize and regiment animal life under the approving rule of children (cf. the transference of the Boy Scout ideal onto animals in all his comics, as for example in TR 119).

appearance (a device also used to distort the nature of women and children) is not all. Disney's obsession with "nature" and his compulsion to exonerate a world he conceives as profoundly perverse and guilty, leads him to extraordinary exaggerations.

All the characters yearn for a return to nature. Some live in the fields and woods (Grandma Duck, the chipmunks, the little wolves), but the majority live in cities, from which they set off on incessant jaunts to nature: island, desert, sea, forest, mountain, lake, skies, and stratosphere, covering all continents (Asia, America, Africa, and Oceania), and very occasionally some non-urban corner of Europe. While a substantial proportion of the episodes take place in the city or in closed environments, they only serve to emphasize the absurd and catastrophic character of urban life. There are stories devoted to smog, traffic jams, noise pollution, and social tensions (including some very funny fights between neighbors), as well as to the omnipresence of bureaucracy and policemen. The city is actually portrayed as an inferno, where man loses control over his own personal life. In one episode after another, the characters become embroiled with objects. On one occasion, Donald gets stuck on a roller skate during a shopping expedition (DD 9/66). He embarks upon a crazy solitary collision course through the city, experiencing all the miseries of contemporary living: trash barrels, jammed thoroughfares, road repairs, loose dogs, terrorized mailmen, crowded parks (where, incidentally, a mother scolds her offspring: "Sit quietly, Junior, so you won't scare the pigeons!"), police, traffic controls, obstructions of all kinds (in knocking over the tables of an outdoor cafe, Donald wonders helplessly "if my charge card will still be honored there!"), car crashes, teeming shops, delivery trucks, and drains: chaos everywhere.

This is not a unique episode, there are other snares which trap people in that great urban whirligig of misfortune: candies (D 185), a lost ticket (D 393), or Scamp's uncontrollable motorcycle (D 439). In this kind of *suffrenture* (suffering coated with adventure), Frankenstein, the legendary robot who escaped from his inventor, rears his ugly head. The city-as-monster reaches its nerve-wracking peak when Donald, in order to get some sleep at night in the face of heavy traffic and the hooting, roaring and screaming of brakes, closes off the road in front of his house (D 165). He is fined by the police. He protests: "I don't have any written authorization, but I do have the right to some peaceful sleep." "You're wrong!" interrupts the policeman. So Donald embarks on a crazy hunt for the necessary authorization: from the police station to the home of the police chief, and then to the town hall to speak to the mayor, who, however, can only sign "orders approved by the city council." (note the hierarchical inflexibility of this bureaucratic world full of prohibitions and procrastinations). Donald has to bring to the council a petition signed by all the residents of his block. He sets out to explore his neighborhood jungle. Never does he find anyone to support him, to help him, to understand that his struggle for peace is a communal one. He is driven off with kicks, blows, and pistol shots: he is made to pay for scratching a car (fifty dollars), has to go to Miami for a single signature, and having fainted when he hears that the neighbor he was seeking has just returned home to Duckburg, he is revived by the hotel manager: "Sir, I must inform you that the rate for sleeping on the carpet is thirty dollars a night." Another neighbor won't sign until he has consulted his attorney (another twenty dollars out of Donald's pocket). He is bitten by a dog while a dear little

old lady is signing. He has to buy spectacles for the next person who signs (three hundred dollars, because the person chose to have them with pure gold frames), and finally, he has to pursue him to a waterfall where he performs acrobatic feats. He falls into the water, and the ink on his petition is washed out. He reconstructs the list ("some sleep at night is worth all the pains I have suffered"), only to be informed that the city council cannot pronounce on the matter for twenty years. In desperation, Donald buys another house. But even here he is out of luck: the council has decided, in view of his difficulties, to move the road from his old street – to his new one. Moral: don't try to change anything! Put up with what you have, or chances are you will end up with worse.

We shall return later to this type of comic, which demostrates the uselessness of persisting in the face of destiny, and Disney's brand of social criticism. But it was necessary to stress the nightmarish and degraded character of the city, for this motivates, in part, the return to nature. The metropolis is conceived as a mechanical dormitory or safe deposit box. A base of operations from which one has to escape. An uncontrollable technological disaster, which if endured, would make existence absurd.

On the other hand, the "peace and quiet of the countryside" is such that only willful interference can disturb it. For example, Gus Goose, in order to persuade the rustic Grandma Duck to spend a few days in the city, has artificially to induce successive plagues of mosquitoes, mice and bees; a fire; and a cow trampling over her garden. She is glad for what has happened, for the day of plagues has prepared her to "put up with the inconveniences of modern city life."

Urban man can only reach the countryside once he has left behind him all the curses of technology: ships are wrecked, airplanes crash, rockets are stolen. One has to pass through Purgatory in order to attain Paradise. Any contemporary gadget one brings to the countryside will only cause problems, and wreak its revenge by complicating and contaminating one's life. In an episode titled "The Infernal Bucket" (note the religious association), Donald has his vacation ruined by this simple object. Another time (D 433), when the duckling scouts try to change the course of nature by asking Gyro Gearloose to invent something to stop a rainstorm, the only little clearing in the forest which remains dry soon becomes crowded, like a replica of a city, bringing all the corresponding urban conflicts. "I think that one shouldn't force nature," says one. Adds the other: "In the long run, it just doesn't pay."

Superficially considered, what we have here is simply escapism, the common mass culture safety valve necessary for a society in need of recreation and fantasy to maintain its mental and physical health. It is the Sunday afternoon walk in the Park, the weekend in the country, and the nostalgia for the past annual vacation. Not surprisingly, those who consider the child as living a perpetual holiday, also seek a spatial equivalent to this carefree existence: the peace of the countryside.

This thesis might appear exhaustive, were it not for the fact that the places where are heroes venture are far from being abandoned and uninhabited. If the adventures took place in pure uncontaminated nature, the relationship would be only between man and inorganic matter. Were there no natives, there would be no human relations other than those which we analyzed in the previous chapter. But this is not the case. A simple statistic: out of the total of one hundred magazines we studied, very nearly half – 47 percent – showed the heroes confronting beings from other continents and races. If one includes comics dealing with creatures from other planets, the proportion rises well over 50 percent. Our sample includes stories covering the remotest corners of the globe.*

*To start with our *American hemisphere*: Peru (Inca-Blinca in TB 104, the Andes in D 457); Ecuador (D 434); Mexico (Aztecland, Azatlán and Southern Ixtiki in D 432, D 455 and TB 107 respectively); an island off Mexico (D 451); Brazil (F 155); the Chilean and Bolivian plateaux (Antofagasta is mentioned in TB 106); and the Caribbean (TB 87).

North America: Indians in the United States (D 430 and TB 62); savages of the Grand Canyon (D 437); Canadian Indians (D 379 and TR 117); Eskimoes of the Arctic (TR 110), Indians in old California (D 357).

Africa and the Near East: Egypt (Sphinxonia in D 422 and TR 109); some corner of the black continent (D 431, D 382, D 364, F 170, F 106); Arab countries (Aridia, archipelago of Frigi-Frigi, the other three nameless – TR 111 and 123, two episodes D 453 and F 155).

Asia: Faroffistan (Hong Kong? D 455); Franistan (a bizzarre mixture of Afghanistan and Tibet); Outer Congolia (Mongolia? D 433); Unsteadystan (Vietnam, TR 99).

Oceania: islands inhibited by savages (D 376, F 68, TR 106, D 377); uninhabited islands (D 439, D 210, TB 99, TR 119); to which one may add a multitude of islands visited by Mickey and Goofy, but of lesser interest and therefore omitted from this list.

In these lands, far from the Duckburg metropolis, casual landing grounds for adventurers greedy for treasure and anxious to break their habitual boredom with a pure and healthy form of recreation, there await inhabitants with most unusual characteristics.

No globe-trotter could fail to thrill to these countries and the idea of taking home with him a real live savage. So here, on behalf of all you eager trippers, is our brochure to tell you exactly what is on the bill of fare (extracted from "How to Travel and Get Rich", as you might find it in *Reader's Digest* as condensed from the *National Geographic*):

1. IDENTITY. Primitive. Two groups: one quite barbaric (Stone Age), habitat Africa, Polynesia, outlying parts of Brazil, Ecuador or U.S.A.; the other group much more evolved but degenerating, if not actually in course of extinction. Sometimes, the latter group is the repository of an ancient civilization with many monuments and local dishes. Neither of these two groups has reached the age of technology.

2. DWELLINGS. The first group has no urban centers at all, some huts at the most. The second group has towns, but in a ruined or useless state. You are advised to bring lots of film, because everything, absolutely everything, is jam-packed with folklore and the exotica.

3. RACE. All races, except the white. Color film is indispensable, because the natives come in all shades, from the darkest black to yellow via cafe-au-lait, ochre and that lovely light orange peculiar to the Redskins.

4. STATURE. Bring close-up and wide-angle lenses. The natives are generally enormous, gigantic, gross, tough, pure raw matter, and pure muscle; but sometimes, they can be mere pygmies. Please don't step on them; they are harmless.

5. CLOTHING. Loincloths, unless they dress like their most distant ancestor of royal blood. Our friend Disney, creater of the "Living Desert," would no doubt have coined the felicitous term "Living Museum."

6. SEXUAL CUSTOMS. By some strange freak of nature, these countries have only males. We were unable to find any trace of the female. Even in Polynesia, the famous tamuré dance is reserved to the stronger sex. We did discover, however, in Franestan, a princess, but were unable to see her because no male is allowed near her. It is not yet sufficiently understood how these savages reproduce. We do, however, hope to come up with an answer in our next issue, since the International Monetary Fund is financing an investigation of the Third World demographic explosion, with a view to determining the nature of whatever (exceedingly efficient) contraceptive device is in use.

7. MORAL QUALITIES. They are like children. Friendly, carefree, naive, trustful and happy. They throw temper tantrums when they are upset. But it is ever so easy to placate them and even, how shall we say, deceive them.

Translator's Note: The following list, culled from Michael Barrier's Barks bibliography will further illuminate the preoccupation of the Ducks with peoples of the Third World (Indians living in the U.S. are not included). Note that this list covers only one writer's Duck stories, and excludes all Mickey Mouse adventures, which are also often set in foreign lands. There may be some duplication with the Chilean edition list.

Canada and Alaska: Alaska (Point Marrow, DD 1/45; Mines in, DD 12/49; US 9–11/58; US 9/65). Canada: North West (Kikmiquick Indians DD 2/50); Eskimoes CS 8/63; Labrador DD 7–8/52; Peeweegah Pygmy Indians US 6–8/57; Gold mines in, US 9–11/61.

Central America: CS 5/61; Aztecland DD 9/65; Yucatan (Mayan ruins, US 8/63); Hondorica DD 3–4/56; West Indies DD 7/47; Caribbean Islands CS 4/60; Cuba 4/64.

South America : War in, US 3–5/59; Emerald in, US 9–11/60; Amazon jungle DD 7–8/57, US 12–2/61; British Guiana DD 9–10/52; Andes (Incan ruins DD 4/49; Incan mines US 6–8/59); Chiliburgeria DD 1/51; Cura de Coco Indians ("Tutor Corps" in, US 9–11/62); Volcanovia (Donald sells warplanes to, DD 5/47); Brutopia US 3–5/57 (Bearded communists in, CS 11/63; Spies from, US 5/65).

Africa: CS 4/62; Gold mine in, US 1/66; Egypt DD 9/43, US 3–5/59; Pygmy Arabs US 6–8/61; Red Sea Village (King Solomon's mines US 9–11/57); Bantu US 9–11/60; Congo (Kachoonga US 3–5/64); Oasis of Nolssa DD 9/50; Kooko Coco (Wigs in, US 9/64); Foola Zoola DD 8/49; South Africa US 9–11/56, US 3–5/59.

Asia: Arabia US 2/65; Persia (Ancient city of Itsa Faka DD 5/50; Oil in, US 3–5/62); Baghdad US 7/64; Sagbad (Capital of Fatcatstan US 10/67); India (Jumbostan US 12/64; Maharajah of Backdore CS 4/49, Maharajah of Swingingdore US 3–5/55, Rajah of Footsore, Maharajah of Howduyustan CS 3/52); Himalayas (Unicorn in, DD 2/50; Moneyless paradise of Tralla La US 6–8/54; Abominable Snowman in Hindu Kush mountains, US 6–8/56).

Southeast Asia: Farbakishan ("Brain Corps" in, GG 11–2/62); Siambodia (Civil War in, CS 6/65); Gung Ho river (Ancient city of Tangkor Wat, US 12–2/58); Unsteadystan (Civil War in, US 7/66); South Miserystan US 7/67.

Others: Australia (Aborigines) DD 5/47, CS 9–11/55, US 3/66; South Sea Islands US 3/63, CS 12/64, CS 9/66; Hawaiian Islands 12–1/54; Jungle of Faceless People US 3/64; Aeolian Mountains GG 3–6/60.

The prudent tourist will bring a few trinkets which he can readily exchange for quantities of native jewelry. The savages are extraordinarily receptive; they accept any kind of gift, whether it be some artifact of civilization, or money, and they will even, in the last resort, accept the return of their own treasures, as long as it is in the form of a gift. They are disinterested and very generous. Clergy who are tired of dealing with spoiled juvenile delinquents, can relax with some good old-fashioned missionary work among primitives untouched by Christianity. Yet they are willing to give up everything material. EVERYTHING. EVERYTHING. So they are an inexhaustible font of riches and treasures which they cannot use. They are superstitious and imaginative. Without pretensions to erudition, we may describe them as the typical *noble savage* referred to by Christopher Columbus, Jean-Jacques Rousseau, Marco Polo, Richard Nixon, William Shakespeare and Queen Victoria.

8. AMUSEMENTS. The primitives sing, dance, and sometimes for a change, have revolutions. They tend to use any mechanical object you might bring with you (telephone, watch, guns) as a toy.

9. LANGUAGE. No need for an interpreter or phrase book. Almost all of them speak fluent Duckburgish. And if you have a small child with you, don't worry, he will get on fine with those other little natives whose language tends to the babyish kind, with a preference for gutturals.

10. ECONOMIC BASE. Subsistence economy. Sheep, fish, and fruit. Sometimes, they sell things. When the occasion arises they manufacture objects for the tourist trade: don't buy them, for you can get them, and more, for free, by tricking them. They show an extraordinary attachment to the earth, which renders them even more *natural*. Abundance reigns. They do not need to produce. They are model consumers. Perhaps their happiness is due to the fact that they don't work.

11. POLITICAL STRUCTURE. The tourist will find this very much to his taste. In the paleolithic, barbaric group of peoples, there is a natural democracy. All are equal, except the king who is more equal than the others. This renders civil liberties nugatory: executive, legislative and judical powers are fused into one. Nor is there any necessity for voting or newspapers. Everything is shared, as in a Disneyland club, if we may be permitted the comparison; and the king does not have any real authority or rights, beyond his title, any more than a general in a Disneyland club, if we may be permitted another comparison. It is this democracy which distinquishes the paleolithic group from the second group, with its ancient, degenerate cultures, where the king holds unlimited power, but also lives under the constant fear of overthrow. Fortunately, however, his native subjects suffer from a rather curious weakness: always wanting to reinstitute the monarchy.

12. RELIGION. None, because they live in a *Paradise Lost*, or a true Garden of Eden before the Fall.

13. NATIONAL EMBLEM. The mollusk, of the invertebrate family.

14. NATIONAL COLOR. Immaculate white.

15. NATIONAL ANIMAL. The sheep, as long as it is not lost or black.

16. MAGICAL PROPERTIES. Those who have not had the great good fortune to have been there, may find this perhaps the most important and most difficult aspect of all, but it represents the very essence of the noble savage and the reason why he has been left by preference in a relatlvely backward state, free from the conflicts besetting contemporary society. Being in close communion with the natural environment, the savage is able to radiate natural goodness, and absolute ethical purity. Unknown to himself, he constitutes a source of permanent or constantly renewable sanctity. Just as there exist reserves of Indians and of wilderness, why should there not be reserves of morality and innocence? Somehow, this morality and innocence will succeed, without changing the technologized societies, in saving humanity. They are redemption itself.

17. FUNERAL RITES. They never die.

Our observant reader will have noticed the similarities between the noble savage and those other savages called children. Have we at last encountered the true child in Disney's comics, in the guise of the innocent barbarian? Is there a parallel between the socially underdeveloped peoples who live in these vast islands and plateaux of ignorance, and the children who are underdeveloped because of their young age? Do they not both share magical practices, innocence, naivete, that natural disposition of a lost, chastened, benevolent humanity? Are not both equally defenseless before adult force and guile?

The comics, elaborated by and for the narcissistic parent, adopt a view of the child-reader which is the same as their view of the inferior Third World adult. If this be so, our noble savage differs from the other children in that he is not a carbon copy aggregate of paternal, adult values. Lacking in the intelligence, cunning, discipline, encyclopedic knowledge, and technological skills possessed by the little city folk (and the chipmunks, Little Wolf, Bongo, and other denizens of Duckburg's metropolitan wilderness), the primitive assumes the qualities of childhood as conceived by the comics (innocence, ignorance, etc.) without having access to the gateways and ladders leading to the adult world.

Here the going becomes heavy, the fog descends. In the whirl of this fancy dress ball, perception is blurred as to who is who; when and where the child is adult, and the adult, a child.

If we accept that the savage is the true child, then what do the little folk of Duckburg represent? What are the differences and similarities between them?

The city kids are only children in appearance. They possess the physical shape and stature of children, their initial dependency, their supposed good faith, their schoolroom obligations, and sometimes, their toys. But as we have seen, they really represent the force which judges and corrects adult errors with adult rationales. In thirty-eight out of the forty-two episodes in which Donald quarrels with his nephews, it is the latter who are in the right. Only in four, on the other hand (e.g. in the "Tricksters Tricked") is it the little ones who transgress the laws of adult behavior, and are properly punished for having acted like children. Little Wolf, in thirty episodes, can do no wrong, in view of the fact that his father is big and bad, black and ugly: he always teaches his father a lesson whenever the latter falls instinctively into the path of weakness and crime. This physical father, the only true male parent in the comics, confirms our thesis once more: he is the vagabond whose power, not being legitimated by Disney's "proper" adult values, will always be mocked. Equally significant is the name of Scamp's natural father: Tramp. But, the true father of Scamp is his human owner. In eighteen out of twenty adventures, we find the chipmunks Chip and Dale making fun of the blunders and frauds of all the adults (Donald, Big Bad Wolf, Brer Bear, Brer Fox, and Brer Ass). In the other two, where they misbehave, they get a drubbing. Gus and Jaq, Bongo, Peter Pan: one hundred percent in the right. Goofy is the eternal and foremost target of adult lessons in childish mouths: he is always wrong, because he lacks adult intellectual maturity. But it is in Mickey Mouse, Disney's premier creation, that childish and mature traits are best reconciled. It is this perfect miniature adult — this child-detective, this paladin of law and decency, ordered in his judgements and disordered in his personal habits (remember Jiminy Cricket, the awkward keeper of Pinocchio's conscience) — who exemplifies the synthesis and symbiosis which Disney hoped, unconsciously, to transmit. But as other characters appeared the synthesis split apart, giving rise to the circular pattern of substitution of the child taking over from the adult.*

Disney did not invent this structure: it is rooted in the so-called popular tales and legends, in which researchers have detected a central cyclical symmetry between father and son. The youngest in the family, for instance, or the little wizard or woodcutter, is subject to paternal authority, but possesses powers of retaliation and regulation, which are invariably linked to his ability to *generate ideas*, that is, his cunning. See Perrault, Andersen, Grimm.**

Now that we have seen the adult role of the child, we are in a better position to understand the presence of the savages within this world.

Their permanent role is to fill the gap left by the small child-shaped urbans, just as the latter are required to fill the gap left by the adult-shaped urbans when they cease to act responsibly.

So there are two types of children. While the city-folk are intelligent, calculating, crafty, and superior; the Third Worldlings are candid, foolish, irrational, disorganized and gullible (like Cowboys and Indians). The first are spirit, and move in the sphere of ideas; the second are body, inert matter, mass. The former represent the future, the latter the past.

Now we understand why the urban kids are constantly on the move, overthrowing the grown-

*This pattern is repeated in Disney films with juvenile actors (e.g. those starring Hayley Mills).

**For an interpretation free of the formalism of Vladimir Propp's structural analysis (*Morphologie du Conte*, Seuil, Paris, 1970), see, among others, the discoveries of Marc Soriano, *Les Contes de Perrault: culture savante et traditions populaires,* Gallimard, Paris, 1968, and "Table Ronde sur les contes de Perrault" *Annales* (Paris), mai-juin 1970.

ups every time they show signs of infantile relapse. The replacement is legitimate and necessary, because this ensures that there be no real change. Everything continues as before. It doesn't matter if one part be in the right and the other in the wrong, as long as the rules stay the same. This can only happen in the self-contained land of Duckburg.

The iron unity of these city people, children and adults alike with respect to the ideals of civilization; the maturity and technical skill with which each time they confront the world of nature is proof anew of the pre-eminence of adult values in Duckburg. The child-savages have no chance to criticize, and thus replace the monolithic bloc of strangers from the city. The former can only accept the generosity of the latter and give them the wealth of their lands. These prehumans are destined to remain in their islands, arrested in an eternal state of pure infancy, children who are not like the nephew-ducks, a pretext for the projection of adult values. Their natural virtue, which is uniform and fixed, represents the beginning and end of time, the pre-Fall and post-judgement Paradise, the font of goodness, patience, joy and innocence. The existence of the noble savage constitutes a guarantee that there will always be children, and that the nephews will have someone to replace them as they grow up (even if the new children have to be born by non-sexual means).

In their assimilation of "superior" values, the urban youngsters automatically lose many of the qualities which adults most admire in children. Intelligence and cunning threaten the traditional image of the immune and trusting child who transforms adult nightmares into purified and perfumed dreams. The children's tricks, although they are dismissed as pranks, also darken the image of original perfection, of a world (and ultimately a salvation) beyond the taint of sex and money. The father wants the child to be his own reflection, to be made in his own image. While he tries to achieve immortality through offspring who never contradict him (and are monopolized by him, just as Disney monopolizes his "monos")*, he simultaneously wants them to be creatures who correspond to his idealized image of open and submissive childhood; which he then can immobilize and freeze into a photograph on the mantlepiece. The adult wants a child who when he/she grows up, will faithfully reproduce and depend upon the past.

Thus the child-reader has two alternatives before him/her, two models of behavior: either follow the duckling and similar wily creatures, choosing adult cunning to defeat the competition, coming out on top, getting rewards, going up; or else, follow the child noble savage, who just stays put and never wins anything. The only way out of childhood is one previously marked out by the adult, and camouflaged with innocence and instinct. It's the only way to go, son.

This division is not grounded in mysticism or metaphysics. The yearning for purity does not arise from any need for a salvation one might term religious. It is as if the father did not wish to continue dominating his own flesh, his own heirs. Sensing that his son is none but himself, the father perceives himself simultaneously as dominator and dominated, in a manifestation of his own unrelenting internal repression. In his attempt to break the infernal circle, to flee from himself, he searches for another being to dominate – someone with whom he can enjoy a guilt-free polarization of feeling, and a clear definition of who is the dominated and who is the dominator. While the son safely grows up and adopts his father's values, he continues to repress the other child who never changes and never protests: the noble savage. In order to escape from the sado-masochistic conflict with his own son and his own being, he establishes a purely sadistic relationship with that other being, the "harmless," "innocent" "noble" savage. He bequeathes to his son a satisfactorily immutable world: his own values and well-behaved savages who will accept them without complaining.

But it is time, lest our own analysis fall victim to circularity, to look beyond the confines of the family structure. Does there not lurk perhaps something else behind this father-noble savage relationship?

*"monos" = monkeys, or cartoon characters (Trans.)

III. FROM THE NOBLE SAVAGE TO THE THIRD WORLD

Donald (talking to a witch doctor in Africa): "I see you're an up to date nation! Have you got telephones?"

Witch doctor: "Have we gottee telephones! ... All colors, all shapes ... only trouble is only *one* has wires. It's a hot line to the world loan bank."

(TR 106, US 9/64)

Where is Aztecland? Where is Inca-Blinca? Where is Unsteadystan?

There can be no doubt that Aztecland is Mexico, embracing as it does all the prototypes of the picture-postcard Mexico: mules, siestas, volcanoes, cactuses, huge sombreros, ponchos, serenades, machismo, and Indians from ancient civilizations. The country is defined primarily in terms of this grotesque folklorism. Petrified in an archetypical embryo, exploited for all the superficial and stereotyped prejudices which surround it, "Aztecland," under its pseudo-imaginary name becomes that much easier to Disnify. This is Mexico recognizable by its commonplace exotic identity labels, not the real Mexico with all its problems.

Walt took virgin territories of the U.S. and built upon them his Disneyland palaces, his magic kingdoms. His view of the world at large is framed by the same perspective; it is a world already colonized, with phantom inhabitants who have to conform to Disney's notions of it. Each foreign country is used as a kind of model within the process of invasion by Disney-nature. And even if some foreign country like Cuba or Vietnam should dare to enter into open conflict with the United States, the Disney Comics brand-mark is immediately stamped upon it, in order to make the revolutionary struggle appear banal. While the Marines make revolutionaries run the gauntlet of bullets, Disney makes them run a gauntlet of magazines. There are two forms of killing: by machine guns and saccharine.

Disney did not, of course, invent the inhabitants of these lands; he merely forced them into the proper mold. Casting them as stars in his hit-parade, he made them into decals and puppets for his fantasy palaces, good and inoffensive savages unto eternity.

According to Disney, underdeveloped peoples are like children, to be treated as such, and if they don't accept this definition of themselves, they should have their pants taken down and be given a good spanking. That'll teach them! When something is *said* about the child/noble savage, it is really the Third World one is *thinking* about. The hegemony which we have detected between

the child-adults who arrive with their civilization and technology, and the child-noble savages who accept this alien authority and surrender their riches, stands revealed as an exact replica of the relations between metropolis and satellite, between empire and colony, between master and slave. Thus we find the metropolitans not only searching for treasures, but also selling the native *comics* (like those of Disney), to teach them the role assigned to them by the dominant urban press. Under the suggestive title "Better Guile Than Force," Donald departs for a Pacific atoll in order to try to survive for a month, and returns loaded with dollars, like a modern business tycoon. The entrepreneur can do better than the missionary or the army. The world of the Disney comic is self-publicizing, ensuring a process of enthusiastic buying and selling even within its very pages.

Enough of generalities. Examples and proofs. Among all the child-noble savages, none is more exaggerated in his infantilism than Gu, the Abominable Snow Man (TR 113, US 6-8/56, "The Lost Crown of Genghis Khan"): a brainless, feeble-minded Mongolian type (living by a strange coincidence, in the Himalayan Hindu Kush mountains among yellow peoples). He is treated like a child. He is an *"abominable* housekeeper," living in a messy cave, "the worst of taste," littered with "cheap trinkets and waste." Hats etc., lying around which he has no use for. Vulgar, uncivilized, he speaks in a babble of inarticulate baby-noises: "Gu." But he is also witless, having stolen the golden jewelled crown of Genghis Khan (which belongs to Scrooge by virtue of certain secret operations of his agents), without having any idea of its value. He has tossed the crown in a corner like a coal bucket, and prefers Uncle Scrooge's watch: value, one dollar ("It is his favorite *toy*"). Never mind, for "his stupidity makes it easy for us to get away!" Uncle Scrooge does indeed manage, magically, to exchange the cheap artifact of civilization which goes tick-tock, for the crown. Obstacles are overcome once Gu (innocent child-monstruous animal – underdeveloped Third Worldling) realizes that they only want to take something that is of no use to him, and that in exchange he will be given a fantastic and mysterious piece of technology (a watch) which he can use as a plaything. What is extracted is gold, a raw matercal; he who surrenders it is mentally underdeveloped and physically overdeveloped. The gigantic physique of Gu, and of all the other marginal savages, is the model of a physical strength suited only for physical labor.*

Such an episode reflects the barter relationship established with the natives by the first conquistadors and colonizers (in Africa, Asia, America and Oceania): some trinket, the product of technological superiority (European or North American) is exchanged for gold (spices, ivory, tea, etc.). The native is relieved of something he would never have thought of using for himself or as a means of exchange. This is an extreme and almost anecdotic example. The common stuff of other types of comic book (e.g. in the internationally famous *Tintin in Tibet* by the Belgian Hergé) leaves the abominable creature in his bestial condition, and thus unable to enter into any kind of economy.

But this particular victim of infantile regression stands at the borderline of Disney's noble savage cliche. Beyond it lies the foetus-savage, which for reasons of sexual prudery Disney cannot use.

*For the theme of physical superdevelopment with the connotation of sexual threat, see Eldridge Cleaver, *Soul on Ice*, 1968.

Lest the reader feel that we are spinning too fine a thread in establishing a parallel between someone who carries off gold in exchange for a mechanical trinket, and imperialism extracting raw material from a mono-productive country, or between typical dominators and dominated, let us now adduce a more explicit example of Disney's strategy in respect to the countries he caricatures as "backward" (needless to say, he never hints at the causes of their backwardness).

The following dialogue (taken from the same comic which provided the quotation at the beginning of this chapter) is a typical example of Disney's colonial attitudes, in this case directed against the African independence movements. Donald has parachuted into a country in the African jungle. "Where am I," he cries. A witch doctor (with spectacles perched over his gigantic primitive mask) replies: "In the new nation of Kooko Coco, fly boy. This is our capital city." It consists of three straw huts and some moving haystacks. When Donald enquires after this strange phenomenon, the witch doctor explains: "Wigs! This be hairy idea our ambassador bring back from United Nations." When a pig pursuing Donald lands and has the wigs removed disclosing the whereabouts of the enemy ducks, the following dialogue ensues:

Pig: "Hear ye! hear ye! I'll pay you kooks some hairy prices for your *wigs*! Sell me all you have!"

Native: "Whee! Rich trader buyee our old head hangers!"

Another native: "He payee me six trading stamps for my beehive hairdo!"

Third native (overjoyed): "He payee me two Chicago streetcar tokens for my Beatle job."

To effect his escape, the pig decides to scatter a few coins as a decoy. The natives are happy to stop, crouch and cravenly gather up the money. Elsewhere, when the Beagle Boys dress up as Polynesian natives to deceive Donald, they mimic the same kind of behavior: "You save our lives . . . We be your servants for ever." And as they prostrate themselves, Donald observes: "They are natives too. But a little more civilized."

Another example (Special Number D 423): Donald leaves for "Outer Congolia," because Scrooge's business there has been doing badly. The reason is that "the King ordered his subjects not to give Christmas presents this year. He wants everyone to hand over this money to him." Donald comments: "What selfishness!" And so to work. Donald makes himself king,

being taken for a great magician who flies through the skies. The old monarch is dethroned because "he is not a wise man like you [Donald]. He does not permit us to buy presents." Donald accepts the crown, intending to decamp as soon as the stock is sold out: "My first command as king is . . . buy presents for your families and don't give your king a cent!" The old king had wanted the money to leave the country and eat what he fancied, instead of the fish heads which were traditionally his sole diet. Repentant, he promises that given another chance, he will govern better, "and I will find a way somehow to avoid eating that ghastly stew."

Donald (to the people): "And I assure you that I leave the throne in good hands. Your old king is a good king . . . and wiser than before." The people: "Hurray! Long Live the King!"

The king has learned that he must ally himself with foreigners if he wishes to stay in power, and that he cannot even impose taxes on the people, because this wealth must pass wholly out of the country to Duckburg through the agent of McDuck. Furthermore, the strangers find a solution to the problem of the king's boredom. To alleviate his sense of alienation within his own country, and his consequent desire to travel to the metropolis, they arrange for the massive importation of consumer goods: "Don't worry about that food," says Donald, "I will send you some sauces which will make even fish heads palatable." The king stamps gleefully up and down.

The same formula is repeated over and over again. Scrooge exchanges with the Canadian Indians gates of rustless steel for gates of pure gold (TR 117). Moby Duck and Donald (D 453), captured by the Aridians (Arabs), start to blow soap bubbles, with which the natives are enchanted. "Ha, ha. They break when you catch them. Hee, hee." Ali-Ben-Goli, the chief says "it's real magic. My people are laughing like children. They cannot imagine how it works." "It's only a secret passed from generation to generation," says Moby, "I will reveal it if you give us our freedom." (Civilization is presented as something incomprehensible, to be administered by foreigners). The chief, in amazement, exclaims "Freedom? That's not all I'll give you. Gold, Jewels. My treasure is yours, if you reveal the secret." The Arabs consent to their own despoliation. "We have jewels, but they are of no use to us. They don't make you laugh like magic bubbles." While Donald sneers "poor simpleton,"

Moby hands over the Flip Flop detergent. "You are right, my friend. Whenever you want a little pleasure, just pour out some magic powder and recite the magic words." The story ends on the note that it is not necessary for Donald to excavate the Pyramids (or earth) personally, because, as Donald says, "What do we need a pyramid for, having Ali-Ben-Goli?"

Each time this situation recurs, the natives' joy increases. As each object of their own manufacture is taken away from them, their satisfaction grows. As each artifact from civilization is given to them, and interpreted by them as a manifestation of magic rather then technology, they are filled with delight. Even our fiercest enemies could hardly justify the inequity of such an exchange; how can a fistful of jewels be regarded as equivalent to a box of soap, or a golden crown equal to a cheap watch? Some will object that this kind of barter is all imaginary, but it is unfortunate that these laws of the imagination are tilted unilaterally in favor of those who come from outside, and those who write and publish the magazines.

But how can this flagrant despoliation pass unperceived, or in other words, how can this inequity be disguised as equity? Why is it that imperialist plunder and colonial subjection, to call them by their proper names, do not appear as such?

"We have jewels, but they are of no use to us."

There they are in their desert tents, their caves, their once flourishing cities, their lonely islands, their forbidden fortresses, and they *can never leave them*. Congealed in their past-historic, their needs defined in function of this past, these underdeveloped peoples are denied the right to build their own future. Their crowns, their raw materials, their soil, their energy, their jade elephants, their fruit, but above all, their gold, can never be turned to any use. For them the progress which comes from abroad in the form of multiplicity of technological artifacts, is a mere toy. It will never penetrate the crystallized defense of the noble savage, who is forbidden to become civilized. He will never be able to join the Club of the Producers, because he does not even understand that these objects have been produced. He sees them as magic elements, arising from the foreigner's mind, from his word, his magic wand.

Since the noble savage is denied the prospect of future development, plunder never appears as such, for it only eliminates that which is trifling, superfluous, and dispensable. Unbridled capitalist despoliation is programmed with smiles and coquetry. Poor native. How naïve they are. And since they cannot use their gold, it is better to remove it. It can be used elsewhere.

Scrooge McDuck gets hold of a twenty-four carat moon in which "the gold is so pure that it can be molded like butter." (TR 48, US 12-2/59). But the legitimate owner appears, a Venusian called Muchkale, who is prepared to sell it to Scrooge for a fistful of earth. "Man! That's the biggest *bargain* I ever heard of in all history," cries the miser as he closes the deal. But Muchkale, who is a "good native," magically transforms the fistful of earth into a planet, with continents, oceans, trees, and a whole environment of nature, "Yessir! I was quite impoverished here, with only atoms of *gold* to work with!" he says. Exiled from his state of primitive innocence, longing for some rain and volcanoes, Muchkale rejects his gold in order to return to the land of his origin and content himself with life at subsistence level. "Skunk Cabbage! [his favorite dish on Venus] I live again .... Now I have a *world* of my own, with *food* and *drink* and *life*!" Far from robbing him, Scrooge has done Muchkale a favor by removing all that corrupt metal and facilitating his return to primitive innocence. "He got the dirt he wanted, and I got this fabulous twenty-four carat moon. Five hundred miles thick! Of *solid gold*! But doggoned if I don't think he got the *best* of the bargain!" Poor, but happy, the Venusian is left devoting himself to the celebration of the simple life. It's the old aphorism, the poor have no worries, it is the rich who have all the problems. So let's have no qualms about plundering the poor and underdeveloped.

Conquest has been purged. Foreigners do no harm, they are building the future, on the basis of a society which cannot and will not leave the past.

But there is another way of infantilizing others and exonerating one's own larcenous behavior. Imperialism likes to promote an image of itself as being the impartial judge of the interests of the people, and their liberating angel.

The only thing which cannot be taken from the noble savage is his subsistence living, because losing this would destroy his natural economy, forcing him to abandon Paradise for Mammon and a production economy.

Donald travels to the "Plateau of Abandon" to look for a silver goat, which his Problem Solving Agency has contracted to find for a rich customer. He finds the goat, but breaks it while trying to ride it, and then discovers that this animal – and nothing else – stands between life and death by starvation (forbidden word) for the primitive people who live near the plateau. What had brought this to pass? Some time ago, an earthquake cut off the people and their flocks from their ancient pasturelands. "We would have died of hunger in this patch of earth if a generous white man had not arrived here in that mysterious bird over there [i.e. an aircraft] . . . and made a white goat with the metal from our mine." It is this mechanical goat which leads the flocks of sheep through the dangerous ravine to pasture in the outlying plains, and without it, the sheep get lost. The natives admire the way Donald & Co. decide to venture back through perilous precipices "which only you and the sheep have the courage to cross. Our people have never had a head for heights." Once through the ravine, Donald and nephews mend the goat and bring the sheep safely back to their owners.

Enter at this point the villains: the rich Mr Leech and his spoiled son who had contracted and sent Donald off in search of the goat. "You signed the contract and must hand over the goods." But the evil party is defeated and the ducks reveal themselves as disinterested friends of the natives. Trusting the ducks as they did their Duckburg predecessor, the natives enter into an alliance with the good foreigners against the bad foreigners. The moral Manichaeism serves to affirm foreign sovereignty in its authoritarian and paternalist role. Big Stick and Charity.* The good foreigners, under their ethical cloak, win with the native's confidence, the right to decide the proper distribution of wealth in the land. The villains; course, vulgar, repulsive, out-and-out thieves, are there purely and simply to reveal the ducks as defenders of justice, law, and food for the hungry, and to serve as a whitewash for any further action. Defending the only thing that the noble savage can use (their food), the lack of which would result in their death (or rebellion, either of which would violate their image of infantile innocence), the big city folk establish themselves as the spokesman of these submerged and voiceless peoples.

The ethical division between the two classes of predators, the would-be robbers working openly, and the actual ones working surreptitiously, is constantly repeated. In one episode (TB 62), Mickey and company search for a silver mine and unmask two crooks. The crooks, disguised as Spanish conquistadors, who had originally stolen the mineral, are terrorizing the Indians, and are now making great profits from tourists by selling them "Indian ornaments." The constant characteristic of the natives – irrational fear and panic when faced with any phenomenon which disrupts their natural rhythm of life – serves to emphasize their cowardice (rather like children afraid of the dark), and to justify the necessity that some superior being come to their rescue and bring daylight. As reward for catching the crooks, the heroes are given ranks within the tribe: Minnie, princess; Mickey and Goofy, warriors; and Pluto gets a feather. And, of course, Duckburg gets the "Indian ornaments." The Indians have been given the "freedom to sell their goods on the foreign market." It is only direct and open robbery without offering a share in the profits, which is to be condemned. Mickey's imperialist despoliation is a foil for that of the Spaniards and those who, in the past, undeniably robbed and enslaved the natives more openly.

Things are different nowadays. To rob without payment is robbery undisguised. Taking with payment is no robbery, but a favor. Thus the conditions for the sale of the ornaments and their importation into Duckburg are never in question, for they are based on the supposition of equality between the two negotiating partners.

An isolated tribe of Indians find themselves in a similar situation (D 430, DD 3/66, "Ambush at Thunder Mountain"). They "have declared war on all Ducks" on the basis of a Previous historical experience. Buck Duck, fifty years before (and nothing has changed since then) gypped them doubly: first stealing the natives' land, and then, selling it back to them in a useless condition. So it is a matter of convincing them that not all ducks (white men) are evil, that the frauds of the past can be made good. Any history book – even Hollywood, even television – admits that the native were violated. The history of fraud and exploitation of the past is public knowledge and cannot be buried any longer, and so it appears over and done with. But the present is another matter.

*Original: Garrote y Caritas. Caritas is an international organization under the auspices of a sector of the North American and European Catholic Church (Trans.)

In order to assure the redemptive powers of present-day imperialism, it is only necessary to measure it against old-style colonialism and robbery. Example: Enter a pair of crooks determined to cheat the natives of their natural gas resourses. They are unmasked by the ducks, who are henceforth regarded as friends.

"Let's bury the hatchet, let's collaborate, the races can get along together." What a fine message! It couldn't have been said better by the Bank of America, who, in sponsoring the mini-city of Disneyland in California, calls it a world of peace where all peoples can get along together.

But what happens to the lands?

"A big gas company will do all the work, and pay your tribe well for it." This is the most shameless imperialist politics. Facing the relatively crude crooks of the past and present (handicapped, moreover, by their primitive techniques), stands the sophisticated Great Uncle Company, which will resolve all problems equitably. The guy who comes in from the outside is not necessarily a bad 'un, only if he fails to pay the "fair and proper price." The Company, by contrast, is benevolence incarnate.

This form of exploitation is not all. A Wigwam Motel and a souvenir shop are opened, and excursions are arranged. The Indians are immobilized against their national background and served up for tourist consumption.

The last two examples suggest certain differences from the classic politics of bared faced colonialism. The benevolent collaboration figuring in the Disney comics suggests a form of neocolonialism which rejects the naked pillage of the past, and permits the native a minimal participation in his own exploitation.

Perhaps the clearest manifestation of this phenomenon is a comic (D 432, DD 9/65, "Treasure of Aztecland") written at the height of the Alliance for Progress program about the Indians of Aztecland who at the time of the Conquest had hidden their treasure in the jungle. Now they are saved by the Ducks from the new conquistadors, the Beagle Boys. "This is absurd! Conquistadors don't exist any more!" The pillage of the past was a crime. As the past is criminalized, and the present purified, its real traces are effaced from memory. There is no need to keep the treasure hidden: the Duckburgers (who have already demonstrated their kindness of heart by charitably caring for a stray lamb) will be able to defend the Mexicans. Geography becomes a picture postcard, and is sold as such. The days of yore cannot advance or change, because this would damage the tourist trade. "Visit Aztecland. Entrance: One Dollar." The vacations of the big city people are transformed into a modern vehicle of supremacy, and we shall see later how the natural and physical virtues of the noble savage are preserved intact. A holiday in these places is like a loan, or a blank check on purification and regeneration through communion with nature.

All these examples are based upon common international stereotypes. Who can deny that the Peruvian (in Inca-Blinca, TB 104) is somnolent, sells pottery, sits on his haunches, eats hot peppers, has a thousand-year-old culture – all the dislocated prejudices proclaimed by the tourist posters themselves? Disney does not invent these caricatures, he only exploits them to the utmost. By forcing all peoples of the world into a vision of the dominant (national and international) classes, he gives this vision coherency and justifies the social system on which it is based. These cliches are also used by the mass culture media to dilute the realities common to these people. The only means that the Mexican has of knowing Peru is through caricature, which also implies that Peru is incapable of being anything else, and is unable to rise above this prototypical situation, imprisoned as it is made to seem, within its own exoticism. For Mexican and Peruvian alike, these stereotypes of Latin American peoples become a channel of distorted self-knowledge, a form of self-consumption, and finally, self-mockery. By selecting the most superficial and singular traits of each people in order to differentiate them, and using folklore as a means to "divide and conquer" nations occupying the same dependent position, the comic, like all mass media, exploits the principle of sensationalism. That is, it conceals reality by means of novelty, which not incidentally, also serves to promote sales. Our Latin American countries become trash cans being constantly repainted for the voyeuristic and orgiastic pleasures of the metropolitan nations. Every day, this very minute, television, radio, magazines, newspapers, cartoons, newscasts, films, clothing, and records, from the dignified gab of history textbooks to the trivia of daily conversation, all contribute to weakening the international solidarity of the oppressed. We Latin Americans are separated from each other by the vision we have acquired of each other via the comics and the other mass culture media. This vision is nothing less than our own reduced and distorted image.

This great tacit pool overflowing with the riches of stereotype is based upon common cliches, so that no one needs to go directly to sources of information gathered from reality itself. Each of us carries within a Boy Scout Handbook packed with the commonplace wisdom of Everyman.

Contradictions flourish, however, and this is fortunate. When they become so blatant as to constitute, in spite of metropolitan press, *news*, it is impossible to maintain the same old unruffled storyline. The open conflict can no longer be concealed by the same formulas as the situation which, although inherently conflictive, is not yet explosive enough to be considered newsworthy.

The diseases of the system are manifest on many levels. The artist who shatters the habits of vision imposed by the mass media, who attacks the spectator and undermines his stability, is dismissed as a mere eccentric, who happens to cast colors or words in the wind. The genius is isolated from real life, and all his attempts to reconcile reality with its aesthetic representation, are neutralized. He is caricatured in Goofy, who wins the first prize in the "pop" art contest, by sliding crazily through a parking lot overturning paint cans and creating chaos (TB 99, DD 11/67). Amidst the artistic trash that he has generated, Goofy cries: "Me [the winner]! Gawrsh! I wasn't even trying!" And art loses its offensive character: "This sure is easy work. At last I can earn money and have fun at the same time, and no one gets mad at me." The public has no reason to be disconcerted by these "masterpieces": they bear no relation to their lives, only the weak and stupid devote themselves to that kind of sport. The same thing happens with the "hippies," "love-ins," and peace marches. In one episode (TR 40, US 12/63) a gang of irate people (observe the way they are lumped together) march fanatically by, only to be decoyed by Donald towards his lemonade stand, with the shout "There's a thirsty-looking group. Hey people, throw down your banners and have free lemonades!" Setting peace aside, they descend upon Donald like a herd of buffa-

loes, snatching his money, and slurping noisily. Moral: see what hypocrites these rioters are; they sell their ideals for a glass of lemonade.

In contrast, there stands another group also drinking lemonade, but in orderly fashion — little cadets, disciplined, obedient, clean, goodlooking, and truly pacific; no dirty, anarchic "rebels" they.

This strategy, by which protest is converted into imposture, is called *dilution*: banalize an unusual phenomenon of the social body and symptom of a cancer, in such a way that it appears as an isolated incident removed from its social context, so that it then can be automatically rejected by "public opinion" as a passing itch. Just give yourself a scratch, and be done with it. Disney did not, of course, get this little light bulb all on his own. It is part of the metabolism of the system, which reacts to the facts of a situation by trying to absorb and eliminate them. It is part of a strategy, consciously or unconsciously orchestrated.

For example, the adoption by the fashion industry of the primitive dynamite of the hippie is designed to neutralize its power of denunciation. Or, the attempts of advertising, in the U.S., to liquify the concept of the women's liberation movements. "Liberate" yourself by buying a new mixer or dishwasher. This is the real revolution: new styles, low prices. Airplane hijacking (TR 113) is emptied of its social-political significance and is presented as the work of crazy bandits, "From what we read in the papers, hijacking has become very fashionable." Thus, the media minimize the matter and its implications, and reassure the public that nothing is really going on.

But all these phenomena are merely potentially subversive, mere straws in the wind. Should there emerge any phenomenon truly flouting the Disney laws of creation which govern the exemplary and submissive behavior of the noble savage, this cannot remain concealed. It is brought out garnished, prettified, and reinterpreted for the reader, who being young, must be protected. This second strategy is called *recuperation*: the utilization of a potentially dangerous phenomenon of the social body in such a way that it serves to justify the continued need of the social system and its values, and very often justifies the violence and repression which are part of that system.

Such is the case of the Vietnam War, where protest was manipulated to justify the vitality and values of the system which produced the war, not to end the injustice and violence of the war itself. The "ending" of the war was only a problem of "public opinion."

The realm of Disney is not one of fantasy, for it does react to world events. Its vision of Tibet is not identical to its vision of Indochina. Fifteen years ago the Caribbean was a sea of pirates. Disney has had to adjust to the fact of Cuba and the invasion of the Dominican Republic. The buccaneer now cries "Viva the Revolution," and has to be defeated. It will be Chile's turn yet.

Searching for a jade elephant, Scrooge and his family arrive in Unsteadystan, "where every thug wants to be ruler," and "where there is always someone shooting at someone else." (TR 99, US 7/66, "Treasure of Marco Polo"). A state of civil war is immediately turned into an incomprehensible game of someone-or-other against someone-or-other, a stupid fratricide lacking in any ethical direction or socio-economic *raison d'etre*. The war in Vietnam becomes a mere interchange of unconnected and senseless bullets, and a truce becomes a siesta. "Wahn Beeg Rhat, yes, Duckburg, no!" cries a guerilla in support of an ambitious (communist) dictator, as he dynamites the Duckburg embassy. Noticing that his watch is not working properly, the Vietcong (no less) mutters "Shows you can't trust these watches from the 'worker's paradise.'" The struggle for power is purely personal, the eccentricity of ambition: "Hail to Wahn Beeg Rhat, dictator of all the happy people," goes the cry and *sotto voce* "happy or not." Defending his conquest, the dictator gives orders to kill. "Shoot him, don't let him spoil my *revolution.*" The savior in this chaotic situation is Prince Char Ming, also known [in the Spanish version] as Yho Soy ["I am" – the English is Soy Bheen], names expressive of his magical egocentricity. He comes to reunify the country and "pacify" the people. He is destined to triumph, because the soldiers refuse to obey the orders of a leader who has lost his charisma, who is not "Char Ming." So one guerrilla wonders why they "keep these silly revolutions going forever." Another denounces them, demanding a return to the King, "like in the good old days."

In order to close the circuit and the alliance between Duckburg and Prince Char Ming, Scrooge McDuck presents to Unsteadystan the treasure and the jade elephant which once had belonged to the people of that country. One of the nephews observes: "They will be of use to

the poor." And finally, Scrooge, in his haste to get out of this parody of Vietnam, promises "When I return to Duckburg, I will do even more for you. I will return the million dollar tail of the jade elephant."

But we can bet that Scrooge will forget his promises as soon as he gets back. As proof we find in another comic book (D 445) the following dialogue which takes place in Duckburg:

Nephew: "They got the asiatic flu as well."

Donald: "I've always said that nothing good could come out of Asia."

A similar reduction of a historical situation takes place in the Republic of San Bananador, obviously in the Caribbean or Central America (D 364, CS 4/64, "Captain Blight's Mystery Ship"). Waiting in a port, Donald makes fun of the children playing at being shanghaied: These things just don't happen any more; shanghai-ing, weevly beans, walking the plank, pirate-invested seas — these are all things of the past. But it turns out that there are places where such horrors still survive, and the nephew's game is soon interrupted by a man trying to escape from a ship carrying a dangerous cargo and commanded by a captain who is a living menace. Terror reigns on board. When the man is forcibly brought back to the ship, he invokes the name of liberty ("I'm a *free* man! Let me *go*!"), while his kidnappers treat him as a *slave*. Although Donald, typically, makes light of the incident ("probably only a little rhubarb about wages," or "actors making a film"), he and his nephews are also captured. Life on board is a nightmare; the food is weevly beans, even the rats are prevented from leaving the ship, and there is forced labor, with slaves, slaves, and more slaves. All is subject to the unjust, arbitrary and crazy rule of Captain Blight and his bearded followers.

Surely these must be pirates from olden days. Absolutely not. They are revolutionaries (Cuban, no less) fighting against the government of San Bananador, and pursued by the navy for trying to supply rebels with a shipment of arms. "They'll be scouting with *planes*! Douse all lights! We'll give 'em the slip in the *dark!*" And the radio operator, fist raised on high, shouts: "Viva the Revolution!" The only hope, according to Donald, is "the good old navy, symbol of law and order." The rebel opposition is thus automatically cast in the role of tyranny, dictatorship, totalitarianism. The slave society reigning on board ship is the replica of the society which they propose to install in place of the legitimately established regime. Apparently, in modern times it is the champions of popular insurgency who will bring back human slavery.

The political drift of Disney is blatant in these few comics where he is impelled to reveal his intentions openly. It is also inescapable in the bulk of them, where he uses animal symbolism, infantilism, and "noble savagery" to cover over the network of interests arising from a concrete and historically determined social system: U.S. imperialism.

The problem is not only Disney's equation of

the child with the noble savage, and the noble savage with the underdeveloped peoples. It is also — and here is the crux of the matter — that what is said, referred to, revealed and disguised about all of them, has, in fact, only one true object: the working class.

The imaginative world of the child has become the political utopia of a social class. In the Disney comics, one never meets a member of the working or proletarian classes, and nothing is the product of an industrial process. But this does not mean that the worker is absent. On the contrary: he is present under two masks, that of the noble savage and that of the criminal-lumpen. Both groups serve to destroy the worker as a class reality, and preserve certain myths which the bourgeoisie have from the very beginning been fabricating and adding to in order to conceal and domesticate the enemy, impede his solidarity, and make him function smoothly within the system and cooperate in his own ideological enslavement.

In order to rationalize their dominance and justify their privileged position, the bourgeoisie divided the world of the dominated as follows: first, the peasant sector, which is harmless, natural, truthful, ingenuous, spontaneous, infantile, and static; second, the urban sector, which is threatening, teeming, dirty, suspicious, calculating, embittered, vicious, and essentially mobile. The peasant acquires in this process of mythification the exclusive property of being "popular," and becomes installed as a folk-guardian of everything produced and preserved by the people. Far from the influence of the steaming urban centers, he is purified through a cyclical return to the primitive virtues of the earth. The myth of the people as noble savage — the people as a child who must be protected for its own good — arose in order to justify the domination of a class. The peasants were the only ones capable of becoming incontrovertible vehicles for the permanent validity of bourgeois ideals. Juvenile literature fed on these "popular" myths and served as a constant allegorical testimony to what the people were supposed to be.

Each great urban civilization (Alexandria for Theocritus, Rome for Virgil, the modern era for Sannazaro, Montemayor, Shakespeare, Cervantes, d'Urfé) created its pastoral myth: an extra-social Eden chaste and pure. Together with this evangelical bucolism, there emerged a picturesque literature teeming with ruffians, vagabonds, gamblers, gluttons, etc., who reveal the true nature of urban man; mobile, degenerate, irredeemable. The world was divided between the lay heaven of the shepherds, and the terrestrial inferno of the unemployed. At the same time, a utopian literature flourished (Thomas More, Tommaso Campanella), projecting into the future on the basis of an optimism fostered by technology, and a pessimism resulting from the breakdown of medieval unity, the ecstatic realm of social perfection. The rising bourgeoisie, which gave the necessary momentum to the voyages of discovery, found innumerable peoples who theoretically corresponded to their pastoral-utopian schemata; their ideal of universal Christian reason proclaimed by Erasmian humanism. Thus the division between positive-popular-rustic and negative-popular-proletarian was overwhelmingly reinforced. The new continents were colonized in the name of this division; to prove that removed from original sin and mercantilist taint, these continents might be the site for the ideal history which the bourgeoisie had once imagined for themselves at home. An ideal history which was ruined and threatened by the constant opposition of the idle, filthy, teeming, promiscuous, and extortionary proletarians.

In spite of the failure in Latin America, in spite of the failure in Africa, Oceania and in Asia, the myth never lost its vitality. On the contrary, it served as a constant spur in the only country which was able to develop it still further. By opening the frontier further and further, the United States elaborated the myth and eventually gave birth to a "Way of Life," and ideology shared by the infernal Disney. A man, who in trying to open and close the frontier of the child's imagination, based himself precisely on those now-antiquated myths which gave rise to his own country.

The historical nostalgia of the bourgeoisie, so much the product of its objective contradictions — its conflicts with the proletariat, the difficulties arising from the industrial revolution, as the myth was always belied and always renewed — this nostalgia took upon itself a twofold disguise, one geographical: the lost paradise which it could not enjoy, and the other biological: the child who would serve to legitimize its plans for human emancipation. There was no other place to flee, unless it was to that other nature, technology.

The yearning of a McLuhan, the prophet of

the technological era, to use mass communications as a means of returning to the "planetary village" (modelled upon the "primitive tribal communism" of the underdeveloped world), is nothing but a utopia of the future which revives a nostalgia of the past. Although the bourgeoisie were unable, during the centuries of their existence, to realize their imaginary historical design, they kept it nice and warm in every one of their expeditions and justifications. Disney characters are afraid of technology and its social implications; they never fully accept it; they prefer the past. McLuhan is more farsighted: he understands that to interpret technology as a return to the values of the past is the solution which imperialism must offer in the next stage of its strategy.

But our next stage is to ask a question which McLuhan never poses: if the proletariat is eliminated, who is producing all that gold, all those riches?

IV. THE GREAT PARACHUTIST

"If I were able to produce money with my black magic, I wouldn't be in the middle of the desert looking for gold, would I?"

Magica de Spell (TR 111)

What are these adventurers escaping from their claustrophobic cities really after? What is the true motive of their flight from the urban center? Bluntly stated: in more than seventy-five percent of our sampling they are looking for gold, in the remaining twenty-five percent they are competing for fortune – in the form of money or fame – in the city.

Why should gold, criticized ever since the beginning of a monetary economy as a contamination of human relations and the corruption of human nature, mingle here with the innocence of the noble savage (child and people)? Why should gold, the fruit of urban commerce and industry, flow so freely from these rustic and natural environments?

The answer to these questions lies in the manner in which our earthly paradise generates all this raw wealth.

It comes, above all, in the form of hidden treasure. It is to be found in the Third World, and is magically pointed out by some ancient map, a parchment, an inheritance, an arrow, or a clue in a picture. After great adventures and obstacles, and after defeating some thief trying to get there first (disqualified from the prize because it wasn't his idea, but filched from someone else's map), the good Duckburgers appropriate the idols, figurines, jewels, crowns, pearls, necklaces, rubies, emeralds, precious daggers, golden helmets etc.

First of all, we are struck by the *antiquity* of the coveted object. It has lain buried for thousands of years: within caverns, ruins, pyramids, coffers, sunken ships, viking tombs etc. – that is, any place with vestiges of civilized life in the past. Time separates the treasure from its original owners, who have bequeathed this unique heritage to the future. Furthermore, this wealth is left without heirs; despite their total poverty, the noble savages take no interest in the gold abounding so near them (in the sea, in the mountains, beneath the tree etc.). These ancient civilizations are envisioned, by Disney, to have come to a somewhat catastrophic end. Whole families exterminated, armies in constant defeat, people forever hiding their treasure, for . . . for whom? Disney conveniently exploits the supposed total destruction of past civilizations in order to carve an abyss between the innocent present-day inhabitants and the previous, but non-ancestral

inhabitants. The innocents are not heirs to the past, because that past is not father to the present. It is, at best, the uncle. There is an empty gap. Whoever arrives first with the brilliant idea and the excavating shovel has the right to take the booty back home. The noble savages have no history, and they have forgotten their past, which was never theirs to begin with. By depriving them of their past, Disney destroys their historical memory, in the same way he deprives a child of his parenthood and genealogy, with the same result: the destruction of their ability to see themselves as a product of history.

It would appear, moreover, that these forgotten peoples never actually produced this treasure. They are consistently described as warriors, conquerors and explorers, as if they had seized it from someone else. In any event, there is no reference at any time – how could there be, with something that happened so long ago? – to the making of these objects, although they must have been handcrafted. The actual origin of the treasure is a mystery which is never even mentioned. The only legitimate owner of the treasure is the person who had the brilliant idea of tracking it down; he creates it the moment he thinks of setting off in search of it. It never really existed before, anywhere. *The ancient civilization is the uncle of the object, and the father is the man who gets to keep it.* Having discovered it, he rescued it from the oblivion of time.

But even then the object remains in some slight contact with the ancient civilization; it is the last vestige of vanishing faces. So the finder of the treasure has one more step to take. In the vast coffers of Scrooge there is never the slightest trace of the handcrafted object, in spite of the fact that, as we have seen, he brings treasure home from so many expeditions. Only banknotes and coins remain. As soon as the treasure leaves its country of origin for Duckburg, it loses shape, and is swallowed up by Scrooge's dollars. It is stripped of the last vestige of that crafted form which might link it to persons, places and time. It turns into gold without the odor of fatherland or history. Uncle Scrooge can bathe, cavort, and plunge in his coins and banknotes (in Disney these are no mere metaphors) more comfortably than in spiky idols and jewelled crowns. Everything is transmuted mechanically (but without machines) into a single monetary mold in which the last breath of human life is extinguished. And finally, the adventure which led to the relic fades away, together with the relic itself. As treasure buried in the earth, it pointed to a past, however remote it may be, and even as treasure in Duckburg (were it to survive in its original form) it would point to the adventure experienced, however remote that may be. Just as the historical memory of the original civilization is blotted out, so is Scrooge's personal memory of his experience. Either way, history is melted down in the crucible of the dollar. The falsity of all the Disney publicity regarding the educational and aesthetic value of these comics, which are touted as journeys through time and space and aids to the learning of history and geography etc., stands revealed. For Disney, history exists in order to be demolished, in order to be turned into the dollar which gave it birth and lays it to rest. Disney even kills archeology, the science of artifacts.

Disnification is Dollarfication: all objects (and, as we shall see, actions as well) are transformed into gold. Once this conversion is completed *the adventure is over*: one cannot go further, for gold, ingot or dollar bill, cannot be reduced to a more symbolic level. The only prospect is to go hunting for more of the same, since once it is invested it becomes active, and it will start taking sides and enter contemporary history. Better

cross it out and start afresh. Add more adventures, which accumulate in aimless and sterile fashion.

So it is not surprising that the hoarder desires to skip these productive phases, and go off in search of pure gold.

But even in the treasure hunt the productive process is lacking. On your marks, ready, go, collect; like fruit picked from a tree. The problem lies not in the actual extraction of the treasure, but in discovering its geographical location. Once one has got there, the gold — always in nice fat nuggets — is already in the bag, without having raised a single callous on the hand which carries it off. Mining is like abundant agriculture, once one has had the genius to spot the mine. And agriculture is conceived like picking flowers in an infinite garden. There is no effort in the extraction, it is foreign to the material of which the object is made: bland, soft, and unresistant. The mineral only plays hide and seek. One only needs cunning to lift it from its sanctuary, not physical labor to shape its content and give it form, changing it from its natural physical-mineral state into something useful to human society. In the absence of this process of transformation, wealth is made to appear as if society creates it by means of the spirit, the idea, the little light bulbs flashing over the characters' heads. Nature apparently delivers the material ready-to-use, as in primitive life, without the intervention of workman and tool. The Duckburgers have airplanes, submarines, radar, helicopters, rockets; but not so much as a stick to open up the earth. "Mother Earth" is prodigal, and taking in the gold is as innocent as breathing in fresh air. Nature feeds gold to these creatures: it is the only sustenance these aurivores desire.

Now we understand why it is that the gold is found yonder in the world of the noble savage. It cannot appear in the city, because the normal order of life is that of production (although we shall see later how Disney eliminates even this factor in the cities). The origin of this wealth has to appear natural and innocent. Let us place the Duckburgers in the great uterus of history: all comes from nature, nothing is produced by man. The child must be taught (and along the way, the adult convince himself) that the objects have no history; they arise by enchantment, and are untouched by human hand. The stork brought the gold. It is the immaculate conception of wealth.

The production process in Disney's world is natural, not social. And it is magical. All objects arrive on parachutes, are conjured out of hats, are presented as gifts in a non-stop birthday party, and are spread out like mushrooms. Mother earth gives all: pick her fruits, and be rid of guilt. No one is getting hurt.

Gold is produced by some inexplicable, miraculous natural phenomenon. Like rain, wind, snow, waves, an avalanche, a volcano, or like another planet.

"What is that falling from the sky?"

"Hardened raindrops . . . Ouch! Or molten metal."

"It can't be. It's gold coins. Gold!"

"Hurray! A rain of gold! Just look at that rainbow."

"We must be having visions, Uncle Scrooge. It can't be true."

But it is.

Like bananas, like copper, like tin, like cattle. One sucks the milk of gold from the earth. Gold is claimed from the breast of nature without the mediation of work. The claimants have clearly acquired the rights of ownership thanks to their native genius, or else, thanks to their accumulated suffering (an abstracted form of work, as we explain below).

It is not superhuman magic, like that of the

witch Magica de Spell, for example, which creates the gold. This kind of magic, distilled from the demon of technology, is merely a parasite upon nature. Man cannot counterfeit the wealth. He has to get it through some other charmed source, the natural one, in which he does not have to intervene, but only deserve.

Example. Donald and nephews, followed by Magica (TR 111, DD 1/66), search for the rainbow's end, behind which, according to the legend, is hidden a golden pot, the direct fruit of nature (TR 111, US 38, 6-8/62). Our heroes do not exactly find the mythical treasure, but return with another kind of "pot of gold": fat commercial profits. How did this happen? Uncle Scrooge's airplane, loaded with lemon seeds, accidently inseminated the North African desert, and when Magica de Spell provoked a rainstorm, within minutes the whole area became an orchard of lemon trees. The seeds (i.e. ideas) come from abroad, magic or accident sows them, and the useless, underdeveloped desert soil makes them grow. "Come on, boys!" cries Donald, "let's start picking lemons. And take them to the town to sell." Work is minimal and a pleasure; the profit is tremendous.

This does not happen only in distant places, but also in Duckburg, on its beaches, woods, and mountains. Donald and Gladstone, for example (D 381, CS 5/59), go on a beachcombing expedition, to see who comes up with the most valuable find to give to Daisy and win her company for lunch. The sea washes up successively, huge seashells, a giant snail, a "very valuable" ancient Indian seashell necklace, rubber boats (one each for Gladstone and Donald), a rubber elephant loaded with tropical fruits, papayas and mangoes, an Alaskan kayak, a mirror, and an ornamental comb. The sea is a cornucopia; generous nature showers abundance upon man, and in the Third World, nature does so in a particularly exotic form. In and beyond Duckburg, it is always nature that mediates between man and wealth.

It is surely undeniable nowadays that all man's real and concrete achievements derive from his effort and his work. Although nature provides the raw materials, man must struggle to make a living from them. If this were not so, we would still be in Eden.

In the world of Disney, no one has to work in order to produce. There is a constant round of buying, selling and consuming, but to all appearances, none of the products involved has required any effort whatsoever to make. Nature is the great labor force, producing objects of human and social utility as if they were natural.

The human origin of the product – be it table, house, car, clothing, gold, coffee, wheat, or maize (which, according to TR 96, comes from *granaries*, direct from warehouses, rather than from the fields) – has been suppressed. The process of production has been eliminated, as has all reference to its genesis; the actors, the objects, the circumstances of the process never existed. What, in fact, has been erased is the paternity of the object, and the possibility to link it to the process of production.

This brings us back to the curious Disney family structure with the absence of natural paternity. The simultaneous lack of direct biological production and direct economic production, is not coincidental. They both coincide and reinforce a dominant ideological structure which also seeks to eliminate the working class, the true producer of objects. And with it, the class struggle.

Disney exorcises history, magically expelling the socially (and biologically) reproductive element, leaving amorphous, rootless, and inoffensive products – without sweat, without blood, without effort, and without the misery which they inevitably sow in the life of the working class. The object produced is truly fantastic; it is purged of unpleasant associations which are relegated to an invisible background of dreary, sordid slumland living. Disney uses the imagination of the child to eradicate all reference to the real world. The products of history which "people" and pervade the world of Disney are incessantly bought and sold. But Disney has appropriated these products and the work which brought them into being, just as the bourgeoisie has appropriated the products and labor of the working class. The situation is an ideal one for the bourgeoisie: they get the product without the workers. Even to the point when on the rare occasion a factory does appear (e.g. a brewery in TR 120) there is never more than one workman who seems to be acting as caretaker. His role appears to be little more than that of a policeman protecting the autonomous and automated factory of his boss. This is the world the bourgeoisie have always dreamed of. One in which a man can amass great wealth, without facing its producer and product: the worker. Objects are cleansed of guilt. It is a world of pure surplus without the slightest suspicion of a worker demanding the slightest reward. The proletariat, born out of the contradictions of the bourgeois regime, sell their labor "freely" to the highest bidder, who transforms the labor into wealth for his own social class. In the Disney world, the proletariat are expelled from the society they created, thus ending all antagonisms, conflicts, class struggle and indeed, the very concept of social class. Disney's is a world of bourgeois interests with the cracks in the structure repeatedly papered over. In the imaginary realm of Disney, the rosy publicity fantasy of the bourgeoisie is realized to perfection: wealth without wages, deodorant without sweat. Gold becomes a toy, and the characters who play with it are amusing children; after all, the way the world goes, they aren't doing any harm to anyone . . . within *that* world. But in *this* world there is harm in dreaming and realizing the dream of a particular class, as if it were the dream of the whole of humanity.

There is a term which would be like dynamite to Disney, like a scapulary to a vampire, like electricity convulsing a frog: social class. That is why Disney must publicize his creations as universal, beyond frontiers; they reach all homes, they reach all countries. O immortal Disney, international patrimony, reaching all children everywhere, everywhere, everywhere.

Marx had a word — fetishism — for the process which separates the product (accumulated work) from its origin and expresses it as gold, abstracting it from the actual circumstances of production. It was Marx who discovered that behind his gold and silver, the capitalist conceals the whole process of accumulation which he achieves at the worker's expense (surplus value). The words "precious metals" "gold," and "silver" are used to hide from the worker the fact that he is being robbed, and that the capitalist is no mere accumulator of wealth, but the appropriator of the product of social production. The transformation of the worker's labor into gold, fools him into believing that it is gold which is the true generator of wealth and source of production.

Gold, in sum, is a *fetish*, the supreme fetish, and in order for the true origin of wealth to remain concealed, all social relations, all people are *fetishized.*

Since gold is the actor, director and producer of this film, humanity is reduced to the level of a thing. Objects possess a life of their own, and humanity controls neither its products nor its own destiny. The Disney universe is proof of the internal coherence of the world ruled by gold, and an exact reflection of the political design it reproduces.

Nature, by taking over human production, makes it evaporate. But the products remain. What for? To be consumed. Of the capitalist process which goes from production to consumption, Disney knows only the second stage. This is consumption rid of the original sin of production, just as the son is rid of the original sin of sex represented by his father, and just as history is rid of the original sin of class and conflict.

Let us look at the social structure in the Disney comic. For example, the professions. In Duckburg, everyone seems to belong to the tertiary sector, that is, those who sell their services: hairdressers, real estate and tourist agencies, salespeople of all kinds (especially shop assistants selling sumptuary objects, and vendors going from door-to-door), nightwatchmen, waiters, delivery boys, and people attached to the entertainment business. These fill the world with objects and more objects, which are never produced, but always purchased. There is a constant repetition of the act of buying. But this mercantile relationship is not limited to the level of objects. Contractual language permeates the most commonplace forms of human intercourse. People see themselves as buying each other's services, or selling themselves. It is as if the only security were to be found in the language of money. All human interchange is a form of commerce; people are like a purse, an object in a shop window, or coins constantly changing hands.

"It's a deal," " 'What the eye doesn't see . . . you can take for free' — I should patent that saying." "You must have spent a fortune on this party, Donald." These are explicit examples, it is generally implicit that all activity revolves around money, status or the status-giving object, and the

competition for them.

The world of Walt, in which every word advertises something or somebody, is under an intense compulsion to consume. The Disney vision can hardly transcend consumerism when it is fixated upon selling itself, along with other merchandise. Sales of the comic are fostered by the so-called "Disneyland Clubs," which are heavily advertised in the comics, and are financed by commercial firms who offer cut prices to members. The absurd ascent from corporal to general, right up to chief-of-staff, is achieved exclusively through the purchase of Disneyland comics, and sending in the coupons. It offers no benefits, except the incentive to continue buying the magazine. The solidarity which it appears to promote among readers simply traps them in the buying habit.

Surely it is not good for children to be surreptitiously injected with a permanent compulsion to buy objects they don't need. This is Disney's sole ethical code: consumption for consumption's sake. Buy to keep the system going, throw the things away (rarely are objects shown being enjoyed, even in the comic), and buy the same thing, only slightly different, the next day. Let money change hands, and if it ends up fattening the pockets of Disney and his class, so be it.

Disney creatures are engaged in a frantic chase for money. As we are in an amusement world, allow us to describe the land of Disney as a carrousel of consumerism. Money is the goal everyone strives for, because it manages to embody all the qualities of their world. To start with the obvious, its powers of acquisition are unlimited, encompassing the affection of others, security, influence, authority, prestige, travel, vacation, leisure, and to temper the boredom of living, entertainment. The only access to these things is through money, which comes to symbolize the good things of life, all of which can be bought.

But who decides the distribution of wealth in the world of Disney? By what criteria is one placed at the top or the bottom of the pile?

Let us examine some of the mechanisms involved. Geographical distance separates the potential owner, who takes the initiative, from the ready-to-use gold which passively awaits him. But this distance in itself is insufficient to create obstacles and suspense along the way. So a *thief* after the same treasure, appears on the scene. Chief of the criminal gangs are the Beagle Boys, but there are innumerable other professional crooks, luckless buccaneers, and decrepit eagles, along with the inevitable Black Pete. To these we may add Magica de Spell, Big Bad Wolf, and some lesser thieves of the forest, like Brer bear and Brer Fox.

They are all oversize, dark, ugly, ill-educated, unshaven, stupid (they never have a good idea), clumsy, dissolute, greedy, conceited (always toadying each other), and unscrupulous. They are lumped together in groups and are individually indistinguishable. The professional crooks, like the Beagle Boys, are conspicuous for their prison identification number and burglar's mask. Their criminality is innate: "Shut up," says a cop seizing a Beagle Boy, "you weren't born to be a guard. Your vocation is jailbird." (F 57).

Crime is the only work they know; otherwise, they are slothful unto eternity. Big Bad Wolf (D 281) reads a book all about disguises (printed by Confusion Publishers): "At last I have found the perfect disguise: no one will believe that Big Bad Wolf is capable of working." So he disguises himself as a worker. With his moustache, hat, overalls, barrow, and pick and shovel, he sees himself as quite the southern convict on a road gang.

As if their criminal record were not sufficient to impress upon us the illegitimacy of their ambitions, they are constantly pursuing the treasure already amassed or pre-empted by others. The Beagle Boys versus Scrooge McDuck are the best example, the others being mere variations on this central theme. In a world so rich in maps and badly kept secrets, it is a statistical improbability and seems unfair that the villains should not occasionally, at least, get hold of a parchment first. Their inability to deserve this good fortune is another indication that there is no question of them changing their status. Their fate is fruitless robbery or intent to rob, constant arrest or constant escape from jail (perhaps there are so many of them that jail can never hold them all?). They are a constant threat to those who had the idea of hunting for gold.

The only obstacle to the adventurer's getting his treasure, is not a very realistic one. The sole purpose of the presence of the villain is to legitimatize the right of the other to appropriate the treasure. Occasionally the adventurer is faced with a moral dilemma: his gold or someone else's life. He always chooses in favor of the life, although he somehow never has to sacrifice the gold (the choice was not very real, the dice were loaded). But he can at least confront evil temptations, whereas the villains, with a few exceptions, never have a chance to search their conscience, and to rise above their condition.

Disney can conceive of no other threat to wealth than theft. His obsessive need to criminalize any person who infringes the laws of private property, invites us to look at these villains more closely. The darkness of their skin, their ugliness, the disorder of their dress, their stature, their reduction to numerical catagories, their mob-like character, and the fact that they are "condemned" in perpetuity, all add up to a stereotypical stigmatization of the bosses' real enemy, the one who truly threatens his property.

But the real life enemy of the wealthy is not the thief. Were there only thieves about him, the man of property could convert history into a struggle between legitimate owners and criminals, who are to be judged according to the property laws he, the owner, has established. But reality is different. The element which truly challenges the legitimacy and necessity of the monopoly of wealth, and is capable of destroying it, is the working class, whose only means of liberation is to liquidate the economic base of the bourgeoisie and abolish private property. Since the moment the bourgeoisie began exploiting the proletariat, the former has tried to reduce the resistance of the latter, and indeed, the class struggle itself, to a battle between good and evil, as Marx showed in his analysis of Eugene Sue's serial novels.* The moral label is designed to conceal the root of the conflict, which is economic, and at the same time to censure the actions of the class enemy.

In Disney, the working class has therefore been split into two groups: criminals in the city, and noble savages in the countryside. Since the Disney worldview emasculates violence and social conflicts, even the urban rogues are conceived as naughty children ("boys"). As the anti-model, they are always losing, being spanked, and celebrating their stupid ideas by dancing in circles, hand in hand. They are expressions of the bourgeois desire to portray workers' organizations as a motley mob of crazies.

Thus, when Scrooge is confronted by the possibility that Donald has taken to thieving (F 178), he says "My nephew, a robber? Before my own eyes? I must call the police and the lunatic asylum. He must have gone mad." This statement

*Karl Marx, *The Holy Family* (1845), cf. Marcelin Pleynet, "A propos d'une analyse des *Mystères de Paris*, par Marx dans *La Sainte Famille*," in *La Nouvelle Critique*, Paris, numéro spécial, 1968.

reflects the reduction of criminal activity into a psychopathic disease, rather than the result of social conditioning. The bourgeoisie convert the defects of the working class which are the outcome of their exploitation, into moral blemishes, and objects of derision and censure, so as to weaken them and to conceal that exploitation. The bourgeoisie even impose their own values upon the ambitions of the enemy, who, incapable of originality, steal in order to become millionaires themselves and join the exploiting class. Never are they depicted as trying to improve society. This caricature of workers, which twists every characteristic capable of lending them dignity and respect, and thereby, identity as a social class, turns them into a spectacle of mockery and contempt. (And parenthetically, in the modern technological era, the daily mass culture diet of the bourgeoisie still consists of the same mythic caricatures which arose during the late nineteenth century machine age).

The criterion for dividing good from bad is honesty, that is, the respect for private property. Thus in "Honesty Rewarded"(D 393, CS 12/45), the nephews find a ten dollar bill and fight for it, calling each other "thief," "crook," and "villain." But Donald intervenes: such a sum, found in the city, must have a legal owner, who must be traced. This is a titanic task, for all the big, ugly, violent, dark-skinned people try to steal the money for themselves. The worst is one who wants to steal the note in order to "buy a pistol to rob the orphanage." Peace finally returns (significantly, Donald was reading *War and Peace* in the first scene), when the true owner of the money appears. She is a poor little girl, famished and ragged, the only case of social misery in our entire sample. "This is all my mom had left, and we haven't eaten all day long."

Just as the "good" foreigners defended the simple natives of the Third World, now they pro-

tect another little native, the underprivileged mite of the big city. The nephews have behaved like saints (they actually wear haloes in the last picture), because they have recognized the right of each and all to possess the money they already own. There is no question of an unjust distribution of wealth: if everyone were like the honest ducklings rather than the ugly cheats, the system would function perfectly. The little girl's problem is not her poverty, it is having *lost* the only money her family had (which presumably will last forever, or else they will starve and the whole house of Disney will come tumbling down). To avoid war and preserve social peace, everyone should deliver unto others what is already theirs. The ducklings decline the monetary reward offered by Donald: "We already have our reward. Knowing that we have helped make someone happy." But the act of charity underlines the moral superiority of the givers and justifies the mansion to which they return after their "good works" in the slums. If they hadn't returned the banknote, they would have descended to the level of the Beagle Boys, and would not be worthy enough to win the treasure hunt. The path to wealth lies through charity which is a good moral investment. The number of lost children, injured lambs, old ladies needing help to cross the street, is an index of the requirements for entry into the "good guys club" — after one has been already nominated by another "good guy." In the absence of active virtue, Good Works are the proof of moral superiority.

Prophetically, Alexis de Tocqueville wrote in his *Democracy in America*, "By this means, a kind of virtuous materialism may ultimately be established in the world, which would not corrupt, but enervate the soul, and noiselessly unbend its springs of action." It is a pity that the Frenchman who wrote this in the mid-nineteenth century did not live to visit the land of Disney, where his words have been burlesqued in a great idealistic cock-a-doodle-doo.

Thus the winners are announced in advance. In this race for money where all the contestants are apparently in the same position, what is the factor which decides this one wins and the other one loses? If goodness-and-truth are on the side of the "legitimate" owner, how does someone else take ownership of the property?

Nothing could be more simple and more revealing: they can't. The bad guys (who remember behave like children) are bigger, stronger, faster and armed; the good guys have the advantage of superior intelligence, and use it mercilessly. The bad guys rack their brains desperately for ideas (in D 446, "I have a terrific plan in my head," says one, scratching it like a half-wit, "Are you sure you have a head, 176–716?"). Their brainlessness is *invariably* what leads to their downfall. They are caught in a double bind: if they use only their legs, they won't get there; if they use their heads as well, they won't get there either. Non-intellectuals by definition, their ideas can never prosper. Thinking won't do you bad guys any good, better rely on those arms and legs, eh? The little adventurers will always have a better and more brilliant idea, so there's no point in competing with them. They hold a monopoly on thought, brains, words, and for that matter, on the meaning of the world at large. It's their world, they have to know it better than you bad guys, right?

There can be only one conclusion: behind good and evil are hidden not only the social antagonists, but also a definition of them in terms of soul versus body, spirit versus matter, brain versus muscle, and intellectual versus manual work. A division of labor which cannot be questioned. The good guys have "cornered the knowledge market" in their competition against

the muscle-bound brutes.

But there is more. Since the laboring classes are reduced to legs running for a goal they will never reach, the bearers of ideas are left as the legitimate owners of the treasure. They won in a fair fight. And not only that, it was the power of their ideas which created the wealth to begin with, and inspired the search, and proved, once again, the superiority of mind over matter. Exploitation has been justified, the profits of the past have been legitimized, and ownership is found to confer exclusive rights on the retention and increase of wealth. If the bourgeoisie now control the capital and the means of production, it is not because they exploited anyone or accumulated wealth unfairly.

Disney, throughout his comics, implies that capitalist wealth originated under the same circumstances as he makes it appear in his comics. It was always the ideas of the bourgeoisie which gave them the advantage in the race for success, and nothing else.

And their ideas shall rise up to defend them.

V. THE IDEAS MACHINE

> "It's a job where there is nothing to do. Just take a turn around the museum from time to time to check that nothing is happening."
>
> Donald (D 436)

> "I am rich because I always *engineer* my strokes of luck."
>
> Scrooge (TR 40)

At this point, perhaps our reader is eager to brandish the figure of Donald himself, who, at first sight appears to run counter to our thesis that Disney's is a world without work and without workers. Everyone knows that this fellow spends his life looking for work and moaning bitterly about the overwhelming burdens which he must carry.

Why does Donald look for work? In order to get money for his summer vacation, to pay the final installment on his television set (which he apparently does a thousand times, for he has to do it afresh in each new episode), or to buy a present (generally for Daisy or Scrooge). In all this, there is never any question of need on Donald's part. He never has any problems whith the rent, the electricity bill, food, or clothing. On the contrary, without so much as a dollar to his name, he is always buying. The ducks live surrounded by a world of magical abundance, while the bad guys do not have ten cents for a cup of coffee. But suddenly, in the next picture zap – the ducks have built themselves a rocket out of nothing. The bad guys spend much more money robbing Scrooge than they will ever get from him.

There is no problem about the means of subsistence in this luxurious and prodigal society. Hunger, like some plague from ancient times, has been conquered. When the youngsters tell Mickey that they are hungry; "Doesn't one have the right to be hungry?" (D 401), Mickey replies "You children don't know what hunger is! Sit down and I'll tell you." Immediately the nephews begin to make fun of him, saying "How long is this hunger business, how long is all this nonsense going to last?" But there's no need to worry, kids. Mickey is not thinking how hunger today is killing millions of people around the world, and causing other millions irreparable mental and physical damage. Mickey recounts a prehistoric adventure about Goofy and himself, with a typical contemporary Duckburg plot, to illustrate the problem of hunger. Apparently, for Mickey, nowadays such problems as hunger do not exist – people live in a fantasy world perfection.

So Donald doesn't really need to work, and the proof is that any money he does manage to make always goes towards buying the superfluous. Thus, when Uncle Scrooge deceitfully promises to will his fortune to him, the first thought that occurs to Donald is "At last I can spend all I want." (TR 116). So he orders the latest model of automobile, an eight-berth cruiser, and a color TV set with fifteen channels and remote-control switch. Elsewhere (D 423) he decides "I must get some temporary work somewhere to raise enough money for this gift." Or, he hopes to go on an expensive trip, but "all I have is this half dollar." (F 117).

As need is superfluous, so is the work. Jobs are usually (as we have observed) those which provide services, protection, or transportation to consumers. Even Scrooge McDuck has no workers; when he is brought a list of his personnel, they are all called "employees."

All employment is a means of consumption rather than production. Without needing to work, Donald is constantly obsessed with searching for it. So it is not surprising that the kind of job he prefers should be easy, and undemanding of mental or physical effort. A pastime while he waits for some piece of luck (or piece of map) to fall upon him from who knows where. In short, he wants wages without sweating. It is moreover no problem for Donald (or anyone else) to find a job, because jobs abound. "Wow, that looks like pleasant work! 'Pastry cook wanted, good wages, free pastries, short hours.' That's for me!" (F 82). The Real drama only beings to unfold when, once having got the job, Donald becomes terrified of losing it. This terror of being left in the street is quite inexplicable, given that the job was hardly indispensable to him.

And since Donald is by definition clumsy and careless, he is always getting the boot. "There are jobs and jobs in the world, but Donald never seems to find one that he can do." "You're fired, Duck. That's the third time you've gone to sleep in the dough mixer!" "You're *fired*, Duck! You do too much fiddling around!" "You're fired Duck! Where did you learn barbering — from an Indian warchief?" (CS 12/59). So work becomes for Donald an obsession with not losing work, and not suffering the catastrophes which pursue him wherever he goes. He becomes unemployed through his incompetence, in a world where jobs abound. Getting a job is no problem since the supply of them is far in excess of de-

mand, just, as in Disney, consumption exceeds production. The fact that Donald, like Big Bad Wolf, the Beagle Boys and a host of others, is an inveterate slacker, proves that their unemployment is the result of their free will and incompetence. To the reader, Donald represents the unemployed. Not the real unemployed caused historically by the structural contradictions of capitalism, but the Disney-style unemployment based on the personality of the employee. The socio-economic basis of unemployment is shunted aside in favor of individual psychological explanations, which assume that the causes and consequences of any social phenomenon are rooted in the abnormal elements in individual human behavior. Once economic pressure has been converted into pressure to consume, and jobs are readily available everywhere, Donald's world becomes one in which "true" freedom reigns: the freedom to be out of work.

Industrial entrepreneurs in the present world push the "freedom of labor" slogan: every citizen is free to sell his labor, choose whom he sells it to, and quit if it doesn't suit him. This false "freedom of labor" (in the Disney fantasy world) ceases to be a myth, becomes a reality and takes on the form of the "freedom" of being

unemployed.

But despite all Donald's good intentions, employment slips through his fingers. He has hardly crossed the employment threshold before he becomes the victim of crazy and chaotic commotion. These absurd paroxysms of activity generally end in the hero's rest and reward. Often, however, the hero cannot escape from these apocalyptic gyrations, because the gods do not wish to release him from his eternal sufferings. This means that the reward and punishment do not depend on Donald, and the result of all this activity is unforeseeable. This increases the reader's feeling of dramatic tension. The passivity and sterility of Donald's work point up his lack of positive merit, other than his accumulated suffering. All respite is conferred upon him from above and beyond, despite all his efforts to master his destiny. Fate, in making Donald his favorite plaything, becomes the sole dynamic factor, provoking catastrophes, and bestowing joys. Fate is like a bottomless bucket in which water is constantly churning. It is Donald's job to fill this bucket. As long as no one comes along and benevolently puts back the bottom, Donald will fail, and be doomed to stoop and pour forever.

This type of work, which takes place in the city, is similar to other forms of nervous suffering which occurs outside the city on foreign adventures. As soon as they leave home, the Duckburgers suffer all kinds of accidents: shipwrecks, collisions, and perils — obstacles and misfortunes galore. It is this torture at the hands of fate which separates them from the treasure they are searching. The exertions of their labors appear null because they are a chain of contingencies. Their "labors" become a response to crises. First, bad luck scatters danger and pain in their path; then, at the end, good luck rewards them with gold. This gold is not easily attained. One has first to suffer *deconcretized work*: work in the form of *adventure*. In a similar way, the first Spanish novels of adventure were called "labors."* In this form of novel, the intermediary between the hero and wealth is the process of accumulating misfortune. This process symbolizes work, without actually being work. It

*E.g. Cervantes' *Trabajos de Persiles y Segismunda.*

is a passively consumed form of toil, rather than one which is actively creative and productive. *Just as money is an abstract form of the object, so adventure is an abstract form of labor.* The treasure is attained by a process of adventuring, not producing. Yet another means — as if more were needed — to mask the origin of wealth. But the substance of the adventure is also fraught with moral consequences. In view of the fact that the hero does not propel himself, but is propelled by destiny, he learns the necessity of obeying its designs. In this way, by accepting the slings of misfortune, he puts fate in his debt, and eventually extracts a few dollars therefrom. The diabolical rhythm of the world — its menacing sadism, its crazy and perilous twists and turns, and its vexations and disruptions — *cannot be denied*, because everything answers to *providence.* It is a universe of terror, always on the point of collapse, and to survive in it requires a philosophy of resignation. Man deserves nothing and if he gets anything, it is due to his humble humanity and his acceptance of his own impotence.

Despite all the masks, Donald is sensed as the true representative of the contemporary worker. But the wages essential to the latter are superfluous to Donald. What the real life worker searches desperately, Donald has no trouble finding. While the worker produces and suffers from the material conditions of life and the exploitation to which he is subjected, Donald suffers only the illusion of work, its passive and abstract weight, in the form of adventure.

Donald moves in a world of pure superstructure with a close formal resemblance, however, to its infrastructure, and the stages of its development. He gives the impression of living at the concrete base of real life, but he is only a mimic floating in the air above. Adventure is like work in the realm of quicksands which believe themselves to be upwards-sucking clouds. When the critical moment of payday arrives, the great mystification occurs. The workman of the real world is cheated and takes home only a fraction of what he has produced: the boss steals the rest. Donald, on the other hand, having demostrated his uselessness on the job, is ipso-facto overpaid. In Disney, not having contributed to wealth, the worker has no right to demand a share in it. Anything this "parasite" may be given is a favor granted from outside, for which he should be grateful, and ask no more. Only providence can dispense the grace of survival to one who has not deserved it. How can one go on strike, how can one demand higher wages, if it is all left to providence, and there are no norms governing working conditions? Donald is the bastard representative of all workers. They are supposed to be as submissive as Donald because they are supposed to have contributed as little as he has to the building of this material world. Duckburg is no fantasy, but the *fantasmagoria* Marx spoke of: Donald's "work" is designed to screen off the contradictions in the bosses' mythology of labor, and hide the difference between the value of labor, and the value which labor creates; that is, surplus value. Labor geared to production does not exist for Donald. In his fantasmagorical rhythm of suffering and reward, Donald represents the dominated (mystified) at the same time as he paradoxically lives the life of the dominator (mystifier).

Disney fantasizes contemporary social conflicts into the form of adventure. But even as he reveals these sufferings innocently, he neutralizes them with the implicit assurance that all is for the best. Everything will be rewarded, and will lead to the improvement of the human condition and the paradise of leisure and repose. The imaginative realm of childhood is schematized by Disney in such a way that it appropriates the real life co-ordinates and anguish of contemporary man, but strips them of their power to denounce them, expose their contradictions, and overcome them.

Work, disguised in Duckburg as innocent suffering, is always defined in function of its contrary, leisure. Typically, an episode opens at a

moment emphasizing the boredom and peace in which the heroes are immersed. The nephews yawn: "we are bored to death with everything . . . even television." (D 43).

The opening situation is stressed as normal: "How can so simple a thing as a *bouncing ball* lead our friends to treasures in Aztecland?" (D 432, DD 9/65). "Is there anything so restful as lying stretched out over one's money, listening to the gentle tic-toc of a clock? One feels so secure." (TR 113). "Who would have imagined that a mere invitation to a family reunion would end like this?" Donald asks himself after an adventure (D 448) which "all started innocently one morning . . ." "It is dawn in Duckburg, normally so quiet a town." (D 448). They are always resting; on a bed, on a couch, on a lawn, or in a hammock. "Mickey takes a well-earned rest as a guest of the Seven Dwarfs in the Enchanted Forest." (D 424). The repetition and restful sense of these phrases sets the tone for life in Duckburg. Our hero leaves his habitual everyday existence, which is that of leisure, interrupted by any one of the harmless attributes of that leisure (like a bouncing ball), which leads him to adventure, suffering and gold. Readers are encouraged to identify with the character because they too are resting while reading the comic, and become easily trapped in the confined-excitement of the race. Once baited, they find themselves accompanying him for the rest of the fantastic episode.

The adventure usually ends in the recompense of a vacation, and a return to rest, now well deserved after the weight of so much *deconcretized* labor. Formally, one may observe in the first and last drawings the principles of immobility and symmetry of balanced forces. A pictorial device of renaissance classicism is used to soothe the reader before and after the

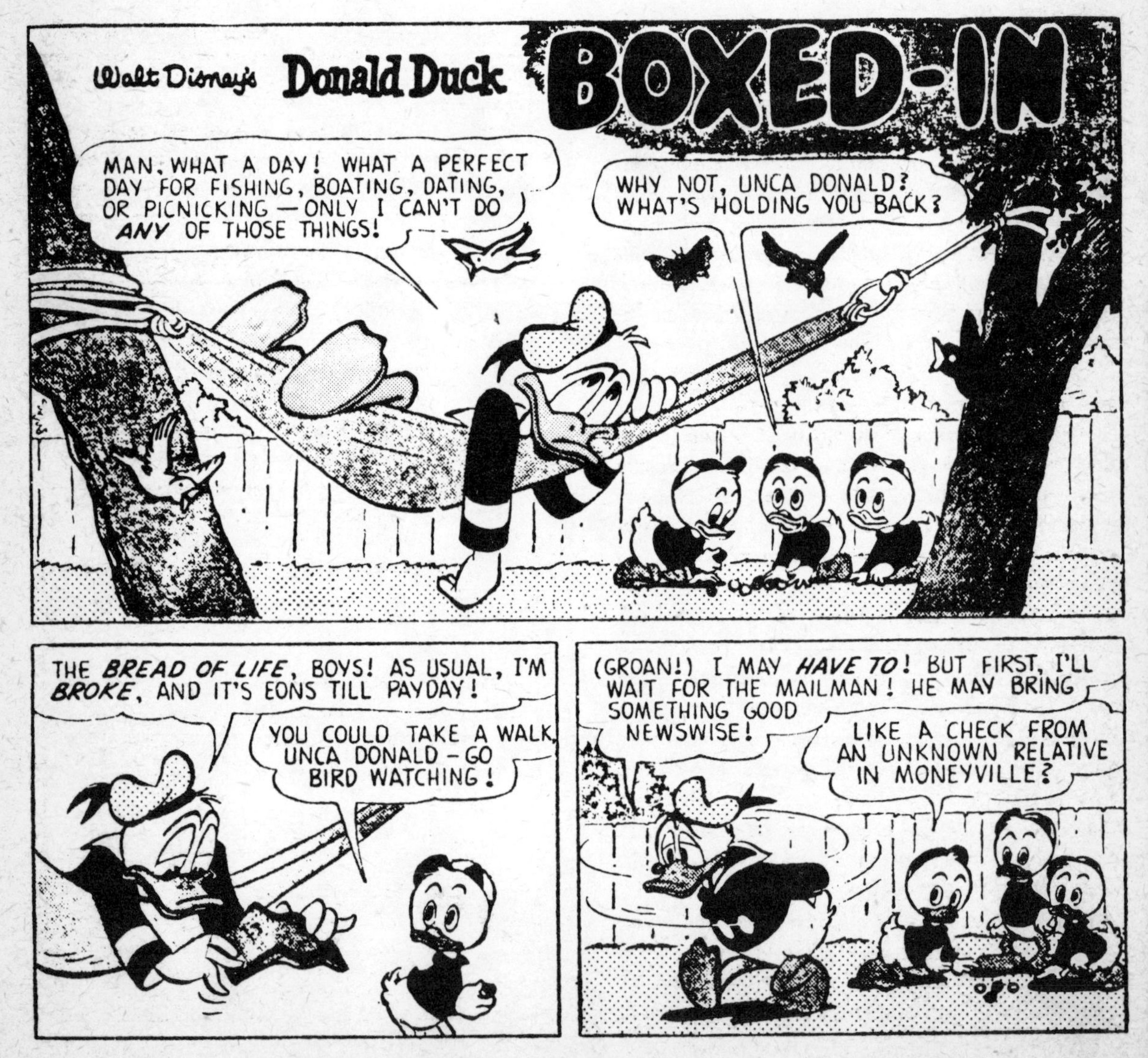

adventure. For its duration, on the other hand, the figures are drawn in constant agitation. They rush, as a rule, from left to right, impelling the eye to follow the heroes' legs flying over the ground. Outstretched fingers point the direction, until peace is restored and the circle closed.

"Ha! Our adventure ends with a tropical vacation." (D 432). After working for Scrooge, Donald is rewarded by his uncle "with a real vacation in Atlantic City." (F 109). "Ha, ha! I have been dreaming for so long of spending the summer in Acapulco. Thanks to my accident insurance, at last I can choose that marvellous place." (F 174). This episode proves clearly how pain provokes good fortune: "Hurray, hurray. I broke my leg." Having been loaned his uncle's property for a month, Donald decides "first of all, I won't work any more. I will forget all my worries and devote myself to leisure." (TR 53). And what were those worries? "You can't imagine how difficult it is, with the cost of living, making it to the end of the month on my wages. It's a nightmare!" What is the great problem? "It's hard to get a decent night's sleep when one knows that the next installment on the TV is due the following day, and one hasn't a cent."

The apparent opposition between work and leisure is nothing but a subterfuge to the advantage of the latter. Leisure invades and imposes its laws upon the whole realm of work. In the "Hard-Working Leisure-Lovers Club" (the description of feminine activity, D 185), work is nugatory, a leisure activity, a vehicle of consumerism, and a means of killing time.

Let us take the most extreme example: Big Bad Wolf and his eternal hunt for the three little pigs. He appears to want to *eat* them. But hunger is not his real motive: his need is really to embellish his life with some simulacrum of activity. Chase the piglets, let them elude him by a trick, so that he can return again, etc. . . . Like the consumer society itself, which by consuming, consumates the adventure of consumption. Seize the object to have it disappear, to have it immediately replaced by the same object in a new guise. This situation is epitomized in D 329, where Practical Pig persuades Big Bad Wolf to let them all go: "What fun can you have, now that you have caught us? You'll have nothing to do, except sit around growing old before your time." Eating them would be to exceed his definition as a character,* beyond which lies the banal or a void. The character becomes self-corrective if ever the constants of his nature are threatened. He cannot, nor does he wish to, face a shortage of pigs, or the invention of some other chaseable object. He feeds upon his own recreation as the manner of his work: "this is more fun than anything else." Practical Pig has convinced him with Madison Avenue persuasiveness: "BUY TO CONTINUE WORKING; BUY TO SECURE YOUR FUTURE; BUY TODAY TO KEEP SOMEONE IN WORK TOMORROW. MAYBE YOU."** The fictitious point of departure is need, which then becomes artificialized, and forgotten. For the wolf, the piglets are "in." Desire is stimulated in order to continue "producing." (the superfluous).

Given *this* pretext that work is indespensible, it enters history in the form of a "repetitious abnormality." Work is regarded as an unusual and eccentric phenomenon, and is emptied of its meaning, which is precisely that it *is* commonplace, habitual, routine and normal. Within the

*See Umberto Eco, *Apocalittici e Integrati,* Bompiani, Milano, 1964 *(Apocalipticos e Integrados ante la cultura de masas*, Editorial Lumen, Barcelona, 1968).

**Quotation from Vance Packard, *The Hidden Persuaders,* New York, 1957. Cf. the advertisement below, from General Motors, for a 1974 variation on this theme:

Cars, Jobs and Progress

Economic progress is like a wheel. When it loses speed it wobbles, and when it stops it falls. Kerplunk.

To keep our economy rolling, Americans must not be afraid to buy what they want and need. Demand means production; more production means more jobs, stronger businesses, and more revenues for our towns and cities, our states and the nation. It adds up to prosperity, and everybody gains.

The automobile is basic to America's economy. It accounts for one-sixth of our Gross National Product. Thirteen million jobs—one in every six—and 800,000 businesses, from steel companies to the corner service station, depend on the automobile.

Right now is the time to buy a new car. Used car values are high. Operating costs on our 1975 cars are reduced, and less scheduled maintenance is required. New cars are a good buy—and buying keeps the wheel of progress rolling.

R.C. Gerstenberg
Chairman
General Motors Corporation

General Motors

See your Chevrolet, Pontiac, Oldsmobile, Buick or Cadillac dealer today.

production process, the stage invariably selected for depiction are those which loosen the bonds of labor. Banal and repetitive work is transformed into free-flowing fantasy, accident and commotion. Labor, in spite of its present coercive character, no longer appears as the daily grind it is, separating all human beings from misery. In a word, daily life becomes *sensationalized.* For Donald, Goofy, Mickey, the chipmunks, the strange and rare are commonplace. Donald, for example, working as a hairdresser (D 329), becomes the genial artist-scientist at the job: "seven inches to the epicranial aponeurosis; nine inches to the splenius capitis; seven inches to the pointus of the proboscis." Routine is refined into a variety of wonders attained "with specially invented tools."

This concept of work is a stratagem for transforming daily life, and all the hard work which is necessary for surviving in it, into a permanent spectacle. Just as a Disney character leaves his normal surroundings to undertake fantasy adventures free of the usual time-space limitations of Duckburg, or undergo the most absurb extravaganzas in the most innocent of urban occuptions, so it is similarly proposed that children transcend the concrete reality of their life, and surrender to the "magic" and "adventure" of the magazines. The segregation of the child's world between the everyday and the enchanted begins in the comics themselves, which take the first step in teaching children, from their tenderest years, to separate work from leisure, and humdrum reality from the play of their imagination. Apparently, their habitual world is that of unimaginative work, whereas the world of the comic is that of fantasy-filled leisure. Children are once again split between matter and spirit, and encouraged to eliminate the imaginary from the real surrounding world. To defend this type of comic on the grounds that it feeds the "overflowing imagination" of the child who tends, supposedly, by his very nature to reject his immediate surroundings, is really to inject into children the escapist needs of contemporary society. A society so imprisoned in its own oppressive, dead-end world, that it is constrained to dream up perversely "innocent" utopias. The adult's self-protective escapist dreams impel the child to abandon its integrated childhood existence. Later, adults use this "natural" fantasy trait of childhood to lessen their own anxiety and alienation from their daily work.

This world of projection and segregation is based upon the role and concept of entertainment as it has developed in capitalist society. The manner in which Donald lives out his leisure, transformed into fantastic multicolor, multimovement and multivision adventure, is identical to the manner in which the twentieth century (fox) consumer lives out his boredom, relieved by the spiritual food of the mass culture. Mickey is entertained by mystery and adventure. The reader is entertained by Mickey entertaining himself.

The Disney world could be revamped and even disappear altogether, without anything changing. Beyond the children's comic lies the whole concept of contemporary mass culture, which is based on the principle that only entertainment can liberate humankind from the social anxiety and conflict in which it is submerged. Just as the bourgeoisie conceive social problems as a marginal residue of technological problems, so they also believe that by developing the mass culture industries, they will solve the problem of people's alienation. This cultural technology reaches from mass communications and its products, to the hucksterism of the organized tour.

Entertainment, as it is understood by the capitalist mass culture, tries to reconcile everything — work with leisure, the commonplace with the imaginary, the social with the extrasocial, body with soul, production with consumption, city with countryside — while veiling the contradictions arising from their interrelationships. All the conflicts of the real world, the nerve centers of bourgeois society, are purified in the imagination in order to be absorbed and co-opted into the world of entertainment. Simply to call Disney a liar is to miss the target. Lies are easily exposed. The laundering process in Disney, as in all the mass media, is much more complex. Disney's social class has molded the world in a certain clearly defined and functional way which corresponds to *its* needs. The bourgeois imagination does not ignore this reality, but seizes it, and returns it veneered with innocence, to the consumer. Once it is interpreted as a magical, marvellous paradigm of his own common experience, the reader then can consume his own contradictions in whitewashed form. This permits him to continue viewing and living these conflicts with the innocence and helplessness of a child. He enters the future without having resolved or even understood the problems of the present.

To put Humpty Dumpty together again, the bourgeoisie have supplied him with the *realm of freedom* without having him pass through the *realm of necessity*. Their fantasy paradise invites participation, not through concretization, but abstraction, of needs and problems. This is not to imply that people should be prevented from dreaming about their future. On the contrary, their real need to achieve a better future is a fundamental ethical motivation in their stuggle for liberation. But Disney has appropriated this urge and diluted it with symbols uprooted from reality. It is the fun world of the Pepsi-generation: all fizz and bubbles.

This conception of redemption by neutralizing contradictions surely has its supreme embodiment in the Disney comic. And in one character in particular we find its ultimate expression. It is, of course – did you guess? – Gladstone Gander. "When I decide to find the best shell on the beach, I don't have to look for it. I'm just lucky." (D 381). He walks around "and never falls into traps. Lucky as always." (F 155).

Gladstone gets all he wants – as long as it is material things – without working, without suffering, and therefore, without deserving a reward. He wins every contest (the dynamo of all Duckburg activity) in advance, and from a position of magical repose. He is the only one who is not ground in the mill of adventure and suffering. "Nothing bad ever happens to him." Donald, by contrast, appears as *real* and deserving, for at least he pretends to work. Gladstone flouts all the principles of puritanical morality. Time and space conspire in his favor, fortune spoils him. His prosperity flows like a pure force of nature. His freedom is not camouflaged in the illusions of necessity. He is Donald without the suffering. One may aspire to him, but one cannot follow him, for there is no path. The reader, simultaneously rejecting and fascinated by Gladstone, learns to respect the necessity of work which gives the right to leisure (as embodied in Donald), and to despise the work-shy "hippie" who is given everything for nothing and is not even grateful.

But what happens when he confronts the Disney gods, those of Genius and Intellect, the supreme idea. "Good luck means so much more than a good brain." observes Gladstone, picking up a banknote that Gyro had overlooked (TR 115). Gyro replies, "Pure coincidence. I still maintain that brains are more important than luck." After an exhausting day of competition, they end in a tie, with a slight advantage to intelligence.

All the other characters not possessing this timeless inexhaustible luck have to earn it with patience, suffering, or intelligence. We have already seen what models of cleverness the little ones are, always ready for their rise to success. Their intelligence is broad, and quick to detect and repress rebellion. They are virtuous Boy Scouts who, subordinate though they are, play the game of deception and adult substitution.

When this Boy Scout grows up and has no one in command over him, he will turn into *Mickey Mouse*, the only creature not involved in the hunt for gold *in and of itself*. He is the only one who always appears as the *helper* of others in their difficulties, and he always helps someone else get the reward. And if he occasionally pockets a few dollars, well, he can hardly be blamed when there is so much money around. In Mickey, intelligence serves to unveil a mystery, and to bring simplicity back to a world disordered by evil men intent on robbing at will. The real life child also confronts a strange world which he too has to explore, with *his mind and his body*. We could call Mickey's manner of approaching the world akin to that of a detective, who finds keys and solves puzzles invented by others. And the conclusion is always the same: unrest in this world is due to the existence of a moral division. Happiness (and holidays) may reign again once the villains have been jailed, and order returns. Mickey is a non-official pacifier, and receives no other reward than the consciousness of his own virtue. He is law, justice and peace beyond the realm of selfishness and competition, open-handed with goodies and favors. Mickey's altruism serves to raise him above the rat-race, in whose rewards he has no share. His altruism lends prestige to his office as guardian of order, public administration, and social service, all of which are supposedly umblemished by the inevitable defects of the mercantile world. One can trust in Mickey as one does in an "impartial" judge or policeman, who stands above "partisan hatreds."

The superior power in Duckburg is always one of intelligence. The power elite is divided into the civil service caste, supposedly above considerations of personal profit, and the economic caste, which uses its intelligence in money-grubbing. The arch-representative of the latter, who has become the acknowledged butt of radical criticism today, is Uncle Scrooge. His outward role is that of the easy target, the tempting bait to divert the reader from all the issues we raise in this study. He is set up so as to leave intact the true mechanisms of domination. Attacking Scrooge is like knocking down the gatekeeper, a manifest but secondary symptom, so as to avoid confronting the remaining denizens of Disney's castle. Could this garishly dramatized Mammon figure be designed to distract the reader's attention, so that they will distrust Scrooge and no one else?

So we shall not start with the avarice, the bath of gold, the good ship "dollar," and the life jacket of penny pinching. We shall not start with the millionaire beggar waiting in the soup line and peering over his nephew's shoulder to get a free glance at his newspaper.

The comic elements in his character, his absurd craftiness, represent a second line decoy. For Scrooge's fundamental trait is *solitude*. Apart from his tyrannical relationship with his nephews and grand nephews, he has no one else. Even when he calls in the police (F 173), he has to solve his problems on his own. Uncle Scrooge's money cannot buy him power. Although it is everywhere, his gold is incapable of making or unmaking anything, or of going to work and moving peoples, armies, and nations. It can only buy moveable, isolated gadgets, to aid him in his crazy chase for money. Stripped of its power to acquire productive forces, money is unable to defend itself or resolve any problem whatsoever. For this reason Uncle Scrooge is unhappy and vulnerable. For this reason nobody wants to be like him (in various episodes, e.g. TR 53 and F 74, Donald flees the opportunity like the plague). Scrooge is obsessed with the fear of losing his money, without being able to use it to defend himself. He has to handle every operation personally. He suffers from the solitude of being

the boss, but without its compensations. But he also cultivates his image of vulnerability in order to blackmail his nephews when they are fed up with his dictatorship; "Confound it," says Donald (TR 113), "we can't leave a weak old duck like Uncle Scrooge locked up all alone in those dreadful mountains."

His vulnerability creates an aura of compassion. He is on the defensive, seeking protection behind primitive weaponry (such as an old blunderbuss). He never rests upon the laurels of his wealth, but continues to suffer from it (and therefore deserves it). For his obsessive suffering is the only way he can be assured of the moral legitimacy of his money; he pays for his gold with worry, and by leaving it uninvested it becomes impotent. Robbing McDuck, however, is no mere theft: it is murder. Gold constitutes an essential element in his life cycle, like the means of subsistence are to the noble savages. Since he never spends anything, Scrooge lives off gold as one breathes air. He is the only truly passionate creature in this world, because he is defending his life. The reader is full of sympathy for him. All the others want money in order to spend it, for base motives. Scrooge loves it for its own sake, and thus sentimentalizes the process of acquiring it. The thieves want to break this pathetic natural bond, depriving him of the only thing left to him in his solitary old age: money. He is a cripple, an invalid, an injured animal demanding the reader's charitable attention.

McDuck is a *poor* man, moreover. All appearances to the contrary, he has no money, no means, and no property. He won't spend; he just relies on family obligations to protect him, and help him go on hoarding. Good fortune has not changed him, and in each adventure he indicates how he got his money in the past, which is exactly the way he is getting it in the present. The story repeats itself endlessly. His avarice serves to bring him down to the same level as the rest of the world. He starts in the race unable to use the wealth he has already amassed. Although he is not invincible, he usually wins, but next time round nothing has changed. In order to add another lot to his massive pile, in order to protect what he already has, he must continuously make fresh efforts. If he triumphs, it is because he proves better at it than the others, time and time again. His wealth confers no advantage, for he never uses it. The gold lies piled up, inert and inoffensive, in the corner; it cannot be used for further enrichment. It is as if it did not exist.

Scrooge gets his last cent as if it were his first, and it is his first. He is the opposite of the arriviste (like Maggie, in *Bringing Up Father*) who wants money in order to change status and rise in the world. Scrooge's every adventure encapsulates his whole career which brought him from poverty to riches, and from slum to mansion. A well-earned career, due to his patient endurance, total self-reliance, solitary genius – guile, intelligence, brain-waves – and his nephews.

Here is the basic myth of social mobility in the capitalist system. The self-made man. Equality of opportunity. Absolute democracy. Each child starting from zero and getting what he deserves. Donald is always missing the next rung on the ladder to success. Everyone is born with the same chance of vertical ascent by means of competition and work (suffering, adventure, and the only active part, genius). Scrooge has no advantage over the reader in terms of money, because this money is of no use, indeed, it is more of a liability, like a blind or crippled child. It is an incentive, a goal, but never, once it has been attained, does it determine the next adventure. So there is really no *history* in these comics, for gold forgotten from the preceding episode cannot be used for the following one. If it could, it would connote a past with influence over the present, and reveal capital and the whole process of accumulation of surplus value as the explanation of Uncle Scrooge's fortune. In these circumstances, the reader could never empathize with him beyond the first episode. And what's more, they are all the first and last episode. They can be read in any order, and are "timeless": one written in 1950 can be published without any trouble in 1970*.

Scrooge's avarice, then, which seems so laughable, is only a device to make him appear poor. It brings him constantly back to his point of origin, so that he can be eternally proclaiming and proving his worth. His stinginess, moreover, is no more than the defect of a positive quality – thrift, the well-known attribute of the bourgeois entrepreneur. A sign of his predestination for success, thrift was the bourgeoisie's moral instrument for seizing without spending as he invested in business and industry, forgetful of his own person. The bourgeoisie saw his *asceticism* as conferring upon him the moral right to engross the work of others, without spending

money and tainting himself by conspicious consumption. There, the purpose was *re-investment* in business and industry. Here, Scrooge observes this ascetic morality, but without the investment to which it is directed, and the power which accompanies this investment. So he retains our sympathy.

The other quality which assures his supremacy is that he always takes the initiative. He is an ideas machine, and each idea generates unmediated riches. He represents the climax of the segregation between intellectual and manual work. He suffers like a manual worker and creates like an intellectual. But he doesn't fritter away his money like the worker is supposed to (and who, as the capitalist says, ought to save so as to be able to rise out of his subservient position), and he does not invest like the capitalist. He tries – and fails – to reconcile the antagonists in the system.

It is not only the individual businessman who professes to have started low and pulled himself up by his bootstraps. The bourgeoisie-as-a-class also propagates the myth that the capitalist system was established by a small group of individuals along the same lines. The pathetic, sentimental solitude of Scrooge is a screen for the class to which he so obviously belongs. The millionaires reduce themselves by making themselves appear as a random, rootless miscellany with no community of interests, and no sense of solidarity, obeying only "natural" law, as long as this respects the property of others. The story of one eccentric glosses over the fact that he is a member of a class, and, moreover, a class which has seized control of social existence.

Scrooge's individual cycle reproduces in each activity of his life the historical cycle of a class, his social class.

*As indeed is actually happening, as two decades of post-war comics are reprinted. (Trans.)

VI. THE AGE OF THE DEAD STATUES

"History? I don't have the faintest notion of it."

Donald, in the history section of a library (D 455)

"Well, this is real democracy.* A billionaire and a pauper going around in the same circle."

Donald to Uncle Scrooge, caught up in the same whirlpool (TR 106, US 9/64)

If there is no path where you walk, you make it as you go, wrote Antonio Machado. But in the Disney version: if there are nothing but paths where you walk, stay were you are.

For the great wizard, the world is a desert of readymade tracks, beaten by robots in animal form.

How come? Aren't these comics feverishly pulsating, always at boiling point? That charming effervescence, that spark of life, the Silly Sympathies, that electric energy of action, are they not the very soul of Disney?

True, the rhythm never falters. We are projected into a kaleidoscope of constantly shifting patterns. The breathless activity of the characters is even reflected in the colors. For instance, the same kitchen changes in successive frames from blue to green, then yellow and red (D 445). The nephews' bedroom (D 185) is filmed in even more dazzling technicolor effects; pale blue, yellow, pink, violet, red and blue. Similarly, the police chief's office (TB 103) is light blue, green, yellow, pink and red in rapid succession. This sudden switching of colored surfaces reaches its climax with the nephews' caps (D 432). The nephew jumping over the grill has a light blue cap; when he drops over the other side it becomes red, and finally, when he is caught, he is left with a green one. The cap remains thus for the rest of the story, as if it were a pathetic reminder of his need to be rescued, until the three nephews are reunited and the color changes begin all over again.

This change of externals over identical and rigid content, the application of a fresh coat of paint from one picture to the next, is the correlate of technological "innovation." All is in motion, but nothing changes.

Like clothing, transportation inside and outside Duckburg is subject to variations on a standard theme. The Duckburgers will take anything which will get them moving: a roller skate or a jet plane, a space rocket or an infernal

*In the English original, "sociable." (Trans.)

bicycle. The perpetual refurbishing of objects offers a veneer of novelty. Each character's ideas machine uses the most extravagant forms of scientific invention in order to get what he wants. In a world where everyone is dressed in the manner of children at the beginning of this century or in the fashion of a small post-frontier town, the thirst for the new, different and strange is all the more striking. The ease with which these gadgets appear and disappear is amazing. The presentation of novelty and "gadgets" in the Disney comic provides a model for the readers during their childhood experience, which later in life is amplified by the mass culture industries into a principle of reality. What is new today is old tomorrow. The products of science, the inventions of Gyro Gearloose, and the latest genial idea on the market are objects of immediate consumption; perishable, obsolescent, and replaceable.

Science becomes a form of sensationalism and technological gimmickry. It is a branch of the patent office opened in the lunatic asylum. It performs dazzling quick-change acts. A vehicle for novelty-hunting intercontinental tourists, and for novelty-hunting comic book script-writers. There is not even any progress: these gadgets are only used for transportation or external variation, and in the next number they have already been forgotten. For there to be progress, there must be memory, an interrelated chain of inherited knowledge. In Disney, the object serves only the moment, and that moment alone. This isolation of the object is the power of control over its production, which in the last analysis, renders it sterile and meaningless. The climax is reached in "Useless Machine" (TR 109), a machine which is mass produced because it serves no purpose except entertainment, as if to parody the Disney comic itself. "Who can resist useless, costly and noisy things? Just look at the success of transistor radios, motorbikes and television sets." This is incitement to the consumption of artificial abundance, which in turn, stimulates the sale of ancillary and other useless products. "The consumption of high grade gasoline by the 'Useless Machines' makes it more expensive to run than jet planes," the secretary informs proprietor McDuck. "They are run all day long, and cause lines at every gas station. And they are all mine," chuckles the unscrupulous millionaire. The gadgets which appear on the scene only to be immediately abandoned and replaced, are usually in the field of communications. Either tourist-transport (airplanes, submarines, ships, launches, and the whole congeries of marvellous stupidities concocted by Gyro), or cultural (television sets, radios and records). The dual tactic of the Disney industry is reinforced through the self-publicizing consumption within the magazines, which promote the mass media and the tourist trade. See the Disneylandia show on Santiago de Chile's channel 13.* Visit Disneyland and Walt Disney World, capitals of the children's world in the U.S.A.

*The television channel belonging to the Catholic University and controlled by the Christian Democratic Party, who in 1971 expelled, most democratically, all their opponents. The Sunday afternoon Disney show has an audience rating of 87%.

Technology, isolated once more from the productive process, passing from the head of the inventor to the manufactured state without the intermediary of manual labor, is used as a subterfuge to conceal the absence of real change. Conceived as a form of *fashion*, it gives a false impression of mutability. The first circle closes in.

Just as the objects are painted over with a fresh color without changing in function, so they are refurbished by technology without altering the nature and thrust of the heroes' activity. Technology is the maid dressed up to look like a fashion model.

The destiny of technology-as-actor is no different from that of the human animal-as-actor: no matter how many bubbles they put into the soda-pop fantasy world, the taste is always the same, unbeatable. Science is pulled out of the toy closet, played with for a while, and put back again. Similarly. the hero of the comic is pulled out of his routine, knocks around in an absurdist dramatization of his daily life, goes off like a firecracker, and then returns to his well-earned rest (his normal condition, and the starting point for the next boring adventure). Thus the beginning and end are the same, and movement becomes circular. One passes from one comic to the next, and the passive achievement of rest becomes the background and spring-board for still another adventure. Even the adventure itself is an exaggerated repetition of the same old material.

The action in each separate adventure is essentially identical to its predecessor, and the predecessor to its antecedent, and dum-titty-dum-titty-dum, chorus, repeat. The least detail describes the major circumference to the epicenter-episode itself. They are the variously colored concentric circles on the archery target: same shapes, but different colors. The hero turns around in the adventure, the adventure turns between identical beginning and end of the episode, the episode revolves within the copy-cat dance of the comics as a whole, the comics revolve within the orbit of reading which induces boredom, boredom induces the purchase of another comic, reading induces more boredom-titty-dum-titty-dum. ,Thus any overflow of fantasy, or movement which might appear eccentric and break the rigid chain, is nothing but a serpent biting its tail, Donald Duck marking time within the closed frame of the same *Order*. The formal breakdown of the Disney world into fragments (a mechanism characteristic of capitalist life in general), into "different" comic strips, serves to deceive the reader, who is but another little wheel in the great grinding mill of consumption.

Boredom and fear of change is held at bay by the physical mobility of the characters. But not only in their epileptic daily activity, in their perpetual travelling, and in their constant decamping from their homes. They also are allowed to cross over from their pre-assigned sector to meet other members of the Disney reality, like the figures dressed as Disney characters who patrol the streets of Disneyland, California, lending cohesion to the crowd of visitors. Madame Mim and Goofy visit Scrooge. Big Bad Wolf converses with the duckling. Mickey helps out Grandma Duck. In this fake tower of Babel, where all speak the same language of the established repressive order, the ingredients are always thrown together to concoct the same old mental potion: curiosity. How will Snow White react towards Mickey? Familiarity is preserved through the maintanance of the traditional character traits. The reader, who is attracted by the adventure, does not notice that beneath the

novelty of the encounter, the characters are continually repeating themselves.

The characters are over active and appear flexible; the magic wand sends off a lot of sparks, but despite all the magic they still remain straight and rigid. There is an *unholy* terror of change. Trapped in the strict limitations of the personality drawn for him — a catalogue assortment with very few entries — anytime a character tries to articulate himself differently, he is doomed to stupendous failure. Donald is under constant attack for his forgetfulness, but as soon as Gyro transplants the memory of an elephant into his brain, the world around him begins to break up (DD 7/67). Almost immediately, everyone — and Donald especially — demands that he be returned to his original state, the good old Donald we all love. The same happens when Uncle Scrooge uses a magic ink to shame his nephew into paying a debt. Not only does it work on Donald, but on Scrooge as well, so that he feels ashamed of himself and heaps costly gifts on Donald. Better not change another person's habitual psychological mechanisms; it is better to be satisfied with the way one is. Great danger lurks behind very sudden changes. Although usually provoked by some microbe or magical device, changes such as revolutions, which pose external threats to a personality structure, and individual psychological disturbances, which threaten a character's escape from his past and present stereotype, also pose a threat. Disney subjects his characters to a relentless slimming course: they pedal away on fixed bicycles, shed a pound, gain a pound, but the same old skelton remains under the New You. If this remedy seems directed only to the privileged classes who can indulge in such sport, it is equally mandatory for the savages, both good and bad.

In any individual hero, it is the tentacles of competition which provoke these formal paroxysms. In ninety percent of our sample, the explicit theme is a race to get to some place or object in the shortest possible (and therefore, most frantic) time. In this (always public) contest, this obstacle race and test of athletic prowess, the goal is usually money ("Time is Money" as the title of one story tells us). But not always: sometimes it is a hankering for prestige, and to stand out from the common herd. Not only because this automatically means dollars, and women to admire and cater to the winner, but also because it represents the happy conclusion to the suffering, the "work" leading

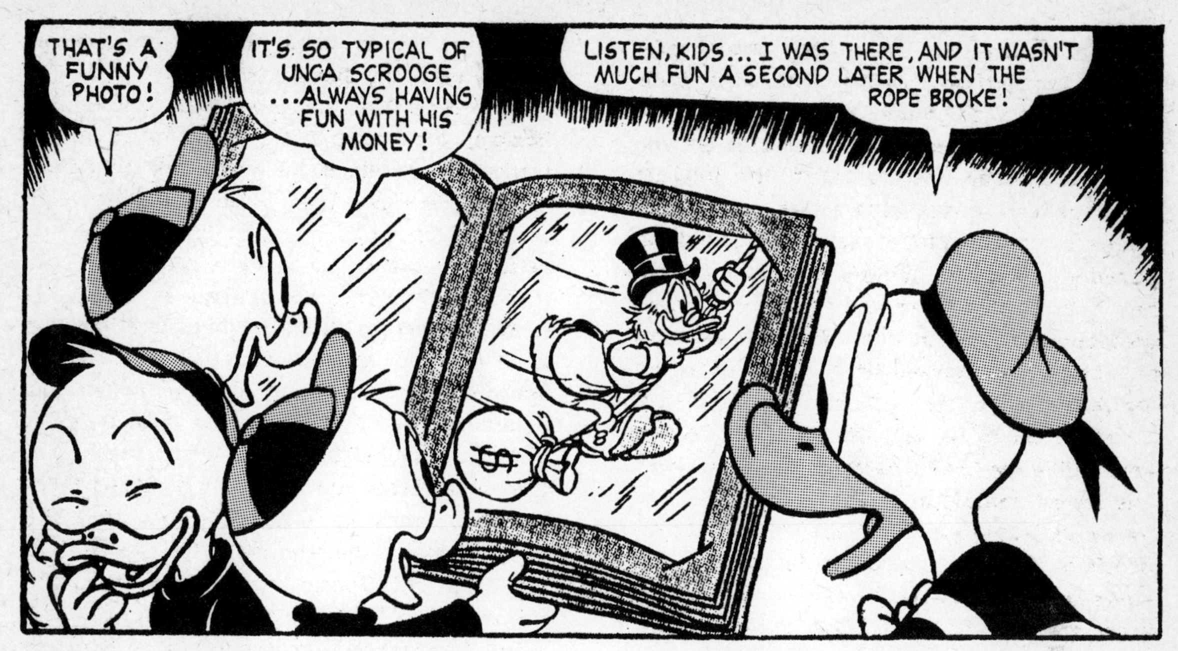

to the halls of fame.

Fame is being able to enjoy, in leisure, all the benefits of productive work. The image radiating from the celebrity assures his livelihood; he can sell himself forever. It is like having found the gold of personality. Converting fame itself into a source of income, it is the business of selling one's own super-self.

But the pre-requisite to all this is to have become a *news item*, broadcast by the mass media, and recognized by "public opinion." To the Disney hero, the adventure in and of itself is not sufficient reward. Without an audience it makes no sense, for the hero must play to the gallery. The importance of the exploit is measured by the degree to which others know that he has surpassed them. Thus, from the television, radio and newspaper he is able to impress other people of his importance and dominate them. A powerful figure may be able to help them become famous themselves. On one occasion (D 443, CS 2/61), Donald is worried because he seems to be one of those people "just born to be nobodies," and wants to do something about it. He asks an actor how he started on the road to fame. Reply: "I was playing *golf* and made a hole-in-one . . . a rich producer saw me do it, and he was so impressed he made me a star." Donald tries the same, but fails because the television cameras were aimed at someone else. "I *would* hit a hole-in-one as *everybody* turned to watch Brigitte van Doren walking by." A politico tells Donald how he found the way to make people notice him. So Donald twice climbs a flagpole, but falls down each time without getting his photograph taken. Finally, he succeeds by accident. "Success did not come easily, but it came," he says to the ducklings, "with this start, Unca Donald, you can become a *movie* star or a Senator . . . or even President!" But the newspaper (*Tripe*) misspells the name under the photograph: Ronald Dunk. Final and total defeat.

It is not truth, but appearance, that matters. The hero's reputation rests entirely upon the gossip column. When his party is a flop (also D 443) Donald says "I can only hope that no reporter gets to hear about this. An article on that party would finish me for good." But naturally there was a reporter there, and the owner and social editor (of the *Evening Tattler*) as well.

With this obsession for the successful propagation of one's own image, it is not surprising that a common trick for getting an episode going is by means of a photograph album. If there is no evidence, it never happened. Every adventure is viewed by its protagonist as a photograph in an album, in a kind of *self-tourism*. The camera is only a means to can and preserve the past. When the photo fails to come out (D 440), it is a disaster, for the guarantee of self-reproduction (in the mass media) has been lost, the bridge of memory has been broken. Immortality has been forfeited; indeed, history itself has been mislaid.

But there is something even better than a photograph: a statue. If a character can get a statue made of himself, immortality is his.

Statue, Statute, Status, Static. Time and time again, someone is rewarded with the prize of a statue standing in a public place or museum. "The secret ambition of Donald: to be the local hero, with a right to a statue in the park." (D 441, DD 7/68). This he achieves by defeating the Martians (sic): "We are thinking of hiring a famous sculptor, so that your likeness may stand among the other "Greats" in the city park!" Every corner a record of the climatic moment of personal past histories. Time, far from being a curse, as in the Bible, is stopped, turned to stone and made immortal. But the family photograph and the statue are not only "souvenirs" brought back from a "tour" of the past. They also validate the past and present importance of one's ancestors, and guarantee their future importance. King Michael the First, "except for the moustache" (D 433), is just like Mickey. The fame of the multitude of uncle ducks can only be proven through the image which they leave behind. Fear of time and competition come to an end when a consensus is reached over an individual's reputation: "I am leaving before they have time to change their opinion of me," explains Goofy (TB 99).

Fame and prize-winning turn an individual into a *product* – that is, in the etymological sense of the word, a finished object, cut off from any other productive process, ready to be consumed or consummated.

Once again, change leads to immobility.

In the first chapter, we have seen that the same static relationships occurred in the supposed conflict between adults and youngsters. There, the poles were apparently in opposition, divided and mobile. But in reality (whether expressed negatively or positively), they were turning around the same central standard, and constantly switching roles; two masks over the same face. In fusing father and son with the same ideals, the adult projects into his offspring the perpetuation of his own values, so that he can pass the baton to himself. The movement generated from the confrontation between the two people or strata, was tautological and illusory. The antagonism disappeared as soon as the two agreed on the rules which put one on top and the other below. Each was himself and his double.

This false dialogue, which is the monologue of the dominant class and its taped playback, is repeated at all levels of the socially stratified cast of characters. Here the age-old concept of twins enters the picture. This folk-motif, which also figures prominently in elite literature (for example, in the work of Poe, Dostoievsky, Cortázar), is often used to express the contradiction people suffer inside their own personality, that is to say, against the rebellious and demonical layer of their being; as in that ambiguous part of them which threatens established order, saving their souls and destroying their lives. The cultural monopolists have flattened and exploited this duality in which one is both commended and condemned, and served it up in simplified form as the collective vision to all the people.

In the two levels in Disney – the dominators, most of the little denizens of Duckburg; and in the dominated, the noble savages and the delinquents – this duality is present on both sides, but is conveyed in a most symbolic manner. In folklore, as we all know, one twin is good and the other bad, with nothing in between. Similarly, among the *dominated* of Disney there are those who happily accept their innocent and subject condition (good guys), and those who attack their bosses' property (bad guys). The sharpness of the division, and the lack of mobility from one side to the other is absolute. The bad guys run around crazily within the prison of their stereotype, with no chance of ever escaping into the realm of the good guys. To such an extent that in one episode, when disguised as (neutral and passive) natives, the bad guys are still punished by having to pick up Uncle Scrooge's money for him. The noble savages, for their part, have to stay quietly *in situ*, so as not to risk being cheated in the city. Each stratum of the dominated is frozen in its goodness or wickedness, for apparently in the plains of the people there are no communication channels between the two. There is no way to be both good *and* attack property. There is no way to be bad if you obey the rules. "Become what you are" goes an old popular saying, coined by the bourgeoisie. Change is prohibited in these sectors. The noble savage cannot become a criminal, and the criminal cannot become innocent. So whether they be actively wicked or passively virtuous, the role of the dominated is fixed, and history, it seems, is made somewhere else.

Contrast this with the dynamism of the *dominant* classes, where mobility reigns and anything is possible. There are rich and poor within the same family. Among friends, one is lucky, the other not. Among the rich, there are good and bad, and intelligent and stupid. The capitivating and craggy land of the dominant tolerates discordance and dilemma. There are no one-hundred-percenters, that is, completely polarized characters. Donald tends to lose, but he wins twenty percent of the time. Uncle Scrooge is often defeated. Even Mickey occasionally behaves like a coward (in D 401 the children frighten him and supplant him. Says Minnie: "You really are sometimes worse than the children. I don't know what to do with you. The children are right." And Mickey replies: "Those doggone kids always get the best of it."). Gladstone Gander is not always the winner, and the Boy Scout ducklings sometime slip up. Only the prodigy Little Wolf escapes this rule, but he needs to, with such a rotten, stupidly wicked father. The realm of the dominant Duckburgers is one of refined nuances, and marked by small contradictions. Over the mass sunk in its collective determinism (that's the way it is, whether you like it or not, you get screwed), rises the dominant personality who can "freely" choose and determine his course in life.

His liberty lies in having a personality, in flourishing through statuary, in holding a monopoly over the voice of history.

Once the adversary is disqualified in advance (and that disqualification is systematic), he is then beaten in a race that he cannot even run. History acquires the face that the dominant class chooses to give it.

Need we stress further how closed and suffocating this world of Disney really is?

Just as the subject classes are deprived of voice and face, and the possibility to open the prison door (notice how easy it is to eliminate

them when production is performed magically, and they are not needed), so the past is deprived of its real charcter and is made to appear the same as the present. Past history in its entirety is colonized by the anxieties and values of the present moment. Historical experience is a huge treasure chest full of hallowed moral tags and recipes, of the same old standards and doctrines, all defending the same old thesis of domination. Donald is supicious of Uncle Scrooge's preoccupation with money, but the miser can always demonstrate that his fortune was justly acquired, since it is liable suddenly to disappear, and is subject to potential disasters. For which a historical precedent from ancient Greece is adduced (F 174): King Dionysus spins his servant Damocles the same yarn.

This analogy underlines the repetitive character of history in Disney. A history in which any earlier epoch is seen as the pioneer of present-day morality. To see the world as a ceaseless prefiguration of Disney you just look back. It may not be true, but at least chronology is protected.

In reality, the past is known through (and in) the present, and as such it exists as a function of the present, as a support for prevailing ideas. Disney's mutilation of the relationship between the past and present accounts for his schematization and moralization of Third World history. Many years ago the conquistadors (like the Beagle Boys) tried to take away the property of the Aztec natives (ducks) who hid it. History is portrayed as a self-repeating, constantly renascent adventure, in which the bad guys try, unsuccessfully, to steal from the good guys (D 432, DD 9/65). The pattern is repeated in many other episodes in which the struggles of contemporary Duckburg are projected onto the history of past cultures. From time to time the

heroes are transported, by a dream, hypnosis or time machine, into another era. Old California (D 357) is the scene of the well-worn formula; the search for gold with hardship, the struggle between cops and robbers, and then the return to leisure and order. The same thing happens in their journeys to ancient Rome, Babylon and prehistory. There are also micro-ducks who come from outer space (TR 96, US 9/66), with traumatic adventures identical to those of our heroes. It's a sure bet that the "future time and infinite space" market will be cornered and colonialized by Disney.

By invading the past (and the future) with the structures of the present, Disney takes possession of the whole of human history. In Egypt there is a sphinx with the face of Uncle Scrooge (D 422, DD 3/64): "When he discovered the Sphinx, some years back, it didn't have a face, so he put his on it." It is only proper that the face of McDuck should be transposable everywhere. It is the trademark of U.S. history. It fits everywhere. At the end of the above story, he adds his likeness to the giant sculptures of Washington, Lincoln, etc. on Mount Rushmore — now called Mount Duckmore. Thus Scrooge joins the Founding Fathers. His statue is even in outer space (TR 48).

Since the bourgeoisie conceive their epoch to be the conclusion and perfection of humanity, the culmination of culture and civilization, they arrogate to themselves the exclusive right to re-interpret, from their particular viewpoint, the history of their own rise to power. Anything which denies the universality and immortality of the bourgeoisie is considered a trivial and eccentric deviation. Any contradictions are a matter of minor, subjective interpersonal disputes. Disney, the bourgeoisie's eulogist and flattering mirror, has distorted history so that the dominant class sees its rise as a natural, not social, phenomenon. The bourgeoisie have taken possession of an apartment which they pre-leased from the moment humanity appeared on earth.

The comic-as-history turns the unforeseeable into a foregone conclusion. It translates the painful course of time into eternal and premature old age. The causes of the present are not to be sought in the past; just consult Donald Duck, trouble-shooting ambassador-at-large. What a shame Socrates could not buy his comics. Surely he wouldn't have drunk the hemlock.

This fusing of the past with the mires and wastes of the present at least injects an illusion of the dynamism of time. While the major differences are obliterated in the cycle, there persists a certain discrepancy, betrayed by the whimpering nostalgia for an irrecoverable excitement.

But there is another means of anodizing and paralysing history. Time is apprehended as a consumable entity. Ancient lands and peoples are the alibi of history. Inca-Blinca, Unsteadystan, the Egypt of the Pharaohs, the Scandinavia of the Vikings, the piratical Caribbean, and the North America of the Indians (Chief Minimiyo, King of the Buffaloes (D 446), cultivating his pre-reservation lands), all march off under the Disney antiquarian wand to the supermarket of the dead statues. Buy your slice of history now, at cut-rate prices. The notion that time *produces* something is naturally eliminated; after all, it could be active and cause decay of those Pepsodent-white teeth.

The visa of the past for entry into the future through Disneyland Customs and Immigration (and Interpol) is stamped with exoticism and folklore. History becomes a marketplace where ancient civilizations pass by the plebiscite of purchase. The only difference among past civilizations lies in the extent of their value today as entertainment and sensation. Unless, of course, it is reduced to the Incan floormat upon which the bourgeoisie admiringly wipe their shoes. Says Daisy, "I made a bargain, I bought this authentic old fry pan for only thirty dollars." Quacks Donald, "But new ones only cost two!" "You don't understand. New ones aren't worth anything. Antique iron is very much the thing nowadays." (F 178). A double irony. The age of the dead statues, where time is suspended or compressed, is like a supermarket-museum. Like Disneyland, California, U.S.A., it is an amusement park, where you can get the bargain of the day, your favorite civilization: "Today and every Tuesday, Chile-with-Indians in Araucanian sauce."

Just as Donald & Co. need a photograph or a statue to guarantee their survival and memory, ancient cultures have to be Disnified in photograph or drawing in order to come back to "life." You. have to be buried alive to order to survive.

Disney approaches an individual existence in the same spirit as he does a foreign civilization, and both compete for success and the propagation of their petrified image. This is suggested in a story where Donald is the nightwatchman in a wax museum (D 436, CS 12/59). One night, while he is at work, a costume ball takes place in the house opposite the museum. The same historical figures (with the same clothes, faces and expressions, etc.) are present at the ball as are petrified in the wax museum. Inevitably, Donald falls asleep, and upon awakening mistakes the moving live figures for the wax ones. He concludes that while he was asleep a "revolution" took place. Apparently, there can be no other explanation for this movement of history. (A similar attitude towards the movement of history emerges from the story cited earlier about Unsteadystan, when the big city folk snuff out a revolution and bring Prince Char Ming (a plastic imitation of the millenary dynasty) back into power. Donald cannot accept any movement of history, real or imaginary). When he awakes he desperately tries to control the real figures with rope and stop the "revolution," yelling that "Queen Elizabeth, Joan of Arc, Attila the Hun, the whole museum is walking around in the street." All this happened because the guests at the costume ball had used as models the same historical figures as are in the museum, turning the past into an oasis of entertainment and tourism. Although it was not his fault, the episode makes Donald a celebrity, and he is rewarded for his work as guardian of the past. He seems to prefer the profession of guardian of the past in the interests of the iron-hard present. "Months have passed, and Unca Donald is making so much money he doesn't *need to work* any more," say the youngsters. "Yes, he's a famous character now . . . *so famous* that he gets *paid* just for allowing his wax dummy to be exhibited at the museum ... Our own Unca

Donald has caused the greatest commotion in the whole history of Duckburg!"

Donald has realized his dreams: easy, well paid and undemanding work. Any civilization, ancient or modern, can model itself on him. Just write Walt Disney Productions.

The Great Duck did nothing to deserve all this. Intelligence may further success and win publicity, but entry to the winter pastures of the dead statues can only be won through a stroke of luck. The movie producer can reconstruct and perpetuate the scene, or can cut it right out. The owners of the mass voice guarantee that the denizens of the cemetery behave themselves according to the rules. If they do not, they will not get a seat on the carrousel of history, they will not be "discovered."

According to Disney, each person, each civilization, in its solitude, imitates and anticipates the vicissitudes of history. History is conceived as being a huge personal organization with each person bearing within himself all the laws which govern change. Therefore, individual norms are valid on both social and individual levels.

Just as disembodied light bulbs are sufficient to send characters off to the discovery of some material or moral treasure, so the super-duper brilliant brain-waves of the magically charged luminaries of history are sufficient to light the paths of progress (D 364). Every creature has his share of genius, deposited in an idea-bank, and in moments of panic he cashes himself in without knowing how much he has on account. But, where do these ideas come from? They come out of nothing, or the previous idea. Disney history is impelled by ideas which do not originate in concrete circumstances or human labor, but are showered on people inexplicably from above. They use up ideas, and pay for them with bodily suffering, but never produce them. The pain of the body is the passive, the play of the soul the active factor. Ideas cannot be invested, because the bank does not receive deposits from humans. One can only draw on the cash benevolently poured by a Supreme Being into one's mental bucket. People are the fuel of the ideas-machine, but not the controls. Every idea is a very special seed, bearing marvellous but seedless fruit. It is governed by the sterile power of *idealist* thinking. Since it does not issue from materiality, from an individual's real existence, the idea serves once and once only. It is a one way street with only one way out: into another one way street. Since they cannot be stored, perceptions are exotic things which are used up at one go and then cast into the trash can, in expectation of another idea to meet the next contigency . . . .

The historic process is "ideated" as a series of unrelated, compartimentalized ideas parading past in single military file. In not acknowledging the origin of ideas in the materiality of humanity, it is as if all our heads were huddled together in a bag, waiting, and trying to overhear some whispered command from the lips of the owner. Since the owner of the bag is placed outside any concrete social situation (like a superhuman, or softhearted moneylender), ideas are conceived as products of a *natural* force. By making ideas appear beyond the control of the passive recipients and extrinsic to them, it takes the motors of history out of history into the realm of *pure nature.* This is called *inversion.* In reality, it is people who make their history, in accordance with concrete conditions, and who, in reciprocal interaction with social forces produce ideas. In Disney the ideas appear to generate this real life process without having any social or material origin, like a Boy Scout manual written in the clouds.

But is this Nature-Computer arbitrary in the distribution of is benefits, as some contemporary literature would suggest? Or is it governed by some law? Surely, for the Disney legal department has all the deeds in order: brains are distributed in a pre-stratified world and the wise and foolish, good and bad, stand there waiting for them. Distribution serves to reinforce damnation or salvation of the predestined, and the values they represent. Apart from the ethical division, people are also differentiated by their talent, so that when Donald puts on Gyro's magic cap (designed "for the mentally deficient," TR 53, GG 4/63), he immediately becomes a genius: "Daniel McDuck founded Duckburg in 1862 . . . Boris Waddle discovered the Waddle Isles in 1609 . . . Hurray! I am a genius in history!" (Note in passing, how the founder is an ancestor of Scrooge, and how the discoverer of the islands attaches his name to them. You are right, Donald, you have learned your lesson well.) He wants to utilize his invention in order to affirm his gentle supremacy: "Huey, Dewey and Louie think they are so bright. I'll show them that their uncle is brighter than they are." The cap is blown off his head and lands "on that crude looking individual." He knows what to do with new ideas: "Wow! Suddenly I know how to rob Scrooge McDuck." And Gyro laments, "Oh no! My Beanie-Brain is aiding his criminal mind!"

As soon as an idea is set in motion towards its happy goal, another factor enters: the imponderable. Talent is not enough, for if it were, the world would be forever predetermined. Chance, fate, and arbitrary forces act beyond the reach of will or talent, and introduce social mobility into the world. It permits individuals to aspire and enjoy a little success from time to time, despite the limitations of their personality. Thus, Donald, defined as a failure, is capable of beating the brilliant McDuck, because he was *lucky:* the idea he got was, for once, superior to his uncle's. Gyro Gearloose, indisputably a genius like Ludwig von Drake, attracts an incredible amount of bad luck. The nephews as a rule combine good luck with intelligence, but if luck lets them down, they will lose.

The mobility between good and bad luck is, however, available only to the dominant sector, that is, the "good guys" from the city who are permitted moral choices, and are always allowed to redeem themselves. For the inferior, criminal class, luck is always terrible and there is not even the glimmer of a good idea. If ever a good idea does appear, it will generally lead the owners to defeat and capture. Thinking is the surest route back to jail. That's fate. Only the class representing order may be governed by chaos, that is, by the law of disorder. The anarchy in the comic action makes it possible to appear to go beyond determinism (in a world which is socially predetermined anyway), and offers the necessary factors of surprise and variety in each episode. An appearance of anarchy in the action endows each character with credibility and suspense, and gives a means of vicarious identification to readers living every day in a constant state of anxiety.

Here is the difference between Disney and other types of comics where a superman operates in a world of order governed by the law of order. Tarzan and Batman cannot deviate from the norm; they are irreducibly good, and represent the physical and mental quintessence of the whole divine law of order. They can have no conflict with the established world or with themselves. Their crusade for moral rectitude against thieves restores the immaculate harmony of the world. As evil is expelled, the world is left nice and clean, and they can take a holiday. The only tension which may arise in this boring and repetitive world derives from the search for the hero's weakness, his Achilles' heel. The reader identifies with this hero because he shares with him his dual personality, the one commonplace, timid and incapable; and the other supreme and omnipotent. The dual personality (Clark Kent/ Superman) is a means for moving from the

everyday to the supernatural and back; there can be no movement within the everyday world itself.

Here lies the novelty of Disney (a product of his historical period), which rejects the clumsy, overdrawn schematism of the adventure strips arising in the same era. The ideological background may be similar, but since he does not reveal the repressive forces openly, Disney is much more dangerous. To create a Batman out of Bruce Wayne is to project the imagination beyond the everyday world in order to redeem it. Disney colonizes reality and its problems with the anagelsic of the child's imagination.

The "magic world of Disney" consists of variations within a circular repressive order. It gives to each character and his ideas, the impression of an autonomous personality, and the freedom of choice. If this freedom were also available to the "lower" strata, and there was no moral predestination at this level, we would be living in another society. The wall separating dominators from dominated would have crumbled, the whole superstructure of repression would have exploded, and this would end up in revolution. Instead of the false dialectic within a closed circuit which we now have in Disney (i.e. the fluid substitution among the "good guys", which we have analysed earlier), there would be a true dialectic, in which those "below" would have the chance to become both rebellious *and* good. The only course now open to the "submissive" peoples, if they leave their state, is revolution, the wrong kind of change, a constant *Unsteadystan* of crime and recrimination. Better be good. And if one is unlucky enough to lack talent, sit tight. Perhaps someday the wheel of fortune will cast some prestige and money your way, so that you can go up, up, up.

Chance is thus a mechanism through which the authoritarian and charitable laws of the universe operate. These laws impose certain rigid catagories of virtue and talent, but, due to an unfathomable will, rewards are afterwards distributed democratically, irrespective of prior classifications. It is a bankrupt welfare state doling out happiness. Luck levels all.

So the readers love these characters, which share all their own degradation and alienation, while remaining innocent little animals. Unable to control their own lives, or even the objects around them, the characters are perfectly closed around the nucleus of their imperfection. The egoism of the little animals, the defense of their individuality, their embroilment with private interests, provides a sense of distance between the characters and their creators, who are projecting their view of the world onto the animals.

The reader as *consumer* of the lives of the animals reproduces the sense of distance by feeling superior to and pity for the little animals. Thus the very act of consumption gives the reader a feeling of "superiority" over the animals and provides the basis for his acceptance of their values.

Only occasionally is a character able to break loose from his egocentric private problems and habits, and identify himself with a struggle other than the race for success. While most of the characters have no regular access to divine, messianic power, they have its plenipotentiary in Mickey Mouse. A character who dedicates his life to the struggle against evil without demanding recompense. He is not a super-anything, but a pacific prophet without judicial or other coercive powers. He does not seek prizes or advantages for himself, and his virtue, when he triumphs, is its own reward. The good luck Mickey merits and cultivates, he uses on behalf of his fellows. It is his disinterest which guarantees success. It raises him above others and their pettiness, and allows him to partake of divine power. He is material, but seems to deny the real, material world. This may help explain his past success in the United States and Europe. He is the tribal chief, and the providential leader who heads the public parades in Disneyland. And he represents Walt himself. In Latin America, on the other hand, Donald is more popular, and is the chosen propagandist for the magazines, although the television programs syndicated from the mother country are called the Mickey Hour or the Mickey Club. We Latin Americans tend to identify more readily with the imperfect Donald, at the mercy of fate or a superior authority, than with Mickey, the boss in this world, and Disney's personal undercover agent.

Through the figure of Mickey, the power of repression dissolves into a daily fact of life. He is at once law and big stick, church lottery, and intelligence agency. His chivalrous generosity, his sense of fair play which distinguishes so acutely between black and white (and the resplendence of his proboscis with its luminous tip lends a reassuringly matter-of-fact air to his gifts of prescience, and guarantees their proper, common-sense application). He never misuses his power. Mickey, standing at a legal boundary which others cannot cross without losing caste or being punished, promotes the messianic spirit at the level of the routine. He makes the spirit the common stuff of life. He turns the unusual, abnormal, arbitrariness of external power, into a commonplace phenomenon which partakes of the natural order. His extraordinary occult powers appear ordinary, and therefore, natural and eternal.

In the Disney world, Mickey is the first and last image of permanence, he is the all encompassing, self-contained law. But the daily life of Mickey is a false daily life, because it is based on the extraordinary. Likewise, his permanence is a false permanence because it, too, is based on the extraordinary. In a certain sense, Mickey's false permanence is a symbol for a false mother.

Perhaps this aspect of Mickey will help us understand the absence of woman as *mother* in Disney.

The only female in the Disney deck is the captive and ultimately frivolous woman, who, subject to courtship and adulation, retains only a fraction of her so-called "feminine nature." Being trapped in this superficial aspect of her being, woman relinquishes that other element which, from time immemorial, has made her a symbol of permanence. A permanence based on a real, physical relationship to existence. One which has made her an integral part of the universe, and part of the natural cycle of life itself. To incorporate into the world of Disney this kind of real permanence and mother image would be to inject an anti-body, a reality which would threaten the return to concrete daily life. The existence of a real mother would exclude the need for the false mother Mickey.

Another turn of the screw, another circle closes.

But is there not a short circuit, a break in the centripetal movement, when Disney criticizes the defects of contemporary society? Does he not:

stigmatize bureaucracy;

ridicule North American tourists (in Inca-Blinca and the Mato Grosso, for example);

attack atmospheric pollution and ecological destruction;

denounce the slaughters committed by inhuman technology;

denounce the solitude of people in the modern city;

attack the unbridled greed of those who exploit the consumer's weakness by selling him useless objects;

denounce the excessive concentration of wealth?

and, isn't the character of Scrooge McDuck a great social satire on the rich; and . . . .?

Wouldn't this vision of Disney's be justified as the best way of teaching children about the evils of today's world and the necessity of overcoming them?

Let us take two examples of Disney's brand of "criticism" and see whether in fact they do alleviate the suffocating atmosphere of the comics. In the Black Forest (TR 119, HDL 7/70) "all days are happy ones for the Junior Woodchucks." There they live in intimate harmony with nature, and even the wildest animals, the bear and the eagle, are affectionate. "Fresh air," "quiet," "health," "goodness" are however soon to be scared off by the true wild beast, the barbarous technology of Uncle Scrooge. An army of bulldozers, trucks, planes and monstrous machines, advances upon the idyllic spot. "Get out, you're holding up progress." Instead of trees, a "model city" and "the city of the future" will be built: "Ten thousand brick houses, with chimneys . . . two million inhabitants, with shops, factories, parking lots and refineries . . ." In reply to the Woodchucks' petition to prevent the construction, comes the infuriating response: "deers, bears, and birds don't pay taxes or buy refrigerators." Technological development is judged to be a harmful natural force, which establishes an authoritarian relationship between itself and those who use it. But there has to be a happy ending. The forces of nature react, at first passively, then with cautious aggressivity, and finally win over the millionaire developer by demonstrating their *utility*. The forest cures him of his colds, his anxieties, and neuroses; he is rejuvenated. Beneath the veneer of attachment to sterile urban progress, there lies a natural moral feeling and simple goodness, the unforgotten child, which permits people to be regenerated from one day to the next. Faced with the curse of contemporary living, one can only flee, turn inward, reconcile social enemies, and regress to the world of nature, where those guilty of provoking such disasters may be redeemed. The conquistador is convinced, and integrates back into nature. Thus the earth, from every flower and tree, regulates and rescues society, and is to be found within the depths of every person. So when McDuck tries to put pure air into cans in order to sell it, the wind drives away the smog and ruins his business (TR 110). Such "criticism" is designed to validate the system, and does not criticize anything. It only proves that it is always possible, in fantasy, to make the magic jump from one type of human being into another one more reconciled with the lost paradise. (It was "the Black Forest, the only one left from the great forests of olden times," which Scrooge wanted to cut down). Moral: one can continue living in the city as long as there remains an ultimate refuge in the country; and as long as there survives the reality and idea of a noble savage. Since a meek people is meek by definition and will never disappear, humanity is saved. The technological revolution is primed by the periodic return to the tribe, as long as it keeps its figleaf or loincloth on. This is cultural regression at its worst. The old natural forces of nature win out against the false natural forces of science.

Disney-style criticism is launched from the viewpoint of the ingenuous child – noble savage third worldling, who is ignorant of the causes of technological excess. It cannot be interpreted as an attack on the system itself, for it does not treat the causes of technological excess.

Once again, science is isolated as a historical factor, and so much so that Gyro Gearloose is always made ridiculous (except when he is able to take on an evil adversary, in which case he instantly becomes a success): "The world today is not ready to appreciate me But I have to live in it and must try to adapt myself." (D 439). Since there are no productive forces, poor Gyro, "the mad scientist" often has to work with primitive, manual methods which testify to his uselessness. In these comics not even scientific rationalism can become subversive.

Disney hopes that by incorporating the weaknesses of the system as well as its strengths, his magazines will acquire an appearance of impartiality. They embody pluralism of motifs and criteria, and liberty of expression, and while promoting sales, creative freedom for writers and artists. Of course, Disney's challenge to the system is stereotyped and socially acceptable. Supposedly, it is composed of conventions shared by all; rich and poor, intelligent and ignorant, big and small. It repeats the common coin of casual street corner and after dinner conversation: deploring inflation (forgetting that it is always the poor who are hardest hit), the decline in social standards (imposed by the bourgeoisie), atmospheric pollution (produced by an irrational system beyond public control), and drug abuse (but not its true causes). This is the facade of democratic debate, which while it appears to open up the problems defined by the bourgeoisie as "socially relevant," really conceals the subtle censorship they impose. This "democratic debate" prevents the ummasking of the fallacy of "free" thought and expression (just consider the treatment in the media of the Vietnam war, the Cuban invasion, the triumphs of the socialist republics, the peace movement, women's liberation, etc.).

But Disney also denounces the mass media themselves. He indulges in the most commonplace and stereotyped criticisms of television: it is the new head of the family, a threat to the harmony of the home, spreading lies and foolishness etc. Television even corrupts Donald's own nephews, who in one episode (D 437, CS 3/61) lose their affection and respect for him because he cannot measure up to a certain boastful television hero called Captain Gadabout. At this moment Donald is in the position of the typical head of the family faced with the comics, Disneyland, and the whole mass culture, as rivals to his authority.

Captain Gadabout has asserted that there are prehistoric savages living in a remote and exotic corner of the Grand Canyon. Donald refuses to believe the story, denouncing the Captain as a "two bit fraud! A pernicious prevaricator! A prince of hokum, and high hipster of hogwash!" and accuses him of brainwashing his nephews. He sets out for the Grand Canyon (not in the spirit of a search for truth, but out of resentment and envy), and discovers that the prehistoric savages exist in reality (just as the Abominable Snow Man did, whose existence he had also challenged). Donald compounds his error by getting trapped by the savages, having to swap clothes with them, and then having to be saved from abandonment (their plane meanwhile has been flown off by the savages) by the arrival of Captain Gadabout himself. Donald, so to speak, is saved by the media; but he is also punished by them. Gadabout films the rescue, so that it is Donald & Co. ("civilized ducks!") who act the part of the savages (who, in the meanwhile, have immediately become civilized) in his adventure series, or face being abandoned in the

Canyon. Later, while watching the television program which broadcasts their humiliation to the world, Donald & Co. ruefully reflect "The irony of it! We not only can't expose Captain Gadabout for the faker he is, we have to sit and watch *ourselves* be the *fakes*!"

Television is the bible of contemporary living. The nephews carry a set umbilically around with them to the Canyon. It is used to give the savages an instant crash course in civilization, teaching them to cook (duck), to practice sport, and even pilot a plane. Following a TV instruction session, the savages depart for civilization, watched by the distraught ducks. "They're going *up* toward the canyon rim!" "To *civilization* — where *we* wanted to go!" "They made it!" "They *landed* up there, all safe and sound — thanks to our portable telly vee!" Only the mass communications media can bring people — and children — out of that desert, that primitive (backward, underdeveloped) plateau, that illiterate childhood.

The whole world of the ducks is a television play, whether they like it or not, there is no escaping it. We all live in an enormous Disney comic, we have bravely to accept the fantasy, and not poison ourselves with the rhetoric of an urgent return to reality. Better to accept the fantasy, even if we secretly know it to be fraudulent, because supposedly it offers plenty of information, healthy amusement, and salvation.

Be satisfied with the role of spectator; otherwise you'll end up as a suffering extra in the great movie of life. Donald, the would-be critic, is vindictively exposed by the media. He is on screen, he is part of the show too. His rebellion led to the most terrible humiliation, and he made himself all the more ridiculous for having attempted to write his own scenario. The mass media, once again, have revealed themselves as messianic, invincible and irrevocable.

Criticism has been incorporated in order to provide a veneer of pluralism and enlightenment. Contradictions in the system are used to feign movement which does not lead anywhere, and to suggest a future which will never come.

The last circle closes in to strangle critical analysis, ours or any other. When the curtain opens on the historical drama of the world of Disney, the only character on stage is a Cement Curtain.

CONCLUSION: POWER TO DONALD DUCK?

Nephews: "We're *saved*, Unca Donald! The gunboat stopped firing!"
Donald: "And I stamped out all the fuses."

(D 364, CS 4/64)

Attacking Disney is no novelty; he has often been exposed as the travelling salesman of the imagination, the propagandist of the "American Way of Life", and a spokesman of "unreality." But true as it is, such criticism misses the true impulse behind the manufacture of the Disney characters, and the true danger they represent to dependent countries like Chile. The threat derives not so much from their embodiment of the "American Way of Life", as that of the "American Dream of Life". It is the manner in which the U.S. dreams and redeems itself, and then imposes that dream upon others for its own salvation, which poses the danger for the dependent countries. It forces us Latin Americans to see ourselves as they see us.

Any social reality may be defined as the incessant dialectical interaction between a material base and the superstructure which reflects it and anticipates it in the human mind. Values, ideas, *Weltanschauung*, and the accompanying daily attitudes and conduct down to the slightest gesture, are articulated in a concrete social form which people develop to establish control over nature, and render it productive. It is necessary to have a coherent and fluid mental picture of this material base, and the emotional and intellectual responses it engenders, so that society can survive and develop. From the moment people find themselves involved in a certain social system — that is, from conception and birth — it is impossible for their consciousness to develop without being based on concrete material conditions. In a society where one class controls the means of economic production, that class also controls the means of intellectual production; ideas, feelings, intuitions, in short — the very meaning of life. The bourgeoisie have, in fact, tried to invert the true relationship between the material base and the superstructure. They conceive of ideas as productive of riches by means of the only untainted matter they know — grey matter — and the history of humanity becomes the history of ideas.

To capture the true message of Disney, we must reflect upon these two components in his fantasy world to understand precisely in what way he represents reality, and how his fantasy may relate to concrete social existence, that is, the immediate historical conditions. The way

Disney conceives the relationship between base and superstructure is comparable to the way the bourgeoisie conceive this relationship in the real life of the dependent countries (as well as their own). Once we have analysed the structural differences and similarities, we will be better able to judge the effects of Disney-type magazines on the condition of underdevelopment.

It is, by now, amply proven that the Disney world is one in which all materiality has been purged. All forms of production (the material, sexual, historical) have been eliminated, and conflict has never a social base, but is conceived in terms of good versus bad, lucky versus unlucky, and intelligent versus stupid. So Disney characters can dispense with the material base underpinning every action in a concrete everyday world. But they are certainly not ethereal angels flying around in outer space. Continually we have seen how purposefully their lives reflect his view of the everyday world. Since Disney has purged himself of the secondary economic sector (industrial production, which gave rise to contemporary society and power to the bourgeoisie and imperialism), there is only one infrastructure left to give body to his fantasies and supply material for his ideas. It is the one which automatically represents the economic life of his characters: the *tertiary* sector. The service sector, which arose in the service of industry and remains dependent upon it.

As we have observed, all the relationships in the Disney world are compulsively consumerist; commodities in the marketplace of objects and ideas. The magazine is part of this situation. The Disney industrial empire itself arose to service a society demanding entertainment; it is part of an entertainment network whose business it is to feed leisure with more leisure disguised as fantasy. The cultural industry is the sole remaining machine which has purged its contents of society's industrial conflicts, and therefore is the only means of escape into a future which otherwise is implacably blocked by reality. It is a playground to which all children (and adults) can come, and which very few can leave.

So there can be no conflict in Disney between superstructure and infrastructure. The only material base left (the tertiary, service sector) is at once defined as a superstructure. The characters move about in the realm of leisure, where human beings are no longer beset by material concerns. Their first and last thought is to fill up spare time, that is, to seek entertainment. From this entertainment emerges an autonomous world so rigid and confined, it eliminates all traces of a productive, pre-leisure type of infrastructure. All material activity has been removed, the mere presence of which might expose the falsity of Disney's fusion of entertainment and "real" worlds, and his marriage of fantasy and life. Matter has become mind, history has become pastime, work has become adventure, and everyday life has become a sensational news item.

Disney's ideas are thus truly material PRODUCTIONS of a society which has reached a certain stage of material development. They represent a superstructure of values, ideas and criteria, which make up the self-image of advanced capitalist society, and facilitate innocent consumption of its own traumatic past. The industrial bourgeoisie impose their self-vision upon all the attitudes and aspirations of the other social sectors, at home and abroad. The utopic ideology of the tertiary sector is used as an emotional projection, and is posed as the only possible future. Their historic supremacy as a class is transposed to, and reflected in, the hierarchy established within the Disney universe; be it in the operations of the industrial empire which sells the comics, or in the relations between the characters created in the comics.

The only relation the center (adult-city folk bourgeoisie) manages to establish with the periphery (child-noble savage-worker) is touristic and sensationalist. The primary resources sector (the Third World) becomes a source of playthings; gold, or the picturesque experiences with which one holds boredom at bay. The innocence of this marginal sector is what guarantees the Duckburger his touristic salvation, his imaginative animal-ness, and his childish rejuvenation. The primitive infrastructure offered by the Third World countries (and what they represent biologically and socially) become the nostalgic echo of a lost primitivism, a world of purity (and raw materials) reduced to a picture postcard to be enjoyed by a service-oriented world. Just as a Disney character flees degenerate city life in search of recreation and in order to justify his wealth through an adventure in paradise, so the reader flees his historic conflicts in search of recreation in the innocent Eden of Donald & Co. This seizure of marginal peoples and their transformation into a lost purity, which cannot be understood apart from the historic contradictions arising from an advanced capitalist society, are ideological manifestations of its economic-

cultural system. For these peoples exist in reality, both in the dependent countries and as racial minorities ("Nature's" bottomless reservoir) within the U.S. itself.

Advanced capitalist society is realizing in Disney the long cherished dream of the bourgeoisie for a return to nature. It the course of the bourgeoisie's evolution this dream has been expressed in a multitude of historic variations in the fields of philosophy, literature, art and social custom. Recently, from the mid-twentieth century, the mass media have assisted the dominant class in trying to recover Paradise, and attain sin-free production. The tribal (now planetary) village of leisure without the conflicts of work, and of earth without pollution, all rest on the consumer goods derived from industrialization. The imaginative world of children cleanses the entire Disney cosmos in the waters of innocence. Once this innocence is processed by the entertainment media, it fosters the development of a class political utopia. Yet, despite the development of advanced capitalist society, it is the historic experience of the marginal peoples which is identified as the center of innocence within this purified world.

The bourgeois concept of entertainment, and the specific manner in which it is expounded in the world of Disney, is the superstructural manifestation of the dislocations and tensions of an advanced capitalist historical base. In its entertainment, it automatically generates certain myths functional to the system. It is altogether normal for readers experiencing the conflicts of their age from within the perspective of the imperialist system, to see their own daily life, and projected future, reflected in the Disney system.

Just as the Chilean bourgeoisie, in their magazines, photograph the latest hyper-sophisticated models in rustic surroundings, putting mini- and maxi-skirts, hot pants and shiny boots into the "natural environment" of some impoverished rural province (Colchagua, Chiloe) or — this is the limit, why not leave them in peace, exterminators — among the Alacalufe Indians; so the comics born in the United States, reflect their obsession for a return to a form of social organization which has been destroyed by urban civilization.* Disney is the conquistador constantly purifying himself by justifying his past and future conquests.

But how can the cultural superstructure of the dominant classes, which represents the interests of the metropolis and is so much the product of contradictions in the development of its productive forces, exert such influence and acquire such popularity in the underdeveloped countries? Just why is Disney such a threat?

The primary reason is that his products, necessitated and facilitated by a huge industrial capitalist empire are imported together with so many other consumer objects into the dependent country, which is dependent precisely because it *depends* on commodities arising economically and intellectually in the power center's totally alien (foreign) conditions. Our countries are exporters of raw materials, and importers of superstructural and cultural goods. To service our "monoproduct" economies and provide urban paraphernalia, we send copper, and they send machines to extract copper, and, of course, Coca Cola. Behind the Coca Cola stands a whole structure of expectations and models of behavior, and with it, a particular kind of present and future society, and an interpretation of the past. As we import the industrial product conceived, packaged and labelled abroad, and sold to the profit of the rich foreign uncle, at the same time we also import the foreign cultural forms of that

*Cf. Michèle Mattelart, "Apuntes sobre lo moderno: una manera de leer el magazine," in *Cuadernos de la Realidad Nacional* (Santiago), No. 9, September 1971.

society, but without their context: the advanced capitalist social conditions upon which they are based. It is historically proven that the dependent countries have been maintained in dependency by the continued international division of labor which restricts any development capable of leading to economic independence.

It is this discrepancy between the social-economic base of the life of the individual reader, and the character of the collective vision concerning this base which poses the problem. It gives Disney effective power of penetration into the dependent countries because he offers individual goals at the expense of the collective needs. This dependency has also meant that our intellectuals, from the beginning, have had to use alien forms to present their vision, in order to express, in a warped but very often revealing and accurate manner, the reality they are submerged in, which consists of the superimposition of various historical phases. It is a bizarre kind of ambiguity (called "barroquismo" in Latin American culture), which manages to reveal reality at the same time as it conceals it. But the great majority of the people have passively to accept this discrepancy in their daily subsistence. The housewife in the slums is incited to buy the latest refrigerator or washing machine; the impoverished industrial worker lives bombarded with images of the Fiat 125; the small landholder, lacking even a tractor, tills the soil near a modern airport; and the homeless are dazzled by the chance of getting a hole in the apartment block where the bourgeoisie has decided to coop them up. Immense economic underdevelopment lies side-by-side with minute mental superdevelopment.

Since the Disney utopia eliminates the secondary (productive) sector, retaining only the primary (raw material) and tertiary (service) sectors, it creates a parody of the underdeveloped peoples. As we have seen, it also segregates spirit and matter, town and countryside, city folk and noble savages, monopolists of mental power and mono-sufferers of physical power, the morally flexible and the morally immobile, father and son, authority and submission, and well-deserved riches and equally well-deserved poverty. Underdeveloped peoples take the comics, at second hand, as instruction in the way they are supposed to live and relate to the foreign power center. There is nothing strange in this. In the same way Disney expels the productive and historical forces from his comics, imperialism thwarts real production and historical evolution in the underdeveloped world. The Disney dream is cast in the same mold which the capitalist system has created for the real world.

Power to Donald Duck means the promotion of underdevelopment. The daily agony of Third World peoples is served up as a spectacle for permanent enjoyment in the utopia of bourgeois liberty. The non-stop buffet of recreation and redemption offers all the wholesome exotica of underdevelopment: a balanced diet of the unbalanced world. The misery of the Third World is packaged and canned to liberate the masters who produce it and consume it. Then, it is thrown-up to the poor as the only food they know. Reading Disney is like having one's own exploited condition rammed with honey down one's throat.

"Man cannot return to his childhood without becoming childish," wrote Marx, noting that the social conditions which gave rise to ancient Greek art in the early days of civilization, could never be revived. Disney thinks exactly the opposite, and what Marx regretfully affirms, Walt institutes as a cardinal rule of his fantasy world. He does not rejoice in the innocence of the child, and he does not attempt, from his "higher" level, to truthfully reflect the child's nature. The childish innocence, and the return to a historic infancy which Disney, as monarch of his creation, elevates, is a defiance of evolution. It is like a dirty, puerile, old man clutching his bag of tricks and traps, as he crawls on towards the lost paradise of purity.

And why, readers may ask, do we rail against this deshelved senility, which for worse or worser has peopled the infancy of us all, irrespective of our social class, ideology or country? Let us repeat once more: the Disney cosmos is no mere refuge in the area of occasional entertainment; it is our everyday stuff of social oppression. Putting the Duck on the carpet is to question the various forms of authoritarian and paternalist culture pervading the relationship of the bourgeoisie among themselves, with others, and with nature. It is to challenge the role of individuals and their class in the process of historic development, and the fabrication of a mass culture built on the backs of the masses. More intimately, it is also to scrutinize the social relations which a father establishes with his son; a father wishing to transcend mere biological determinants will better understand and censure the underhanded manipulation and repression he practices with his own reflection. Obviously, this is equally the case for mothers and daughters as well.

This book did not emanate from the crazied mind of ivory tower individuals, but arises from a struggle to defeat the class enemy on his and our common terrain. Our criticism has nothing anarchic about it. These are no cannon shots in the air, as Huey, Dewey and Louie would have it. It is but another means of furthering the whole process of the potential Chilean and Latin American Revolution by recognizing the necessity of deepening the cultural transformation. Let us find out just how much of Donald Duck remains at all levels of Chilean society. As long as he strolls with his smiling countenance so *innocently* about the streets of our country, as long as Donald is power and our collective representative, the bourgeoisie and imperialism can sleep in peace. Someday, that fantastic laugh and its echoes will fade away, leaving a mere grimace in its stead. But only when the formulae of daily life imposed upon us by our enemy ceases, and the culture medium which now shapes our social praxis is reshaped.

To the accusation that this is merely a destructive study which fails to propose an alternative to the defeated Disney, we can only reply that no one is able to "propose" his individual solution to these problems. There can be no elite of experts in the reformation of culture. What happens after Disney will be decided by the social practice of the peoples seeking emancipation. It is for the vanguard organized in political parties to pick up this experience and allow it to find its full human expression.

SELECTED BIBLIOGRAPHY

The following annotated bibliography has been prepared to assist the reader in locating additional Marxist studies on the two principal themes treated in this book: cultural imperialism, and the comic book.

With few important exceptions, most of the material on cultural imperialism in the bibliography comes from the Latin American countries, particularly Cuba. To our knowledge, there are relatively few Marxist analyses from the United States concerning the reactionary effects of the spread of the "American Dream" and its related cultural merchandise on the other peoples of the world. However, because of the struggles of these peoples, this is changing, and hopefully this change will be reflected in the quantity and quality of United States' Marxist analyses and actions in the domain of cultural imperialism; for our small part, we would welcome additions to this list, either forthcoming or overlooked.

The word "culture" has been understood in the political and broadest sense of the word: it refers to the (mass) communication of all social and economic values which support and shape the word "Culture" in the limited, capitalist "Fine Arts" sense of the word.

The entries follow standard bibliographic form, and have been arranged alphabetically by author, except when more than one relevant essay appears in a book, magazine, or from a conference; in which case it is listed under the main title, alphabetically. Where a text has been reprinted, we have tried to list it each time, but have only annotated it once.

The abbreviations also follow standard bibliographic notation. However, it should be noted that "U.S." means the "United States" and *not* "Uncle Scrooge", whereas the notoriety of some of the other abbreviations, such as CIA, USIA, USIS, USAID, ITT, AP, UPI, ABC, CBS, NBC and RCA, should not require any explanatory note: at this point in history it is well known what they stand for.

The entries have been extracted from the ongoing bibliographic publication *Marxism and the Mass Media: Towards a basic bibliography*, edited by the International Mass Media Research Center, the communications research division of the publisher, International General.

ABEL CASTANO, Ramón. *La Publicidad: Un Freno al Desarrollo.* Bogota: Ediciones Tercer Mundo, 1971. A wide-ranging analysis and description of the manipulatory nature of advertising; its development, place and techniques in the context of capitalist monopoly production, and its role in the retardation of human development. With appendix of statements on the function of advertising by its masters.

"Appareils Idéologiques d'Etat et Luttes de Classes: Chili 1970–73" *Cahiers du Cinéma* (Paris), 254–5, Dec. 1974-Jan. 1975, pp. 5–32. An interview with Armand MATTELART by Serge DANEY and Serge TOUBIANA on the ideological apparatuses during the Chilean Popular Unity government from 1970–3; the press, radio, TV, cinema and education: the "mass" strategy of the Chilean Right and U.S. imperialism in its fascist use of the cultural apparatus, and the contradictions of the Left in its ideological analyses and political practice in opening up the cultural apparatus to the masses and responding to the enemy.

ASSMANN, Hugo. *Evaluación de Algunos Estudios Latinoamericanos sobre Comunicación Masiva, con Especial Referencia a los Escritos de Armand Mattelart.* San Jose, Costa Rica: XI Congreso Latinoamericano de Sociología, June 1974. 43 pp. A 2-part analysis on the study of mass communications in Latin America: the 1st is a review and evaluation of the different schools of Latin American mass communications research since the early 1960s and its domination by European and U.S. imperialist values (particularly scientific faith); and the 2nd is an evaluation of the work of Armand and Michèle Mattelart (from 1967–1973 in Chile), with a series of formulations calling for the politicization of mass media research values.

AUTORENKOLLEKTIV. *Wir machen unsere Comics selber: Erfahrung mit Comics in Unterrichts.* Gulner DUVE, ed. Berlin: Basis Verlag, 1974. A textbook for teachers and students on how to make comics so that children will not be dependent on the products of the mass culture industry. In 2 sections; the 1st is an analysis of the present comic book industry, and their consumption, ideology and passifying function in capitalist society; and the 2nd concerns the planning of classes for teaching children how to make their own comics. Many descriptive illustrations.

BARRAUD, Hervé; S. De SEDE "La Mythologie d'Astèrix" *La Nouvelle Critique* (Paris), 26, Sept. 1969, pp. 35–40. The ideology of the French comic strip "Astèrix": the popularity of the comic strip as an extension of the 19th century serial novel, and Astèrix as expression of the mythic history and values of eternal French bourgeois morality, law and order.

BEGLOW, Spartak. *Millionäre machen Meinung von Millionen.* Frankfurt am Main: Verlag Marxistische Blatter, 1971. A description and analysis of the world-wide capitalist press, radio and TV system, and their interconnections. With a list of 277 trusts, news agencies, and publishers composing the international capitalist network. (Chapter 17 published in English: ______, "The Press and Society" *The Democratic Journalist* (Prague), 1971, pp. 12–16).

BUHLE, Paul. "The New Comics and American Culture" in: *Literature and Revolution*, C. Newman and G.A. White, eds. New York: Holt, Rinehart & Winston, 1973, pp. 367–411. Art, the history of the U.S. comic, and the new underground comics as product and reflection of U.S. culture.

CALVET, Louis-Jean. *Linguistique et Colonialisme: Petit Traité de Glottophagie.* Paris: Payot, 1974. The role of language and the study of language and its use in the process of imperialist expansion; linguistic imperialism and its place as part of ideological domination of oppressed peoples; the "superiority" of colonial language, and the denigration, marginalization and extermination of the "exotic" peoples. Contents: The theory of language and colonialism from the 16th thru 19th centuries; Dialects in the colonial process; The linguistic traces of colonialism; The colonial discourse on language; and Language and National Liberation. With a section of specific studies, and bibliography.

CARABBA, Claudio. *Il Fascismo A Fumetti.* Florence: Guaraldi, 1973. A study and documentation on the fascist comic books produced in Italy from the 1930s to 1944, and certain anti-communist comics from the 1960s and 70s, as seen accross the fascist intrepretation of history, heroes, colonial conquest, and anti-bolshevism, with the reproduction of 3 stories; "I Ragazzi di Portoria", "I Tre di Marcelle", and "Di un'Altra Razza". Illustrated, with a list of fascist comic book titles and characters.

CARMO, Alberto "Doing Business with Latin American Brains" *The Democratic Journalist* (Prague), 6, 1974, pp. 15–18. The importation by imperialist countries, particularly the U.S. of scientists, technicians, and professionals from the Third World.

The Chilean Road to Socialism, Dale L. JOHNSON, ed. Garden City, N.Y.: Anchor, 1973. An anthology of 65 texts, by U.S. and Chileans writers, on all aspects of Chilean development during the Popular Unity government (written and edited before the fascist coup).
Relevant:
.POLLOCK, John C.: David EISENHOWER "The New Cold War in Latin America: The U.S. Press and Chile" (pp. 71–86). The

hostile press coverage in the U.S. of the Popular Unity government as expressed by 6 U.S. daily newspapers during 1970–2, accross 5 general themes: Allende's isolation, Left threats to political stability, the responsible positions of the middle and upper classes, the irrational nature of protest against U.S. multinational corporations, and the aura of crisis around Allende.

HUMBERTO, Máximo. "Yankee Television Control" (pp. 120–4). The U.S. TV networks ABC, CBS, and NBC–RCA and how each has their role in U.S. control of Latin American TV and the creation of the mindless consumer.

Cine Cubano (Habana), 4, 63/65, pp. 80–94. 3 articles on cultural imperialism:

"La Industria Cultural Seduce al Capital Monopolista Yanqui" U.S. economic and governmental infiltration into Latin American culture: the work of the advertising, news, and USIA Agencies.

BARAHONA M., Hernán "Chile Entre Dos Fuegos: Cine y TV" U.S. control of Chilean TV and cinema.

"Publicidad Yanqui en las Elecciones Chilenas" U.S.–financed advertising during the Chilean elections.

_____, 66/67, pp. 68–89, 93.

ALMEYDA Clodomiro. "Hacer de la TV Intrumento de Elevación Moral y Liberación Humana" The humans tasks of the TV in Chilean and Latin American development.

FATRAC (Frente Antimperialista de Trabajadores de la Cultura) "Documento Denuncia: De Cómo USA Usa la Música como Arma de Penetración"A well-documented report and analysis on the infiltration of Latin American musical and cultural life by the U.S. Wide-ranging and specific, with bibliography.

"Cinéma et Multinationales", in: *Ecran* (Paris), 24, April 1974, pp. 38–48.

MATTELART, Armand "Hollywood en Vente?" Brief note on the change of ownership in the U.S. film industry from 1968–1972.

GUBACK, Thomas "Le Cinéma U.S.: Un Business International."

COCKCROFT, Eva "Abstract Expressionism: Weapon of the Cold War" *Artforum* (New York), XII, 10, June 1974, pp. 39-41.Brief, well-researched article on the U.S. avantguard art, and its use in support of U.S. Cold War policy and cultural pentration: the interconnected interests of the Museum of Modern Art (NY), the CIA, and the Rockefellers. (Forthcoming in an expanded version, International General, NY, late 1975).

Communications Technology and Social Policy. G. Gerbner; L. Gross; W.H. Melody, eds. New York: Wiley Interscience, 1973. Anthology, relevant:

NORDENSTRENG, Kaarle, Tapio VARIS "The Non-Homogeneity of the National State and the International Flow of Communications" (pp. 393–412). The historical development of communications and the role of consciousness in a world in transition.

MATTELART, Armand "Mass Media in the Socialist Revolution: The Experience of Chile" (pp. 425–440). The structure of information power during the Popular Unity government, and the problems confronted by the State Publishing House Quimantú in transforming the print media: comics, romance magazines, and the press.

Comunicación y Cultura (Santiago de Chile and Buenos Aires), 1, July 1973. First issue of magazine concerned with the role of the mass media and education in the context of Latin American political struggles. Relevant:

BAZIN, Maurice "La 'Ciencia Pura' Instrumento del Imperialismo Cultural: El Caso Chileno" (pp. 74–88). Abstract science and its role as part of cultural imperialism.

MATTELART, Armand. "El Imperialismo en Busca de la Contrarrevolución Cultural: 'Plaza Sésamo', Prólogo a la Telerepresión del año 2.000" (pp. 146–223). An analysis of the creation, organization and ideological content of the U.S. TV program "Sesame Street" as a model for the development of future U.S. domination of world education. (Published separately: _____, same title, Caracas: Universidad Central de Venezuela, 1974. 88 pp.)

_____, (Buenos Aires only), 2, March 1974.

MATTELART, Michèle; Mabel PICCINI "La Televisión y los Sectores Populares" (pp. 3–76). The TV and its role during the Popular Unity government: as part of ideological struggle; mass culture, distribution and technological myths; the relations between political vanguard and cultural apparatus; and a far-ranging study on the use and effects of the TV on the Chilean working class, with statements and interviews, and many facts and figures.

NOMEZ, Nain "La historieta en el Proceso de Cambio Social: Un Ejemplo de lo Exótico a lo Rural" (pp. 109–124). The problem of mass culture and the comic strip in a period of political change, and the experience of the Chilean State Publishing House Quimantú.

ACOSTA, Leonardo "El Barroco de Indias y la Ideología Colonialista" (pp. 125–158). The role and forms of cultural domination as integral part of colonial conquest of Latin America in the 15th, 16th and 17th centuries.

BARRACLOUGH, Solón "Ideología y Práctica de la Capacitación Campesina" (pp. 159–176). Agrarian development, and the concept of the qualified worker as it is dominated by U.S. criteria.

———, 3, 1975. 230 pp. 6 articles and 6 documents on the USIA in Latin American and Vietnam; the U.S. satellite program for education in Latin America; governmental mass media policy in Argentina and Peru:
"Ficha de Identificación de la Agencia de Información de los EE.UU (USIA)". A who's who of USIA cultural penetration in Latin America.
FRESENIUS, Gerardo; Jorge VERGARA "La Agencia Informativa Norteamericana (USIA) y Sus Boinas Verdes de Papel" A study of the contents in the anti-guerrilla comic book *El Deseñgano* produced anonymously by the USIA in Bolivia, Paraguay, Argentina, Venezuela, Guatamala, Nigaragua, Panama, Costa Rica, San Salvador, Santa Domingo, and Honduras. Many illustrations.
BALLOCHI P., Roberto "Algunas Antecedentes Sobre el Satelite Educativo para América del Sur" The history of the U.S. attempt to sell U.S. education by communications satellite to Latin American.
TORRES, Héctor "Colombia y el Satelite Educativo" A critique of UNESCO's proposals for education by satellite in Colombia and its adverse effect in increasing U.S. cultural dominance.
SANTOS, Enrique "Tecnología, Imperialismo y Educación" A ideological study of the U.S. conception of educational technology: satellites, and audio-visual instruction.
GRAZIANO, Margarita "Los Dueños de la Televisión Argentina" A very detailled analysis of the structure and ownership of Argentine local and national TV, made at the time of the nationalization of the TV channels in 1974.
Plus the following 6 documents: 2 texts by the Peruvian Revolutionary Government on the Expropriation of the Peruvian daily newspapers in 1974; an interview with a U.S. government ex-film official on the work of the USIA in Vietnam; an interview with Frank Shakespeare, the director of the USIA on the U.S. propaganda war during "peaceful coexistence"; the UNESCO satellite proposals; and the position of the Soviet Union regulating the transmission of direct TV satellite broadcasting.

The Democratic Journalist (Prague), 9, 1973.
EPSTEIN, S. "Imperialism and Manipulating with Public Opinion" (pp. 4–5). U.S. propaganda and its language.
CARMO, Alberto "International Telephone and Telegraph – A Gigantic Multinational Octopus" (pp. 15–18). The penetration of ITT into the communications systems in different countries throughout the world, and its effects, particularly in Chile.
VARIS, Tapio "The Changing role of Electronic Media in World Communications" (pp. 15–18). The contents of international TV programs, and the "free" flow of information.

———, 2, 1974.
KREJCI, Jaroslav; Jan CERNAL "Misuse of Information Technology in the Ideology" (pp. 10–16). The development of of U.S. information technology – computers, data banks, etc. – as a growing support for U.S. capitalist society: in its domestic planning and surveillance; foreign military policy; and as basis for "post-industrial" theories and anti-communist propaganda.
CARMO, Alberto "Brazil's Problems Today" (pp. 17–20). The U.S.'s growing control of Brazilian education and culture: the development by U.S. industry of direct satellite communications for educational programming.

———, 3, 1974.
CARMO, Alberto "When they Speak About Freedom of the Press in Chile" (pp. 3–6). The Popular Unity government's policy concerning the right for all newspapers to publish.
ZASURSKY, Y.N. " 'Free Flow of Information': The Cold War and Reducing International Tension" (pp. 7–11). The evolution of the concept of the "free flow of information": from its roots in the Cold War to its present-day use as a means to objectify capitalist values and impose them on the rest of the world; the example of Chile.
GRONBERG, Tom; Kaarle NORDENSTRENG "Approaching International Control of Satellite Communications" (pp. 12–15).

———, 7/8, 1974.
RODRIGUEZ BETHENCOURT, Miriam "Sesame Street – Disseminates New Agression" (pp. 20–21). A brief history of the U.S.–business developed TV program "Sesame Street" and its international penetration.
MATTELART, Armand; Daniel WAKSMAN "Plaza Sesamo and An Alibi for the Author's Real Intentions" (pp. 21–25). The U.S. development of "Sesame Street" as a model for the U.S. creation of a world repressive education system: technology and U.S. business interests; satellite communications; its ideology and its supposed "neutral and educational" character.

———, 9, 1974.
VARIS, Tapio "Global Traffic in Television" (pp. 8–11).
LENT, John A. "Imperialism via Q-Sorts" (pp. 14–17). The monopolization of Asian communications research by the U.S., United Kingdom, France and West Germany by the use of: western communications theories and models, "experts", and conferences.
NORTH, Joseph "Chile: The Sacred Duty of Democratic Journalists" (pp. 19–20). The responsibility of all journalists to speak out against the fascist generals in Chile.

DIAZ RANGEL, Eleazar. *Pueblos Subinformados: Las Agencias de Noticias y América Latina*. Caracas: Universidad Central de Venezuela, 1967. The control of information to and from Latin America by the U.S. news agencies UPI and AP, and their connection to the Latin American and world press, with examples of their coverage of the U.S. invasion of the Dominican Republic, and the Third World in general; and the Third World's fight to develop their own news agencies. Many facts and figures.

von DOETINCHEM, Dagmar; Klaus HARTUNG. *Zum Thema Gewalt in Superhelden-Comics.* Berlin: Basis Verlag, 1974. The superman-type comics, and how they reflect the values of capitalist life and channel its frustrations into fantasy life: the theme of power and its distortion, free will as expression of the free marketplace, the reinforcement of the repressive concept of the State, and the depiction of criminality. Illustrated examples.

DORFMAN, Ariel. *Ensayos Quemados en Chile: Inocencia y Neocolonialismo*. Buenos Aires: Ediciones de la Flor, 1974. Anthology of 11 texts written in Chile on the mass media and revolution: capitalist domination of children's literature (the comic book character Babar the Elephant), *Reader's Digest*, the Lone Ranger, the change of names of the industries nationalized by the Popular Unity government, book production, TV educational programs, and the fascist ideological offensive.

______; Manuel JOFRE. *Superman y sus Amigos del Alma*. Buenos Aires: Ediciones Galerna, 1974. 2 studies on the comics published before and during the Popular Unity government in Chile. The 1st, by Dorfman, analyses the Lone Ranger and other superheroes in relation to the evolution of the capitalist State; and the 2nd, by Jofre, examines the changes in the comics produced by the Chilean State Publishing House Quimantú.

ECO, Umberto. *Apocalittici e Integrati*. Milan: Bompiani, 1965. A critique of mass culture concepts and values; high, middle, low; kitsch; cartoons (Steve Canyon, Superman, Charlie Brown) and their characterization, myths and consumption; and a section on the mass media and the TV. (In Spanish: ______, *Apocalipticos e Integrados Ante la Cultura de Masas.* Barcelona: Editorial Lumen, 1968).

Enciclopedia del Fumetto: 1. Oreste del BUONO, ed. Milan: Milano Libri Edizione, 1969. An anthology of 25 texts by Italian authors tracing the development of the U.S. comic book from the late 19th century through the 1960s. For the most part progressive, with the exception of the last section "Cosa Nostra" on the fantasized depiction of war and police repression in the comics, and particularly the text of Stelio MILLO "Appunti sul fumetto fascista" on the fascist content of Flash Gordon and Mandrake, etc. in Italy under the rule of Mussolini.

FANON, Franz. "This is the Voice of Algeria" in: ______, *A Dying Colonialism*, Harmondsworth, England: Penguin, 1970, pp. 53-80. A study of the change in attitudes towards the radio by Algerians during the fight for liberation: from the French-controlled radio as symbol and reinforcement of colonialist values to its use as an active element of struggle.

FARAONE, Roque. *Mass Media in Latin America*, an issue of: *ISAL Abstracts* (Montevideo), Year 4, IV, 45, 1973. 30 pp. A general introduction to the character and problems of the mass media in Latin America: the structure and ownership of the media and its control by U.S. imperialist interests; entertainment, advertising and anarchy of the capitalist media, and its role as vehicle for the dominant ideology. Extracts from the Peruvian General Telecommunications Law, brief information on the new Argentine Broadcasting Law, with a list of journalism schools in Latin America. Bibliography, by country, of Marxist and progressive studies on the mass media.

______, *Medios Masivos de Comunicación.* Montevideo: Nuestra Tierra, Nov. 1969. 60 pp. The mass media in Uruguay, particularly as distorted and dominated by U.S. advertising. Contents: The common character of all the instruments of social communications; Advertising and Propaganda; Freedom of the Press and the Right of Free Information; and Distribution and Effects.

FRAPPIER, Jon. "Advertising: Latin America" *NACLA* (North American Congress on Latin America) *Newsletter* (New York), III, 4, July-Aug. 1969, pp. 1–11. The purpose, content and organization of U.S. advertising in Latin America.

______, "U.S. Media Empire Latin America" *NACLA Newsletter* (New York), II, 19, March–April 1968. The ownership and control of the Latin American press, radio and TV by U.S. media and business interests.

FRESNAULT-DERUELLE, Pierre "Le récit (ou le scénario-parenthèses) de Bande Dessinée" *La Nouvelle Critique* (Paris), 49, Jan. 1972, pp. 62–65. How economic pressures have effected the development of the comic book storyline: the weekly sale of the comics, and the development of the consumable, closed vision of the world. Brief bibliography.

______, "Une Unité Commerciale de Narration: La Page de Bande Dessinée" *La Nouvelle Critique* (Paris), 44, May 1971, pp. 42–49. The evolution of the comic strip form as effected by capitalist economic pressure: the relation between image and text, from caption to balloons, organization of the story, serial presentation, and the page layout.

I Fumetti di "Unidad Popular": Uno Strumento di Informazione Populare nel Cile di Allende. Milan: Celuc, 1974. Introduction by Umberto ECO. A selection of 13 stories from *La Firme*, a popular education magazine published in comic book format by the Popular Unity government publishing house Quimantú in 1972 and early 1973, treating the subjects of bureacracy, agrarian reform, urban life, and the mass struggle against profiteering. (An English edition will be published in 1976, and will also contain the important work produced in 1970 and 1971).

GIFFORN, Hans "Comics als Lesestoff von Kindern und als Gegenstand politischer Erziehung" in: *Die Heimlichen erzieher: Kinderbucher und politischer lernen*, D. RICHTER; J. VOGT, eds., Hamburg: Rowohlt, Jan. 1974, pp. 142–160. Comics as distraction to encourage fantasy; superheroes and the reinforcement of the values of capitalism.

GARCIA LUPO, Rogelio "El Gobierno Peronista Frente a los Medios de Comunicación de Masas" *Peronismo y Socialismo* (Buenos Aires), I, 1, Sept. 1973, pp. 21–24. The U.S. news agencies AP and UPI during 20 years in Argentina: their control over information (news and advertising), and alliances with the local bourgeois press, particularly *La Nación* and *La Prensa.*

GUBACK, Thomas H. "American Interests in the British Film Industry" *The Quarterly Review of Economics and Business* (Urbana, Ill.), VII, 2, Summer 1967, pp. 7–21. The U.S. film industry's control of British film production and distribution.

______, "Film and Cultural Pluralism" *The Journal of Aesthetic Education* (Urbana, Ill.), V, 2, April 1971, pp. 35–51. The film as economic entity, and the U.S. domination of European film production and distribution.

GUTIERREZ VEGA, Hugo. *Información y Sociedad.* Mexico, D.F.: Fondo de Cultura Económica, 1974. The concepts and contents of North American communications and its allied mass communications research, and their negative effect on Mexican society: the information business and alienation, public opinion manipulation, information consumption, the electronic media, and the Left comic books of Quino, and Rius.

HOROWITZ, Andrew "Domestic Communications Satellites" *Radical Software* (New York), II, 5, 1973, pp. 36–40. The development of the U.S. communications satellite program: the inter-locking interests of the U.S. military and monopoly aircraft and communications industries; externally, profit motivation and joint global penetration; and internally, surveillance and control over the flow of information and the apathy of the FCC.

Ideología y Medios de Comunicación, Manuel A. GARRETON, ed. Buenos Aires: Amorrortu, 1974. Anthology of 6 texts originally published in the Chilean revue *Cuadernos de la Realidad Nacional* during the Popular Unity government, on different aspects of ideological struggle. Relevant here:

MARTINEZ, Jesús "Para Entender los Medios: Medios de Comunicación y Relaciones Sociales" (pp. 94–129). A wide-ranging analysis of the means of communications under capitalist conditions, with a section on the media under conditions of colonialism and dependency.

DORFMAN, Ariel "Inocencia y Neocolonialismo: Un Caso de Dominio Ideológico en la Literatura Infantil" (pp. 170–206).

"L'impérialisme Culturel" *Le Monde Diplomatique* (Paris), 249, Dec. 1974, pp. 7–11.

SCHILLER, Herbert I. "Les Mécanismes de la Domination Internationale" The growth of the U.S. communications and marketing corporations, the closing gap between advertising and information, the spread of the U.S. advertising agency around the world, the public opinion poll, the practice of the "free flow of information", and the promotion of "neutral and inoffensive" entertainment.

MATTELART, Armand "Une Stratégie Globale pour l'Amérique Latine: The tactics of the U.S. multinationals and the U.S. government in the use of cultural penetration as part of their world propaganda campaign: U.S. control of Latin American TV content, "Sesame Street" as important part of U.S. plans for "educating" the world, and Brazil's role in U.S. plans for "educating" Latin America.

______. "Au Chili: Les Armes de la Contre-révolution culturelle" The role of the U.S. advertising agency during the Chilean Popular Unity government: from the promotion of U.S. cultural merchandise to the planning of the overthrow of the Allende Government.

TEXIER, Jean-Claude "Métamorphoses d'une Industrie de la Pensée?" The increasing dominance of U.S. capital and its attendant values in the French press and publishing industry.

RAMONET, Ignacio "Cinéma Francais et Capitaux Américains" U.S. dominance of French film production and distribution.

GOBARD, Henri "Les Gallo-Ricains:Aberrations d'un Nouveau Conformisme" The growing emulation and prestige of U.S. cultural values in France: music, clothing, office habits, language and education.

"Imperialismo y Medios Masivos de Comunicación", a special issue of: *Casa de las Americas* (Habana), Year 13, 77, March-April 1973, 174 pp. Anthology of 8 texts on the capitalist and imperialist mass media; including women's magazines, comic books, mass culture and journalism.

ACOSTA, Leonardo "Medios Masivos e Ideología Imperialista" The development of the mass media in the context of U.S. financial-political-military interests, its concepts of technology, progress, and history as part of imperialist growth: persuasion, advertising and consumption, marketing, press contents, and the "new world" of electronics, technocracy, "mass culture", and "end of ideologies."

MATTELART, Armand "La Industrial Cultural no es una Industria Ligera"

VIEWEG. Klaus: Willy WALTHER "Cambios en la Estructura de Información de la Prensa Imperialista" The effects of scientific-technical change on monopoly capitalism, and its manifestation on its press theory and practice: journalist style, information presentation, types of news stories, objectivity, credibility, and specialists.

DORFMAN, Ariel "Salvación y Sabiduría del Hombre Común: La Teología del *Reader's Digest*"

ERHART, Virginia "Amor, Ideología y Enmascaramiento en Corin Tellado"

MATTELART, Michèle "Apuntes sobre lo Moderno: Una Manera de Leer la Revista Femenina"

VERGARA, Jorge "Comics y Relaciones Mercantiles"

MURARO, Heriberto J. "Ideología en el Periodismo de TV en Argentina"

Imperialismo y Medios Masivos de Comunicación. 2 volumes. Lima: Editorial Causachum, 1973. 150 and 161 pp. Relevent:

Volume I:

ACOSTA Leonardo "Medios Masivos e Ideología Imperialista" (pp. 7–67).

VIEWEG, Klaus, Willy WALTHER "Cambios en la Estructura de Información de la Prensa Imperialista"

PEREZ BARRETO, Samuel "El Caso 'Plaza Sesamo' en el Perú" (pp. 121–150)

Volume II:

DORFMAN, Ariel "Salvación y Sabiduría del Hombre Común: La Teología de Selecciones del *Reader's Digest*" (pp. 5–38).

GARGUREVICH, Juan "Informe sobre Algunas Revistas Alienantes en el Perú" (pp. 88–94). The imperialist press implantation in Peru: The U.S. multinational publishers Hearst, Western Publishing, Reader's Digest, Walt Disney, Time-Life, and Vision, and the reactionary content of their publications.

URIBE, Hernán "La Desinformación: Industria Imperialista" (pp. 121-142). World communications growth, and imperialist communications strategy against Latin America (particularly Chile, Brazil, and Argentina) in the development of *Homus Consumem*: technological penetration, press control, film, comic books, public relations and advertising agencies, news agencies (AP and UPI), and U.S. government agencies (USIA); and the need for Latin American journalists to fight this invasion. Many important facts and figures.

Instant Research on Peace and Violence (Tampere, Finland), 1, 1973. 4 articles on international communications:

GRONBERG, Tom; Kaarle NORDENSTRENG "Approaching International Control of Satellite Communications" (pp. 3–8). A report of actions taken at UNESCO and elsewhere to prevent the spread of U.S.–style "freedom of communications" and imperialism.

MATTELART, Armand "Modern Communications Technologies and New Facets of Cultural Imperialism" (pp. 9–26). The marriage of U.S. mass culture and the U.S. war economy: the U.S. electronics and aerospace corporations and their militarization of world science and education. (Translation of chapter from original Spanish: ______, *La Cultura como Empresa Multinacional*. Mexico, D.F.: Ediciones Era, 1974).

VARIS, Tapio "European Television Exchanges and Connections with the Rest of the World" (pp. 27–43). The flow of TV programs in western Europe and eastern Europe, and their relationship to the developing countries. Facts and figures.

VAYRYNEN, Raimo "Military Uses of Satellite Communications" (pp. 44–49). U.S. development of satellite communications for military uses.

INTERNATIONAL ORGANIZATION OF JOURNALISTS (IOJ), ed. *The Chilean Coup and its Cruel Aftermath*. Prague: IOJ, 1974, 153 pp. Extensive documentation on the fascist coup in Chile, with statements and appeals by the IOJ, and interviews and accounts of the day of Allende's death and subsequent fascist tortures.

TIMOSSI, Jorge "Augusto Olivares: A Revolutionary Journalist" (pp. 29–33). On the director of the national TV who died with Allende at La Moneda.

CARMO, Alberto "When They Speak about Freedom of the Press in Chile" (pp. 43–58).

"The Present Situation of the Press and Journalists in Chile" (pp. 59–86). The control and ownership of the press, radio and TV during the Popular Unity government; the destruction of the Left media at the time of the coup, and its control under the fascist regime; with a list of murdered, imprisoned, and exiled journalists. (This last article published separately: ______, same title, Prague: IOJ, 1974, 16 pp.).

———. *Chile: One Year Later.* Prague: IOJ, 1974. 34 pp. A detailled account of the events concerning journalists and the press in Chile since the fascist coup in September 1973: from U.S. economic support of the anti-Allende press to repression and murder; with information on the 9 known murdered journalists, the 45 known imprisoned journalists, their conditions of imprisonment, police terror, unemployed journalists, press control, the clandestine press, and IOJ actions in support of the Chilean people.

———. *La FIOPP: Instrumento de la Política "Interamericana" de los EE.UU.* Prague: IOJ, 1967. 41 pp. The political role of FIOPP (the Inter American Federation of Professional Journalists' Organizations) in Latin America; as an instrument of the U.S.–based American Newspaper Guild financed with CIA funds.

———. *The Media Today and Tomorrow.* Prague: IOJ, 1974. 131 pp. Anthology of 9 texts on the problems arising from the increasing technological developmet of satellites and their use in international communications, with a series of statements and documents on UNESCO's communications policies.

KOLOSOV, Yuri "Global TV and its Prospects" (pp. 5–10). The possibilities of satellite use in science, culture, and education, and the political and propaganda problems in the peaceful use of technology.

NORDENSTRENG, Kaarle; Tom GRONBERG "Approaching International Control of Satellite Communications" (pp. 11–23).

KOZLUK, Tadeusz "Problems of Television Satellite Broadcasting" (pp. 24–32). The legal and political problems: national sovereignty and peaceful use of satellites.

NALIN, J. "The Scientific and Technological Revolution and Journalism: The Case 'For' and 'Against' " (pp. 33–43). Satellite communications and propaganda: national sovereignty, and USSR proposals to UNESCO for satellite broadcasting.

VARIS, Tapio "The Changing Role of Electronic Media in World Communications" (pp. 44–50).

MATTELART, Armand "Modern Communications Technologies and New Facets of Cultural Imperialism" (pp. 58–83).

ADESANIA, Ade "The Psyche Under the Pressure of Information" (pp. 84–95).

NORDENSTRENG, Kaarle "Prognosis for the Development of Mass Media and Their Uses" (pp. 96–111).

———, "Uruguay and Mass Media Today", an issue of *Journalists' Affairs* (Prague), 15/16/17, 1974, 28 pp. The mass media in Uruguay from 1967 to 1973: the role of the USIA and the CIA in support of the Uruguayan ruling class, and the theoretical support of J.T. Klapper and USIA specialists in the development of the theories, planning, operation and aims of mass persuasion and monopoly propaganda techniques; the ownership of the mass media; and press freedom and the journalist. With a detailled chronology of actions against the freedom of information from 1967–1973.

JANCO, Manuel; Daniel FURJOT. *Informatique et Capitalisme.* Paris: Maspero, 1972. A far-ranging analysis of information science and the computer industry in the process of capitalist reproduction, relations of productions, and its location in the class struggle. In 4 sections; relevant here are the chapters on imperialist expansion, the internationalization of the capitalist mode of production, war and police repression, and the many facts and figures on IBM worldwide.

Journal of Communications (Philadelphia, Pa.) XXIV, 1, Winter 1974.

FAGEN, Patricia W. "The Media in Allende's Chile" (pp. 59–70). The problems in the transformation of the mass media during the Popular Unity government: the overwhelming private ownership, the difficulties of the Left media to compete economically, and problems of changing the old contents of the mass press.

GUBACK, Thomas H. "Film as International Business" The economics of film and TV film productions, and how co-production arrangements are used by the U.S. film industry to dominate the international flow of film and TV programs.

VARIS, Tapio "Global Traffic in Television" (pp. 102–109). International TV programming and distribution: the dominance of the U.S. and Great Britain in the sale of programs (and ideology) to Europe and the developing countries; and the unequal flow of news between Eurovision and Intervision (the Socialist countries).

SCHILLER, Herbert I. "Freedom from the 'Free Flow'" (pp. 110–116). The growing international resistance to the one-way flow of information and values from the few powerful capitalist countries, particularly the U.S., towards the developing countries, and how the U.S. media monopolies use the concept of the "free flow" to continue their economic penetration around the world.

KAHN, Albert E. *The Game of Death: Effects of the Cold War on Our Children.* New York: Cameron & Kahn, 1953. A study of the U.S. Cold War policy in the U.S., particularly concerning the militarization of the U.S. education system during the 40s and 50s in support of U.S. government policy. Relevant is chapter V: "Niagara of Horror" on the violence, war, crime and fantasy content of children's comic books, TV programs and film production.

KOLOSOV, Yuri "TV and International Law"

The Democratic Journalist (Prague), 11, 1974, pp. 21–24. The issues in the UN concerning the control over the use of direct TV broadcast satellites: reactionary broadcasting, national sovereignty, and governmental responsibility for broadcast contents and violations.

KUNZLE, David "Art in Chile's Revolutionary Process: Guerrilla Muralist Brigades" *New World Review* (New York), XLI, 3, 1973, pp. 42–53. The work of the popular mural painting brigades in Chile developed during the Popular Unity government to combat the propaganda of the private press and to disseminate the ideas of the Chilean government.

_____, "Art of the New Chile: Mural, Poster and Comic Book in A 'Revolutionary Process' " California, 1972–4, 48 pp. ms. A study, written before the fascist coup, on the Chilean cultural offensive during the Popular Unity government and its work in developing alternative communications channels, particularly the mural, poster and comic strip, to fight the right wing propaganda machine: the terror tactics of the reactionary press, the politicization of the art institutions, the Ramona Parra mural Brigades, poster production, and the contents of the new comic books produced by the state publishing house Quimantú. (forthcoming in: *Art and Architecture in the Service of Politics*, H. Millon and L. Nochlin, eds., MIT Press).

_____, *The History of the Comic Strip: Volume I. The Early Comic Strip (Narrative Strips and Picture Stories in the Early European Broadsheets 1450–1826).* Berkeley, Calif.: University of California Press, 1973. The development of the predecessor of the modern comic strip, with examples from Great Britain, Italy, Germany, Holland, and Russia, analysing their often progressive social-political role in propaganda and popular struggles. Many Illustrations.

LAWSON, John Howard. *Film in the Battle of Ideas*. New York: Masses and Mainstream, 1953. A study of the U.S.–Hollywood film industry, its ideological content, and role as propaganda arm for U.S. imperialist policy. With many concrete analyses of U.S. film production, and a section on world film production as part of class struggle.

MALPICA, Carlos. *Los Dueños del Perú.* Lima: Ediciones Peisa, 1974 (6th ed.). The power structure of Peruvian economic, political, social and cultural life, and its dominance and ownership by U.S. governmental and business interests. For the most part, the material dates from before 1968. In 8 chapters, relevant here are the analyses of the control of public opinion, news and advertising agencies, communications ownership, police espionage and the telephone, the cultural sector and the universities.

MASS MEDIA GROUP *(Unga Filosofer*, Sweden), ed. "Speeches given at the Seminar on Cultural Imperialism, Stockholm, October 1974" 47 pp. mimeographed. A transcript of the proceeding of the seminar with numerous interventions, brief introduction by Karl-Ola NILSSON, and 4 texts:

SCHILLER, Herbert I. "Mass Media and U.S. Foreign Policy" (pp. 1–16). The relation between the media owners and U.S. foreign policy, from its historical roots from the 1940s through the Cold War, to the use of UNESCO by the U.S., until very recently, in promoting U.S.–style "free flow of information" concepts as a means to expand the dissemination of the U.S. multinational advertising message.

EKBERG, Sven "The U.S.–Imperialism and Europe" (pp. 17–25). Brief resume of U.S. policy regarding Europe during the past 20 years, particularly as effected by U.S. imperialist interests in the Third World.

DeVYLDER, Stefan "The Imperialism and the Dependent Countries" (pp. 26–33). Imperialist propaganda and advertising in the transmission of consumption patterns from the capitalist countries to the Third World; the example of Latin America.

VARIS, Tapio "The Flow of Television Programmes" (pp. 34–47). The concentration of media production in the capitalist centers, the world-wide distribution of U.S. production and ideology, U.S. production in foreign countries, and the use of technology to open up new markets for the U.S.

Mass Media and International Understanding, France VREG, ed. Ljubljana, Yugoslavia: School of Sociology, Political Science, and Journalism, 1969. The proceedings from a conference, of the same name, held in Ljubljana in 1968.

VREG, France. "Structural and Functional Changes in the Public and World Community" (pp. 34–50). The changing relationship between governments and their publics, and the effects on international communications.

SMYTHE, Dallas W. "Conflicts, Cooperation and Communications Satellites" (pp. 51–73). The development of communications satellites and the social-political problems they pose internationally, particularly regarding the ideological invasion of the developing countries by the U.S.

SCHILLER, Herbert I. "International Communications, National Sovereignty and Domestic Insurgency" (pp. 92–107). Technological change and economic power in the mass media: the negative effect of the concentration of this power and control in the capitalist countries on the growth of the underdeveloped countries.

MATTELART, Armand. *Agresión en el Espacio: Cultura y Napalm en la Era de los Satélites.*

Santiago de Chile: Ediciones Tercer Mundo, Sept. 1972. A well-documented analysis of the organization, content and effects of the role of U.S. business and war interests in the development of international satellite communications. (Reprinted:______. *Agresión desde en el Espacio: Cultura y Napalm en la Era de los Satélites.* Buenos Aires: Siglo XXI, 1973).

______. *La Cultura como Empresa Multinacional.* Mexico, D.F.: Ediciones Era, 1974. The civil re-conversion of the U.S. multinational corporations after the Vietnam War, and the new forms of ideological offensive under peaceful co-existence, and the evolution of the mythology of mass culture. Contents: I. Superbombarderos y Superheroes; II. Cultura de Masas y Económia de Guerra; III. Los Nuevos Dueños y Publicos de la Agresión Cultural; IV. La Industria del Turismo en la Reconversión del Imperio; V. Conclusión: La Muerte de Superman.

______; Patricio BIEDMA; Santiago FUNES. *Comunicación Masiva y Revolución Socialista.* Santiago de Chile: Ediciones Prensa Latinoamericana, 1971. 3 texts on the transformation of the mass media and culture as part of Chile's socialist construction.
MATTELART, Armand "Comunicación y Cultura de las Masas" The nature of bourgeois and imperialist communications, and the tasks of the media.
BIEDMA, Patricio "Prensa Burguesa, Prensa Popular y Prensa Revolucionaria" The recuperation of the popular press by the bourgeoisie.
FUNES, Santiago "Escritura, Producción Literaria y Proceso Revolucionario" The problems of literature and writing.

______; Carmen CASTILLO; Leonardo CASTILLO. *La Ideología de la Dominacion en una Sociedad Dependiente.* Buenos Aires: Ediciones Signos, Oct. 1970. An analysis of the structure and content of Chile's ruling class ideology as manifest during its resistance to agrarian reform. Bibliography.

______; Mabel PICCINI; Michèle MATTELART. *Los Medios de Comunicación de Masas: La Ideología de la Prensa Liberal en Chile*, a special issue of: *Cuadernos de la Realidad Nacional* (Santiago de Chile), 3, March 1970 (2nd ed.), 287pp. A series of well-documented studies on the values and contents of the Chilean capitalist press, as effected by U.S. economic and ideological penetration.
MATTELART, Armand. Chap. I "El Marco del Analisis Ideológico", a critique of U.S. "communications research"; II. "Estructura del Poder Informativo y Dependencia", the control of the dependent Chilean mass media; Ch. III. "La Mitología de la Juventud en un Diario Liberal", the myth of youth.
PICCINI, Mabel. Chap. IV. "El Cerco de la Revistas de Idolos" an analysis of the "fan" magazines.
MATTELART, Michèle. Chap. V. "El Nivel Mítico de la Prensa Seudo-Amorosa", an analysis of the concept and contents of the "romance" magazines.

______; Daniel WAKSMAN "Más Allá de la SIP" *Chile Hoy* (Santiago de Chile), 19–20, October 1972, pp. 16–17. An analysis of the structure and control of SIP (the Inter American Press Association), the group which brings together the interests of the U.S. and Latin American mass media owners, with particular emphasis on the Scripps-Howard syndicate.

Medios Masivos de Comunicación, a special issue of: *Referencias* (Habana), III, 1972. 556 pp. Anthology of 25 texts on the mass media. In 4 sections: general writings; theoretical studies; investigations of different media systems; and on the imperialist media. Relevant here:
WOLFE, Catherine M.; Marjorie FISK "Por qué se Leen las Tiras Cómicas"
MARTINEZ, Jesús M. "Para Entender los Medios de Comunicación y Relaciones Sociales"
MATTELART, Armand "Por un Medio de Comunicación de Masas no Mitológico"
ECO, Humberto "Apocalípticos e Integrados Ante la Cultura de Masas"
MATTELART, Michèle "Nivel mítico de la Prensa Seudo-Amorosa"
ICAIC EDICIONES "La Industria Cultural Seduce al Capital Monopolista Yanqui"
ECO, Humberto "El Mito de Superman"
MATTELART, Armand "La Dependencia del medio de comunicación de Masas"

MORALES, Argueles "Panamá: Presencia y Violencia Cultural del Imperialismo" *Cine Cubano* (Habana), 78/79/80, pp. 70–76. The reactionary cultural role of the U.S. controlled mass media as part of imperialist penetration in Panama.

MUJICA, Hector, *Apuntes para una Sociología Venezolana de la Comunicación.* Caracas, 1973, 153 pp. mimeographed. An survey and critique of international mass communications theory and research; and analysis of the structure and content of the mass media in different countries and its relevance for the development of the Venezuelan mass media. Bibliography.

MURARO, Heriberto. "La Manija", a series of 3 articles in: *Crisis* (Buenos Aires), 1, May 1973; 2, June 1973; and 3, July 1973, pp. 48–54; 52–60; and 64–69, respectively. The 1st, "Quienes son los Dueños de los Medios de Comunicación en América Latina" is an analysis of the structure and ownership of the mass media in Latin America, particularly Colombia,

Chile, Mexico and Peru, and their dependence on U.S. business interests; and the policy of the Chilean and Peruvian governments in trying to recover their press and radio. The 2nd "Los Dueños de la Television Argentina" is a study of the power structure of the Argentine TV, and its control by ABC, CBS, and Time-Life. The 3rd "El Negocio de la Publicidad en la Televisión Argentina" is an analysis of the advertising on Argentine TV; the production of TV commercials, their effects, and interrelated economic interests of the U.S. advertising agencies (J. Walter Thompson, McCann-Erickson) and U.S. business sponsors.

NAISON, Mark "Sports and the American Empire" *Radical America* (Cambridge, Mass.), VI, 4, July–Aug. 1972, pp. 95–120. The development of U.S. mass spectator sports since the 2nd World War. In 3 sections. Relevant here is the section on sports in U.S.'s relations to the Third World and U.S. blacks, and its role as vehicle and means of assimulating peoples and cultures into the interests of the U.S.

"New Frontiers of Television" Symposium, Bled, Yugoslavia, June 1971. Relevant papers:

BOJANIC, Ivo "On the Hinderances of the New Frontiers of Television" The social-political problems preventing the international use of the mass media.

SMYTHE, Dallas W. "Cultural Realism and Cultural Screens" (16 pp.). The historical development of "capitalist realism": its "a-political" art, science, ideology and mass communications research, and a series of formulations on socialist culture, emphasizing on the level of international communications, the need for developing countries to protect themselves from "capitalist realism."

NORDENSTRENG, Kaarle; Tapio VARIS "International Inventory of Television Program Structure" *The Democratic Journalist* (Prague), 4, 1974, pp. 6–9. The flow of TV programs: the dominance of the U.S. in the world markets, and the flow between East and West Europe. (A resume of a report published by the University of Tampere, Finland, April 1973).

PASQUALI, Antonio "Le Cas de l'Amérique Latine: Pollution Spontanée?" 10 pp. mimeographed (for the "Communications de Masse et Pollution Mentale" Conference, Paris, 1971). A description and study of the contents and quality of the mass media in Venezuela and Latin America, and its domination by imperialist values.

SANTORO, Eduardo. *La Televisión Venezolana y la Formación de Estereotipos en el Niño.* Caracas: Universidad Central de Venezuela, 1969. An analysis of Venezuelan TV contents and how it effects the development of social and cultural values in children: a critique of mass communications criteria, particularly from the U.S., formulations on the concept of Collective Communications, and an empirical study of Venezuelan TV contents.

SCHILLER, Herbert I. "Madison Avenue Imperialism" in: *Communications in International Politics,* R.L. Merritt, ed. Urbana, Ill.: University of Illinois Press, 1972, pp. 318–338. U.S. multinational corporations, their growing advertising and public relations appendages, and their increasing domination over world mass communications.

_____. *Mass Communications and American Empire.* Boston: Beacon Press, 1971. A well-documented economic and political analysis of the structure and policy of the U.S. mass media and its effect on international communications: the development of U.S. radio and TV; the predominance of military interests; electronics and counter-revolution; the global invasion of the U.S. electronic industry and the commercialization of broadcasting; the developing countries under electronic siege, and communications satellites; and proposals for the democratic re-structuring of the mass media.

_____. *The Mind Managers.* Boston: Beacon Press, 1973. An analysis of the extent and growth of the U.S. mind and information management empire; government, business, and advertising and public relations agencies. Relevant here are the chapters: VI. Mind Management Moves Overseas, Exporting the Techniques of Persuasion; and VII. Mind Management in a New Dimension, From the Laws of the Market to Direct Political Control.

_____. "National Development Requires Some Social Distance" *Antioch Review* (Yellow Springs, Ohio), XXVII, 1, Spring 1967, pp. 63–75. The function and power of the imperialist mass media, and the need for developing countries to control incoming political-cultural messages.

_____. "Waiting for Orders – Some Currents Trends in Mass Communications Research in the United States" *Gazette* (Amsterdam), 1, Winter 1974, pp. 11–21. The intimate (and empirical) relationship between U.S. mass communications research and the economic needs of U.S. business and the development of the consumer: polls and statistics; and the increasing support role of communications research in institutional planning and as a research arm of U.S. foreign and military planning.

_____; Dallas W. SMYTHE "Chile: An End to Cultural Colonialism" *Society* (New Brunswick, N.J.), March 1972, pp. 35–39, 61. A study of the Chilean mass media and the problems confronting the Popular Unity government in changing the media from a U.S. styled and dominated private means of product promotion to a socialized means of communications.

"Science as Cultural Imperialism" in: *Por Qué? Science and Technology in Latin America*, Jamaica Plain, Mass.: Science for the People, Dec. 1972, pp. 19–23. The role of science in U.S. cultural imperialist policy in Latin America: as a means to spread U.S. ideology and substitute it for native cultural forms; the concepts of technology as "progress"; the teaching of U.S. science in Third World education programs and its effects on development; the brain drain; and the need for the U.S. to de-politicize the Latin American university to assure the extension of U.S. business – the example of Brazil.

SILVA, Ludovico. *Teoría y Práctica de la Ideología.* Mexico City: Editorial Nuestro Tiempo, 1971. The Marxist theory of ideology, and a critique of some forms of capitalist ideology and their practical effects in regard to Latin American development. Particularly relevant are the sections "Los Comics y su Ideología", and "El Sueño Insomme: Ideas sobre Televisión, Subdesarrollo, Ideología" on the comics and TV, and underdevelopment.

SIQUEIROS, David A. "Mouvement et 'Remous' de l'Art au Mexique: Cinéma National ou Falsificateur" in:_______, *l'Art et la Révolution,* Paris: Editions Sociales, 1973, pp. 95–108. A brief resume of the character of the Mexican film, the great pressures from Hollywood and capitalist forces, and a call for the nationalization of the film industry and its use in education.

SMYTHE, Dallas W. "Reflections on Proposals for an International Programme of Communications Research", 14 pp. mimeographed (for the International Association for Mass Communications Research, General Assembly and Congress "Communications and Development", Buenos Aires, Sept. 1972). UNESCO's programme for communications research: on the use of technology in the development of communications, and the harmful effects of advanced capitalist consumer technology on the developing countries.

SOLANAS, Fernando E.; Octavio GETINO. *Cine, Cultura y Descolonización.* Buenos Aires: Siglo XXI, 1973. A series of theoretical texts and practical results, by the filmmakers of "La Hora de los Hornos" and members of the Cine Liberación group in Buenos Aires, in which they historically situate the "Cinema of Liberation" or "Third Cinema": from the Hollywood film, through the "Cinema d'auteur", to the film as part of the anti-imperialist struggles of the Third World peoples, and the minorities in the imperialist center.

Textual (Revista del Instituto Nacional de Cultura, Lima), 8, Dec. 1973, 79 pp. Anthology of 10 articles on cultural imperialism, ideology, advertising and TV in Latin America. Relevant:

URRUTIA BOLONA, Carlos "Comunicación Masiva y Agresión Cultural" The role of the mass media and cultural domination in the formation of social values.

DRINOT SILVA, Rafael "Publicidad: Produción y Consumo de lo Cotidiano" The fundamental role of advertising in the structure and reproduction of capitalist society, and the central placement of the U.S. advertising agency in the economy of the Latin American countries.

PEREZ BARRETO, Samuel "El Caso 'Plaza Sésamo' en el Perú". The U.S. developed "educational" TV program Sesame Street as arm of U.S. cultural and economic penetration in Latin America, and the reasons why the program was refused broadcast rights in Peru.

DORFMAN, Ariel "Salvación y Sabiduría del Hombre Común: La Teología del *Reader's Digest*" The ideology of *Reader's Digest*: contents and organization; fragmentation, mystification; and false knowledge.

GONZALES MONTES, Antonio R. "Bugs Bunny en el U.S. Army: Azar o Coincidencia Ideológica" The contents of the U.S. TV program.

TAPIA DELGADO, Gorki "'Los Picapiedra' Aliados del Imperialismo" The U.S. TV series The Flintstones, and the development of the infantile, passive, conformist U.S.–style consumer.

RAMOS FALCONI, Ruben "Medios de Comunicación de Masas: Mito y Realidad" U.S. multinational corporations and their use of the media, and Peruvian revolutionary praxis.

"El Papel Socio-Político de los Medios de Comunicación Masiva" The conclusion from conference, of same name, held in Costa Rica, November 1972, calling for the politicization of Latin American mass media research.

"Transnationales: Le Défi" an issue of: *Politique Aujourd'hui* (Paris), 1–2, Jan.–Feb. 1975. 128 pp. 10 texts on the U.S. multinational corporations, the World Bank and imperialism. Relevant here are the texts on the "Multinational State":

DUBOIS, Jean-Pierre; Paul Ramadier "Le Nouvel Ordre Mondial" The tactics of the U.S. multinational industrials.

COLLINS, Joseph D. "États-Unis et Transnationales Américaines: Retour à l'Envoyeur" The world expansion of the U.S. financial system, with U.S. governmental and military support.

MATTELART, Armand "Vers la Formation des Appareils Idéologiques de l'État Multinational" An analysis of the multinationalization of the major U.S. Advertising, Accounting, Management, Marketing, Think Tank, Public Relations, Public opinion poll

Corporations: their growing take-over of world planning for the U.S.–style "Consumer Society", their increasing involvement in social-political "Corporate State" development (such as in Brazil and Chile) to assure the expansion of the U.S. multinational industrial and financial corporations, and their role as ideological wing and spokesman for U.S. government interests.

Voices of National Liberation, Irwin SILBER, ed. Brooklyn, N.Y.: Central Book Co., 1970. Anthology of 92 texts delivered at the Cultural Congress of Havana, January 1968. Foreward by Irwin SILBER. Organized in 6 sections; with greetings to the Congress; speech of Fidel Castro to closing session; and and appendix of regulations, commission reports, and resolutions of the Congress. All relevant, but noted particularly:

SIERRA, Cainas "Consuming Radio and Television Programs Like Pop Corn, Hot Dogs or Coca Cola"

HUY CAN, Cu "The Obliteration of National Culture is the War Cry of Conquerors"

RAWASH El DIEB, Mohamed "The Brain Drain"

BELAL, Abdelaziz "Cultural Depersonalization Under Colonialism"

PINEDA BARNET, Enrique "Colonization of Taste"

MARTINEZ, José "The Cultural Colonization of Latin American Countries"

CHERIF, Cheick "As Long as the Mass Media are Owned or Controlled by the Capitalist Monopolies, they Cannot Serve the Cause of the Popular Masses"

*Les Tintins de la Ve*, issue number 15 of *Le Point* (Paris). The French children's magazines and their uniformly reactionary contents, and 25 million readers.

WAGNER, Dave "Donald Duck: An Interview" *Radical America* (Cambridge, Mass.), VII, 1, 1973, pp. 1–19. An imaginary interview with Donald Duck on the history of the Disney business, its ideology, T.W. Adorno, and revolutionary culture.

WETTSTADT, Günter. *Technik und Bildung: Zum Einfluss burgerlicher Technikphilosophie auf die imperialistische Bildungsideologie.* Frankfurt am Main: Verlag Marxistische Blätter, 1974. An analysis of the influence of political ideology on technology and how education functions to make science and technology serve the bourgeois. Relevant here is the chapter on capitalist technological ideology in education and its role in imperialist development.

APPENDIX: DONALD DUCK VS. CHILIAN SOCIALISM: A FAIR USE EXCHANGE

John Shelton Lawrence

The new media of mass communications has occasionally stimulated visions of an international community that exchanges its cultural creations and enriches its consciousness through the resultant diversity. Marshall McLuhan's phrase, "the global electronic village", expresses this optimism, as did Thomas Hutchinson's prophecy of 1938 regarding the future of television:

> Television means the world in your home and in the homes of all the people of the world. It is the greatest means of communication ever developed by the human mind. It should do more to develop friendly neighbors, and to bring understanding and peace on earth than any other single material force in the world today.[1]

To such minds, the notion of art as universal language has come of age with the technologies for the world-wide distribution of imagery.

The belief that popular, commercial art and entertainment will advance the cause of humankind found an eloquent proponent in Walt Disney, whose moralism and sense of cultural mission are widely known. More than a decade after his death, the corporation he formed seeks to give embodiment to his visions of commercial entertainments that would have a salutary effect on all the peoples of the world. For example, in announcing the Experimental Prototype Community of Tomorrow (EPCOT) to be constructed in Florida, the Disney Corporation's president Card Walker wrote:

> There never has been a greater need for the communication of information about the diverse peoples of our planet, the new systems evolving to meet the need of those people, and the alternatives we face. . . .
>
> EPCOT Center and its two major themes, Future World and the World Showcase, will be devoted to . . . the advancement of international understanding and the solution of the problems of people everywhere.
>
> Our dedication . . . will extend as far as the Disney ability to communicate can reach, including films, television, educational materials and even the licensing of concepts and products.[2]

Disney's *Annual Report for 1977* provided this view of EPCOT's potential:

> It will be a "communicator to the world", . . . "a permanent international people to people exchange", advancing the cause of world understanding . . . a much needed symbol of hope and optimism. . . .[3]

The tensions between enlightenment and enjoyment, American national and foreign interest, corporate profit and service to mankind are to be dissolved in this last of the great theme parks conceived by Walt Disney before his death.

Turning from the appealing rhetoric of "sharing", "communication", "understanding", and "peace" to examine actual patterns of exchange in the world's popular media, one discovers important inequalities among nations. In film and television, where Disney Productions

---

This text was first published in John Shelton Lawrence and Bernard Timberg, editors, *Fair Use and Free Inquiry: Copyright Law and the New Media*, Norwood, N. J.: Ablex, 1980. It has been slightly updated for publication here. Reprinted by permission of the author.

has had great success, United States dominance is immediately evident. Although there is significant global *distribution* of media products, there is relatively little *exchange*. Some major countries, for example, import as much as 69 percent of their foreign films from the United States.[4] About television, Elihu Katz and George Wedell report in their survey of international programming:

> On Monday, July 15, 1975, at 8:30 p.m. the viewers of Bangkok could choose among three American series: "Manhunt", "The FBI", and "Get Christie Love!". On a Saturday night in Tehran the viewer had a choice of "A Family Affair" and "Days of Our Lives" on one channel and "The Bold Ones" and "Kojak" on the other. The examples are handpicked, of course, for the choice sometimes includes—as in Thailand on Sundays—wrestling (local), a Disney film, or "Hawaii Five-O."[5]

Some countries import as much as 100 percent of their programming, resulting in choices like those just mentioned; the United States imports only 1 percent of its commercial television offerings and a mere 2 percent of its public television.[6]

In the field of children's comics there are similar patterns of dominance by United States exports, led, of course, by Disney, whose publications are translated into eighteen different languages, including Arabic, Flemish, Serbo-Croatian, and Thai.[7] Millions of the Disney comics are distributed monthly, not to mention the additional millions sold by Marvel and DC Comics, but United Stated entrepreneurs import almost nothing from foreign countries for distribution to their own people.[8] Communication in "the global village", then, goes one way: the United States transmits cultural messages but receives very few from those to whom its communications are directed.[9]

DONALD DUCK AND THE CHILEAN REVOLUTION

The relations of dominance and passivity in world cultural exchange have not escaped the attention of observers in host countries for United States media products. One of the more forceful attempts to analyze the influence and values of imported United States culture and of the Disney universe in particular occurred in Chile during its short-lived socialist government under Salvadore Allende (1970–73). Ariel Dorfman and Armand Mattelart wrote *Para Leer al Pato Donald* (translated into English as *How to Read Donald Duck: Imperialist Ideology in the Disney Comic*)[10] which was widely read in Chile, Latin America, and eventually in a number of other countries—the United States excluded. Details of its English translation and attempted importation are an unrecounted episode in the evolving tradition of copyright and fair use. It is a story that turns on the presumed unique status of imagery as understood by image-producing corporations and the correlative timidity of publishers about viewing such images within the fair use tradition.

At the time of the socialist revolution in Chile, the communications industries there exhibited a typical Third World configuration. More than 50 percent of its television programming was imported from foreign countries, with a predominance of United States offerings like "Bonanza", "Mission Impossible", "FBI", "Disneyland", etc.[11] Half-hour episodes that would cost from $3,000 to $5,000 in Japan or West Germany could be obtained for sums like $65–$70. Feature length United States films priced at $24,000 to $60,000 in Japan or Germany were available for $350 to $400. As Jeremy Tunstall has explained,

> The standard American practice in all media fields is initially to undercut the opposition through price competition; this follows from the enormous number of publications and broadcast outlets in the USA. Since an extra "copy" of news agency service, or the use of a feature film or a television series, has no obvious or "rational' price, there is more than the usual scope for price cutting and variation.[12]

Clearly such pricing policies will depress native production in market economies, since the cost of a program or film copy can be held below the costs even for lighting a studio or providing film stock. The virtually free distribution of programs and films at "country prices" is thus a good initial investment in an economy that may rise to greater affluence without ever developing its own media production facilities. Furthermore, United States programs are undeniably popular with foreign audiences and help foreign television networks to fill up programming hours once they have made a commitment to use television as a form of national entertainment.

The Chilean comics market also imported American products like *Superman*, *The Lone Ranger*, and others, as well as the Disney comics.[13]

Responding to these circumstances in December 1969, the Popular Unity party formulated a program for mass communications that received the approval of allied political groups.

> The means of communication (the radio, the press, publishing, television and the cinema) are fundamental aids to the formation of a new culture and of a new man. They should therefore be imbued with an educative spirit and freed from their commercial character. Measures should be taken to make the media available to the social organizations and to cast off the brooding presence of the monopolies.[14]

When the Popular Unity party came to power in 1970, it did make an effort to reshape a culture for the Chilean population, though it left commercial television largely intact. The state took over the largest publishing house in Chile, Zig-Zag, and used it to launch Empresa Editorial Quimantú, an operation that eventually published several million inexpensive books for wide distribution.[15]

It was through Quimantú (meaning literally "Sunshine of Knowledge") that a counteroffensive against the Disney comics was launched. Rather than forbidding further publication of Disney materials, Quimantú created *Cabro Chico (The Little Kid)* as an alternative, progressive-revolutionary comic. Two associates at Quimantú, Ariel Dorfman of the Juvenile and Educational Publications Division and Armand

Mattelart, head of Investigation and Evaluation of the Mass Media Section, collaborated on *The Little Kid* and also wrote *How to Read Donald Duck* (1971), a popular and radical exposé of the values and worldview of Walt Disney material.

How to Read Donald Duck deals with several topics ranging from the peculiar sexual and familial values of Disney's "funny animals" to the political and social values that lie close to the surface in the episodes of Donald, his nephews, and the surpassingly rich but stingy Scrooge McDuck. It analyzes attitudes towards work, ownership, leisure, and the other perpetual themes of conflict in Duckburg. Many of their observations are paralleled by those found in the works of James Agee, Richard Schickel, and other critics of Disney.

But the central weight in the Dorfman-Mattelart critique falls upon the political and economic values of Disney as they relate to peoples of the less developed countries who have fallen into the U.S. orbit of influence—often symbolized by Disney fantasies about the Ducks as global travelers.

Roughly half the Disney comics sampled in their study showed the heroes from Duckburg confronting the peoples of other continents and ethnic groups. Plots in the stories and the imagery used to convey them—images that Quimantú reproduced without authorization from Disney—reveal a population of childlike noble savages on the one hand and political revolutionary thugs on the other. The former are easily tricked out of their wealth by the greedy ducks since they do not understand the value of their assets, and they are perpetually in need of redemption from problems that they cannot solve with their own resources. The political revolutionary thugs terrorize the natives of imaginary countries like Unsteadystan, though they are easily defeated once exposed by the super-intelligent ducks.[16] The Disney comics, which to some extent permit the regional production of Disney material, at times engage freely in antirevolutionary political propaganda. An episode appearing after the seizure of power by the junta featured the Allende government in the form of buzzards named Marx and Hegel, who attack helpless kittens as Jimmy Cricket watches. They are eventually chased away by a farmer with a shot-gun. "Ha! Firearms are the only thing those bloody birds are afraid of." Marx and Hegel (in their Disney-buzzard form) are of course "immune to the voice of conscience".[17]

In generalizing about the implications of Disney materials for a country like Chile, Dorfman and Mattelart suggest

> The threat derives not so much from their embodiment of the "American way of life", as that of the "American dream of life". It is the manner in which the U.S. dreams and redeems itself, and then imposes the dream upon others for its own salvation. . . . It forces us Latin Americans to see ourselves as they see us. . . . The Disney cosmos is no mere refuge in the area of occasional entertainment; it is our everyday stuff of repression.[18]

The socialist critique of Donald Duck found a fairly wide audience in Chile, resulting in twelve separate printings before the military coup that destroyed the Popular Unity government in 1973. Like many other artifacts of the socialist period, the book was burned; the authors were compelled to seek refuge in other countries. A *New York Times* article reported that "after the coup the president of the neighborhood council ripped down the socialist calendars and slogans that hung on the wall of his two-room wooden shack. In their place he put up some posters of Mickey and Donald."[19] In the wake of socialist criticism, the Disney characters had become antirevolutionary symbols.

The book was, however, destined to survive its burning and banning in Chile, and its exiled authors survived the mass executions carried out by the military junta. A Latin American edition had been published in Argentina in 1972. Feltrinelli in Italy published its translation *Come Leggere Paperino* in the same year. By 1975 *Para Ler o Pato Donald* had appeared in Portugal, followed in rapid succession by the French edition, *Donald l'imposteur* (1976); the Swedish, *Konsten All Lasa Kalla Anka* (1977); the German, *Walt Disney's Dritte Welt* (1977); the Danish, *Anders And i den tredje verden* (1978); and the Dutch, *Hoe Lees ik Donald Duck* (1978), with other editions in Greek, Finnish and Japanese. English language edition sales are now in the region of over 20,000, with total world sales around 500,000.[20] In their modest way, these figures rival the global reach of Disney's distribution.

One might have expected that the book would become widely available in the U.S., but here intervened the consideration of copyright. The art historian David Kunzle, who has written a major social history of the comic strip and who has also studied the art of revolutionary Chile, prepared a translation and introduction for *How to Read Donald Duck* while attempting negotiations with American publishers. Random House, which had an option through Feltrinelli, considered publication, as did Beacon Press, which had fearlessly published the Gravel edition of the *Pentagon Papers*. Both were eventually deterred by their fear of litigation from Disney, according to Kunzle.[21] Disney comic book frames provided visual documentation for the book's argument about prominent themes and stereotypes. Disney's reputation suggested that it would never give permission for such a use and that it would cause expensive litigation if these frames were published without permission. Eventually, International General of New York, which specializes in Marxist publications, agreed to publish the book and had it printed in England: 3,950 copies of *How to Read Donald Duck* left England in May 1975 and arrived at the New York docks in June. At that time, Donald Duck in his corporate form began to fight back, confronting the thieving revolutionary thugs of an "Unsteadystan" that no longer existed.

THE DETENTION AND RELEASE OF *HOW TO READ DONALD DUCK*[22]

The Imports Compliance Branch of the Customs department, a subdivision of the Treasury Department, has the authority to review imported material for its "piratical" character. When *How to Read Donald Duck* arrived, Imports Compliance made a preliminary judgment that the book might infringe upon Disney copyrights. The Chief of Imports Compliance, Eleanor M. Suske, informed International General in a letter of July 10, 1975, that the book was being seized and held in custody pending a final determination. Walt Disney Productions was similarly informed in a letter of August 12. Both parties were invited to submit briefs, as the Treasury Department has authority to consider evidence and arguments in such cases.

International General sought legal assistance from the Center for Constitutional Rights (CCR), which argued for the release of the book both on fair use and First Amendment grounds. The letters were vigorous and detailed.[22]

In its response to the notification, Walt Disney Productions was represented by its Eastern counsel, Franklin Waldheim, who declared that the books were piratical infringements of Disney's character copyrights.[23] He anticipated the fair use defense by suggesting that the use of the illustrations was in no way necessary to document what the authors were attempting to prove, since the mere description of the plots and quotation of literary text would have sufficed—a use which Disney did not choose to contest. In interpreting the purposes behind the book's use of the images, he saw the attempt to embellish a book at the expense of Disney. He also suggested that the use of a Disney-like image of Scrooge McDuck on the cover was an effort to deceive unsuspecting parents into believing that they were buying one of the Disney comics—thus depriving Disney of income that rightfully belonged to it.[24]

A central contention in the Waldheim letters is that imagery, unlike the words in the comic text, is not susceptible to fair use; verbal equivalents are in all cases sufficient—except where the nature of the art work itself is discussed. It was this point that the attorneys for International General and the authors confronted in their briefs and rebuttals.

The Center for Constitutional Rights is a nonprofit legal assistance group in New York City that provides counsel in issues related to the Constitution and Bill of Rights. Lawyers for the Center, Peter Weiss, Rhonda Copelon, and William H. Schaap, defended *How to Read Donald Duck* against the accusation of piracy by an appeal to both the fair use concept and the First Amendment. In their letter of August 8, 1975, to the Imports Compliance Branch of Customs, they argued that in relation to recognized fair use questions,[25] Donald Duck could pass traditional tests. They cited Judge Lasker in *Marvin Worth Products v. Superior Films Corp.* (S.D.N.Y. 1970, 319 Fed. Supp. 1269; 168 USPQ 693, 697):

> The cases and commentaries attempting to define the quicksilver concept of "fair use", although varying and overlapping in their definitions, appear to agree that there are at least four tests appropriate to determine whether the doctrine applies: (1) Was there a substantial taking qualitatively or quantitatively? (2) If there was such a taking, did the taking materially reduce the demand for the original copyrighted property? (3) . . . Does the distribution of the material serve the public interest in the free dissemination of information, and (4) Does the preparation of the material require the use of prior materials dealing with the same subject matter?

Taking Judge Lasker's decision as the point of departure, the center's lawyers answered his questions in the following way:

> 1. No.—There is no substantial taking. On the one hand, the cartoons reproduced represent but a very small portion of the entire book. On the other, each representation consists, as a rule, of but one or two frames taken from an entire comic strip or book.
>
> 2. Definitely not.—The taking, such as it is, in no way reduces the demand for the original copyrighted property, since no one would buy "How to Read Donald Duck" as a substitute for the original copyrighted property.
>
> 3. Most certainly.—The public interest in the free dissemination of information—in this case the views of the author-scholars concerning the values and attitudes perceived in Donald Duck comics—can only be served by the publication of their book, complete with representative samples of the comics which are the subject of their criticism and analysis.
>
> 4. Absolutely.—As discussed at greater length in the enclosure [provided by authors and publisher], reproduction of some of the cartoons is a categorical prerequisite to the publication of the book in a meaningful, readable way.

Having formulated the fair use defense, the CCR memorandum turned to the question of the First Amendment and argued as follows:

> . . . we would contend that preferred position of the First Amendment in the spectrum of constitutionally guaranteed rights must be recognized in the field of copyrights as well. The book at issue, while a serious work of scholarship, is also a frankly political statement which is, or should be, of interest to a large number of readers. In view of this, the greatest reticence should characterize its evaluation by an agency of the government, lest property rights be given preference over rights of free speech and political expression. In other words, only the grossest and most unambiguous case of piracy—such as clearly is not present here—could possibly justify an assault on free speech in the guise of copyright protection. On the other hand, given a delicately balanced situation from a pure copyright point of view, First Amendment considerations should always tip the balance in favor of publication (or, in this case, importation).

The CCR lawyers concluded their First Amendment argument with a citation from Judge Wyatt's decision in the *Time v. Bernard Geis* case, where he appealed to the public interest in being permitted to share important information about the assassination of President Kennedy.

An author-editor letter, written immediately upon receipt of the Customs Compliance notification and included with the CCR statement, addresses itself primarily to the question of whether the contested images are necessary to their critical analysis. The text of that letter reads as follows:

6 Reasons Why No Cartoon Matter, No Book

1. The book is a criticism of the Disney *cartoons*; not Disney literary values. Cartoons are a unique mass medium which are an *inseparable* marriage of literary and visual matter. If it is possible for the book to capture the essence of Disney with written language only, we would ask: Why didn't Disney just write a novel? Obviously, he didn't.

2. It is not just the language used, but even more important, the relation between Disney language and graphic matter which is in question. This is particularly the case in the incredible use of racial, ethnic, professional, political slurs and stereotypes which are the very essence of Disney graphic matter. For example, the bearded captain (p. 58) which is obviously an unwritten slur against Fidel Castro. See all cartoons for Disney's family of clichés, particularly of foreign peoples (the Vietnamese, p. 57; Africans, p. 50; Arabs, p. 51, etc.).

Also, the depiction of "villains" throughout as big, black, ugly and stupid; all so cliché-ridden they are literally undescribable without using the cartoon itself.

Similarly, the sexuality and coyness in the visual matter—in opposition to asexuality and prudery in the language.

In brief, the written text is the thesis, and the cartoon reproductions are the evidence and proof.

Just as the essence of Disney is both literary and graphic, the essence of the criticism of Disney is both literary and graphic.

3. Being given the foreign authorship and origin of the book; the US government's and US mass media's well publicized opposition to the Chilean Popular Unity government; the equally well orchestrated promotion of the Disney image of "purity, innocence", etc., etc., the environment in the US has been so poisoned by these well-publicized campaigns, that to criticize Disney without the use of graphic proof would substantially reduce its impact and credibility in the USA.

Furthermore, many of the cartoons were never published in the USA, and thus a written text without cartoon reproductions would further decrease the credibility of the analysis, because the USA audience is not aware of this aspect of Disney, particularly Disney's very political character, which is the very essence of the book's thesis.

4. The changes of language in the translation from the original Spanish are significant in the case of those few original English-language cartoons—often poorly translated and altered in function for Latin American political conditions. An aspect not known to the USA public.

5. Disney comics were a phenomenon of the 40's and 50's in the USA, and for the most part are no longer available and have become "collector's items" (READ: "speculator's"), and thus the average reader would have no public means to find the original comics to check the veracity of just a literary description without the use of the visual matter. The reader would have to rely on his/her memory, which being given No. 3 above, would further decrease the credibility of the book.

6. Last, but certainly not least. The book is EDUCATIONAL. It was written primarily for young students, in Chile, among others, and intended as a simple, popular and readable book—like the Disney comics themselves. If each frame had to be described with language only, its complete popular and mass essence would be changed: instead of a short and popular book which now exists, it would become a long and unpopular tome of 1,000 pages, accessible and readable only by a limited group of (boring?) introverted scholar-types.

Again to repeat, if the essence of Disney can be captured solely by language, why did *they* take the trouble to make graphic matter?

Answer: In reality the verbal and visual matter are inseparable (also insufferable).[26]

As letters from the conflicting parties were received at the Customs Compliance office, they were duplicated and transmitted for response to both Disney Productions and to CCR. The parties reiterated their positions in a variety of ways and engaged in a more detailed debate regarding the necessity to reproduce Disney images. Franklin Waldheim, Disney's attorney, found in Point 6 of the author-editor memorandum, a confirmation of the piratical intent upon which Disney was resting much of its case.[27] It was held to be a concession to the accusation that the taking was designed to enhance the entertainment value of the book. But this taking in its larger context served the ultimate purpose of dissuading anyone from ever buying Disney commodities in the future. The Disney argument thus contained at least three distinct strands:

1. The contention that the unauthorized reproduction was merely illustrative.

2. The claim that International General and the authors had pirated for the purpose of deceiving prospective comics buyers into believing that they were buying the genuine Disney product.

3. The argument that the ultimate purpose of such taking and deception was to deprive Disney of its rightful markets.

Responding to these contentions about the alleged cloaking of its uses behind the mantle of fair use—as opposed to honestly flying the black flag of piracy—the CCR responded to the Customs Department as follows:

As for Disney's statement that inserting copies of the comic book frames is not necessary since the book is not a criticism of artistic style, we submit that the Disney comics primarily convey their message through pictures, not just dialogue or situation. For example, on p. 58 of *How to Read Donald Duck*, the authors discuss the situation of a comic in which Donald becomes involved with revolutionaries. The reproduction of selected frames is necessary in order to demonstrate both Disney's negative portrayal of the revolutionary leader through his pictured actions and to show the strong resemblance he bears to Fidel Castro. These subtle statements cannot be described in mere words, but must be shown in order to discuss their impact intelligently. As in *Time v. Geis*, 293 F. Supp. 130 (S.D.N.Y. 1968) the excerpts from the copyrighted work are necessary to make the author's theory comprehensible.[28]

Thus it is clear that both of the disputing parties held the visual matter of Disney to have a unique status. The authors contended that imagery conveys information that becomes available for discussion only when it is reproduced. The Disney corporation argued, on the other hand, that except in the context of art criticism, copyrighted visual contents are wholly susceptible to evocation through verbal equivalents; images, unlike words, thus have a legal status that prevents their reproduction for the mere purpose of message analysis.

It was probably the failure to produce a specific law or precedent on this point that pushed the Customs Department toward a decision favoring the importation of *How to Read Donald Duck*. On June 9, 1976, Eleanor M. Suske rendered an opinion "that the books do not constitute piratical copies of any Walt Disney copyrights recorded with Customs, within the meaning of Section 106 of the copyright law."[29] Disney challenged the decision by seeking further representation from the firm of Donavan, Leisure, Newton and Irvine of New York. Upon their restatement of the Disney contentions of piratical infringement in a letter of October 6, 1976,[30] the Treasury Department (the parent administrative agency for Customs) articulated the reasons for its decision more fully through a letter from Leonard Lehman, Assistant Commissioner for Regulations and Rulings. "No specific copyright recorded with Customs has been cited as the basis for the exclusive action sought by Walt Disney Productions."[31] There had, in fact, been doubt about whether the Latin American comic book images had ever been copyrighted in the countries where they had been published—a point made by CCR and never addressed by Disney in its representations. But more important, from the standpont of the fair use controversy, was the Treasury Department's acceptance of both the fair use and First Amendment arguments.

> The spotty use of one, two, or three cartoon "frames" throughout the work in question, does not appear to be a substantial appropriation of a material part of any one copyrighted work so as to come within the infringement test of *Arnstein v. Porter*, 154 F.2d 464 (2d Cir. 1946), *cert. denied*, 330 U.S. 851. Furthermore, the total of 68 frames does not constitute a substantial portion of the 112-page book. Finally, we do not believe the questioned item, priced at $3.25, and consisting overwhelmingly of ponderous text, could be confused for a Disney. . . . Most of the issues are related to the sociopolitical "message" of the work in either a specific or general context. We believe the following quotation is very apt for this case:
>
> > The spirit of the First Amendment applies to the copyright laws, at least to the extent that the courts should not tolerate any attempted interference with the public's right to be informed regarding matters of general interest when anyone seeks to use the copyright statute which was designed to protect interests of a quite different nature. (*Rosemont Enterprise, Inc. v. Random House, Inc.* 366 F2d 303, 35 C.O. Bull. 1965–66, p. 683)

This final ruling, of course, represented substantial concurrence with the arguments advanced by CCR. Walt Disney Productions did not choose to protest the matter any further at that time, though it was clear from their final memorandum issued by Donavan, *et al.* that they did not regard the Treasury Department as even having the jurisdiction to render a decision of fair use.

But in spite of sympathy for the arguments of CCR and International General, there was a serious snag for them in the final determination of the Customs Department. In her letter of June 9, 1976, Ms. Suske indicated that the entire shipment of 3,950 copies could not be accepted for importation because of the manufacturing clause of the copyright regulations. Although 1,500 copies could be admitted,

> The balance of 2,450 booklets in this shipment remain prohibited importation under Title 17, United States Code, Section 16, and are subject to seizure and forfeiture, however you may petition for remission of forfeiture and request approval to export this merchandise under Customs supervision.[32].

Somewhat ironically, the manufacturing and importation clause of the copyright law is a vestige of a period in history when American book publishers, newspapers, and magazines, freely pirated the works of foreign authors—to the severe disadvantage of both English and American authors. The final price exacted by the pirate industries in the struggle over international copyright that persisted from 1836 to 1891 was a provision in the copyright law that would prevent more than minimal importation of books manufactured in foreign lands.[33] Thus, the claims of an earlier generation of pirates, combined with the authors' inability to find a wholly American publisher, prevented the widespread circulation of their critique in the land that created and sustained the Disney perception of the world.

CONCLUSIONS

The story of *How to Read Donald Duck* is in important respects unique in the history of visual scholarship and publication. To my knowledge, it is the only case in which a substantial number of images belonging to a major media corporation have been exactly reproduced for purpose of political argumentation—such use being subsequently vindicated by a public decision-making agency. True, a considerable amount of reproduction has occurred surreptitiously, without the asking of permission or resulting challenge by copyright holders. The Donald Duck case squarely confronted the philosophical question regarding the image's status as a prerequisite to informed and precise analysis and proved to be persuasive, even though Dorfman and Mattelart's Marxist point of view about Disney's politics would hardly be considered plausible by the average United States citizen.

It would be a mistake, however, to exaggerate the significance of the Donald Duck affair as legal precedent. Granting that the Treasury Department had jurisdiction to make a determination of fair use—a point that Disney had contested through its counsel[34]—the case can carry little weight for the American legal system. As an affirmation of the rights of critical inquiry, it has a necessarily *ad hoc* rather than generalized implication for future fair use decisions.

A greater value of the Donald Duck case lies in its illumination of the residual powers and uses of copyright—as opposed to its normal justification emphasizing incentive and income for creators. Here we can see censorship in the form of prior restraint with its usual attendant evils. The absence of a domestic edition of *How to Read Donald Duck* and its minimal importation—a mere 1,500 renders it virtually a collector's item—deprives the American audience of a commentary upon the Disney imagery and stories and thereby prevents them from passing their own judgment upon its message. Furthermore, this restraint is exercised in an arbitrary way; the book has been published in twelve other major languages, appearing in countries where Disney maintains branch offices.[35] America alone is chosen as the territory from which the book is to be excluded through administrative or legal action.

The visions of world community promoted by the Disney Corporation could come closer to realization if we could hear more of the world's people as they assess our cultural impact. To the extent that copyright law restricts such a hearing, its functions and privileges need reassessment.[36]

FOOTNOTES

[1]Quoted in Horace Newcomb, *TV: The Most Popular Art* (N.Y. Doubleday, 1974) p. 2.

[2]*Annual Report 1977, Walt Disney Productions*, p. 1.

[3]*Ibid.*, p. 8.

[4]Jeremy Tunstall, *The Media are American* (N.Y.: Columbia, 1977), table 3, pp. 282–83. India is cited as having the 69 percent figure.

[5]Elihu Katz and George Wedell, *Broadcasting in the Third World: Promise and Performance* (Cambridge, Mass.: Harvard University Press, 1977), p. 161. Cf. also table 5.4, pp. 158–60.

[6]Tunstall, table 1, pp. 278–79.

[7]David Kunzle, *How to Read Donald Duck: Imperialist Ideology in the Disney Comics* (N.Y.: International General, 1975), p. 14.

[8]For one study of American comics and their dominance of a foreign market see Dagmar von Doetinchem and Klaus Hartman, *Gewalt in Superhelden Comics* (Berlin: Basis Verlag, 1974), esp. p. 144*ff.*

[9]Herbet Schiller has published several studies, including *Mass Communication and American Empire* (Boston: Beacon Press, 1971); *Communication and Cultural Domination* (White Plains, N.Y.: International Arts and Sciences Press, 1976), which contains "Afterword, Chile: Communications Policies of Reform and Counterrevolution", p. 98–109.

[10]See note 7. Ariel Dorfman has been Professor of Spanish at the University of Amsterdam; Armand Mattelart, a professor and researcher in the Audiovisual Department at the University of Paris.

[11]Cf. Turnstall, table 1, pp. 278–79. Chile is listed at 55 percent of imported programming.

[12]*Ibid.*, p. 43. Cf. table 17, pp. 301–303.

[13]Kunzle's Introduction, p. 12.

[14]Salvador Allende, *Chile's Road to Socialism*, Joan E. Garces (Ed.), (Harmondsworth, England: Penguin, 1973), p. 48.

[15]Mike Gonzalez, "Ideology and Culture under Popular Unity", in Philip O'Brien (Ed.), *Allende's Chile* (N.Y.: Praeger, 1976), p. 117.

[16]A good summary review of themes in the book is provided by J. A. Hoberman, "The Donald Duck Report", *Village Voice*, July 26, 1976.

[17]See the reproduction in Kunzle's Introduction, p. 13.

[18]Dorfman and Mattelart, pp. 95, 98.

[19]Quoted by Hoberman.

[20]Information from the title page of *How to Read Donald Duck* and through correspondence with Seth Siegelaub of International General, Dec. 10, 1978.

[21]Details provided through conversation.

[22]A correspondence file, from which information and quotations are taken, was provided by Peter Weiss and Ellen Seeherman of the CCR.

[23]Waldheim to Suske, Sept. 10, 1975.

[24]Waldheim to Regional Commissioner of Customs, Imports Compliance Branch, Sept. 25, 1975.

[25]CCR, Weiss, Copelon, and Schaap to Suske, Aug. 8, 1975.

[26]Letter "6 Reasons Why No Cartoon Matter, No Book" (slightly edited here for publication) is dated Aug. 12, 1975. It was written by the authors and Seth Siegelaub.

[27]Waldheim to Darrel D. Kast, Acting Director, Entry Procedures and Penalties Division, U.S. Customs Service, Washington, D.C.

[28]CCR, Seeherman, and Weiss to Darrell Kast, Jan. 12, 1976.

[29]Suske to Weiss, June 9, 1976.

[30]Donavan, Leisure, Newton, Irvine to Leonard Lehman, Assistant Commissioner of Customs, Regulations and Rulings, Washington, D.C., Oct. 6, 1976.

[31]Lehman to Donavan, Leisure . . . , July 7, 1977.

[32]Suske to Weiss, June 9, 1976.

[33]Cf. Aubert J. Clark, *The Movement for Copyright in the Nineteenth Century*, (Washington, D.C.: Catholic University Press, 1960), especially chap. 2.

[34]Donavan, Leisure . . . to Lehman, Oct. 6, 1976, raises this point.

[35]Disney has foreign subsidiaries with Principal Marketing Executives in Australia, Belgium, Canada, Denmark, England, France, Germany, Italy, Japan, Spain, and Sweden. *Annual Report 1977*, p. 40.

[36]The Copyright Act of 1976 provides that the manufacturing and import restrictions will be phased out by 1982 (see Section 601). In 1981, however, the Register is to report to Congress on the probable effects of discontinuing the restrictions, at which time the issue may be reexamined.

BOOKS ON COMMUNICATION, CULTURE & IDEOLOGY: 1984

INTERNATIONAL GENERAL pob 350, new york, ny 10013, USA.
IMMRC international mass media research center 173 av de la dhuys, 93170 bagnolet, FRANCE.

NEW TITLES:

Armand Mattelart, Seth Siegelaub, editors

COMMUNICATION AND CLASS STRUGGLE: 1. CAPITALISM, IMPERIALISM

1979, 448pp, Large-format Paper, 178 x 260mm, 0-88477-011-7, $20.95

Armand Mattelart, Seth Siegelaub, editors

COMMUNICATION AND CLASS STRUGGLE: 2. LIBERATION, SOCIALISM

1983, 440pp, Illustrations, Large-format Paper, 178 × 260mm 0-88477-018-4, $20.95

COMMUNICATION AND CLASS STRUGGLE, a two-volume work, is the first general marxist anthology of writings on communications, information and culture. Its purpose is to analyse the relationship between the practice and theory of communication and their development within the context of class struggle. Armand Mattelart and Seth Siegelaub, the editors, have selected 128 essential marxist and progressive texts originating in over 50 countries and written since the mid-nineteenth century to explain three interrelated phenomena: (1) how basic social, economic and cultural processes condition communication; (2) how bourgeois communication practice and theory have developed as part of the capitalist mode of production; and (3) how in the struggle against exploitation and oppression, the popular and working classes have developed their own communication practice and theory, and a new, liberated mode of communication, culture and daily life.

"With its 128 texts and bibliographies, almost 900 pages and 800,000 words, this 2-volume anthology is by far the most impressive attempt to date to lay the groundwork for a critical theory of communication and culture... Destined to be a classic!"

Sakari Hänninen, Leena Paldàn, editors

RETHINKING IDEOLOGY: THE MARXIST DEBATE

1983, 160pp, Paperback, 120 x 190mm, 0-88477-015-X, $7.50

With Gramsci's ground-breaking work over 50 years ago, Louis Althusser's recent "Ideology and Ideological State Apparatuses" (1970), and the present world economic and political crisis, the need to formulate a theory of ideology is increasingly posed as a central element in an analysis of existing society as well as in a political project for its transformation. Developing on the analyses of the research group PIT ("Projekt Ideologie-Theorie"), begun in 1977, *Rethinking Ideology* contains the principal papers presented at the "International Seminar on Problems of Research On Ideology" held in West Berlin in 1982. The contributions range from highly conceptual texts to those on politics, education, aesthetics, fascism and feminism; all together they offer a rare confrontation between a wide spectrum of theoretical positions on questions of ideology.

What is IG/IMMRC?

The International Mass Media Research Center (IMMRC) and International General (IG) are an inter-related information center/library and publisher whose purpose is to contribute to the development of left communication theory and practice. Founded in 1973 by Seth Siegelaub, our work consists in the documentation, production and dissemination of marxist, critical and progressive studies concerning all aspects of communication and culture. Our work, which is independent of any political party or institution, is entirely self-supported.

Research/Library

At our center in Bagnolet, France, we maintain a growing reference library and extensive files of thousands of left books, pamphlets, reviews, articles and manuscripts, covering 44 subjects in more than 7 languages concerning communication in over 50 countries. The library is free and is open by appointment. In addition, we provide special research by arrangement, as well as photocopies of hard-to-find material available in our library.

Books/Publications

The principal publication arising from our research and library is the multi-lingual annotated *Marxism and the Mass Media: Towards a Basic Bibliography,* published irregularly and distributed worldwide to libraries, universities, and media researchers and organisations. In addition, we originate and publish a growing list of related books on communication and culture, the sale of which provides the sole source of economic support for our library and research work.

Response/Exchanges

Keeping up with the evolution of communication and cultural practices and theories, however, requires the constant exchange of left material and information from many people from different countries, areas of work and specialisations. Concretely, these exchanges concern 3 main areas:

(1) for our reference files, we need raw *bibliographic information,* reading lists, and promotional mailings, catalogues from publishers, reviews and groups, etc.;

(2) for our library, we seek *published or unpublished materials* via review copies, gifts and loans etc. from interested political and cultural groups, reviews, publishers, and media researchers, unions and organisations, etc.; and lastly,

(3) for our publishing, we search both *authors* with original manuscripts, as well as editorial *collaborators* to jointly develop special media bibliographies or other book projects of mutual interest.